"European criminal policy is characterized by both inclusive and exclusive tendencies. The heritage of enlightenment and the post-World War II revival of fundamental rights allow elements of inclusive criminal policy survive on the old Continent. That however does not prevent, rather mitigates control societies' exclusive tendencies, which can be traced in occupying territories both upwards by blurring the line between the war against terrorism and criminal justice and downwards, through a remarkable societal readiness to demand legal and – more often than not – penal law solutions for incivilities. The volume edited by Nina Peršak is an elegant attempt to document and analyze these latter disturbing tendencies in contemporary Europe. The multi-layered and interdisciplinary nature of the problem is mirrored by methodology: the volume is scientifically embedded into criminology, political science, sociology and criminal law; is characterized by a balanced representation of European states; and an equally fair proportioning of country analyses, empirical research and theory."

Petra Bárd, *Senior Researcher and Head of the Criminal Law Division, National Institute of Criminology, Hungary; Assistant Professor, ELTE School of Law, Hungary; and Visiting Professor, Central European University, Hungary*

"This book is an important addition to the literature on the control of 'incivilities' – understood broadly as contested uses of, and presences in, public spaces. It reminds us of the fine line between targeting behaviours of others, and targeting others for what or who they are. From homelessness in Hungary to political protest in Spain, the measure of acceptability of behaviour in public increasingly becomes its potential for causing feelings of discomfort in others. Keenly observed trends in different European countries provide illustrative detail of a growing trend of low-level suppression that redraws the boundaries of ownership of public spaces."

Antje du Bois-Pedain, *Senior Lecturer in the Faculty of Law and Deputy Director of the Centre for Penal Theory and Penal Ethics at the Institute of Criminology, University of Cambridge, UK*

Regulation and Social Control of Incivilities

The increasing trend and prevalence of incivilities-targeting punitive regulatory measures across Europe raises important issues regarding the legitimacy, effectiveness and impact of such formal social control. Regulation and Social Control of Incivilities addresses the pertinent issues of current punitive regulation and the social control of incivilities, their trends, criminological explanations, political, spatial, cultural, representational and policing dimensions as well as the underlying behaviour it targets.

Part I explores issues surrounding the regulation of incivilities, drawing examples from several European countries including Spain, Italy, Great Britain, Belgium, Slovenia and Hungary. It inspects the legal form and content of the prohibition of incivilities and the social factors that can help explain it, as well as the effectiveness and societal impact of various anti-nuisance measures. Part II focuses on social control and the representation of incivilities, including the construction and control of public nuisance in Belgium, the spatial and cultural aspects of incivilities and of law enforcement against them, the media representations of incivilities in the British and Flemish press, and the intersections between migration and control of incivilities when policing in the Netherlands.

This book brings together international scholars to examine the ways in which understudied European countries approach the issue of anti-social behaviour. This multidisciplinary text will be of interest to students, scholars and policymakers concerned with issues of social control, incivilities and criminalisation.

Nina Peršak is a research professor at the Faculty of Law, Ghent University, Belgium. She holds a doctorate in law from University of Ljubljana and an LL.M. (Law) and M.Phil. (Social and Developmental Psychology) from University of Cambridge. Her research interests lie in the fields of criminology, criminal law, criminal legal philosophy (in particular criminalisation theory), human rights, victimology, sociology of law and social psychology. She is the author of *Criminalising Harmful Conduct: The Harm Principle, its Limits and Continental Counterparts* (Springer, 2007) and the editor of *Legitimacy and Trust in Criminal Law, Policy and Justice: Norms, Procedures, Outcomes* (Ashgate, 2014).

Routledge Studies in Crime and Society

15 **Criminology and War**
Transgressing the borders
Edited by Sandra Walklate and Ross McGarry

16 **Transitional Justice and Legacies of State Violence**
Talking about torture in Northern Ireland
Lisa White

17 **Why Men Buy Sex**
Examining sex worker clients
Philip Birch

18 **State Crime, Women and Gender**
Victoria E. Collins

19 **Men, Masculinities and Violence**
An ethnographic study
Anthony Ellis

20 **Order and Conflict in Public Space**
Edited by Mattias De Backer, Lucas Melgaço, Georgiana Varna and Francesca Menichelli

21 **Policing, Port Security and Crime Control: An Ethnography of the Port Securityscape**
Yarin Eski

22 **Organised Crime in European Businesses**
Edited by Ernesto Savona, Michele Riccardi and Giulia Berlusconi

23 **Regulation and Social Control of Incivilities**
Edited by Nina Peršak

Regulation and Social Control of Incivilities

Edited by Nina Peršak

Routledge
Taylor & Francis Group
LONDON AND NEW YORK

First published 2017
by Routledge
2 Park Square, Milton Park, Abingdon, Oxon OX14 4RN

and by Routledge
711 Third Avenue, New York, NY 10017

First issued in paperback 2018

Routledge is an imprint of the Taylor & Francis Group, an informa business

British Library Cataloguing-in-Publication Data
A catalogue record for this book is available from the British Library

Library of Congress Cataloging in Publication Data
Names: Peršak, Nina, editor.
Title: Regulation and social control of incivilities / edited by Nina Peršak.
Description: Abingdon, Oxon ; New York, NY : Routledge, 2016. | Series: Routledge studies in crime and society | Includes bibliographical references and index.
Identifiers: LCCN 2016007979 | ISBN 9781138951549 (hardback) | ISBN 9781315668147 (ebook)
Subjects: LCSH: Breach of the peace—Law and legislation—Europe. | Disorderly conduct—Law and legislation—Europe. | Police regulations—Europe. | Nuisances—Europe—Criminal provisions. | Harassment—Law and legislation—Europe—Criminal provisions.
Classification: LCC KJC8779 .R447 2016 | DDC 345.4/0243—dc23
LC record available at https://lccn.loc.gov/2016007979

ISBN 13: 978-1-138-49946-1 (pbk)
ISBN 13: 978-1-138-95154-9 (hbk)

Typeset in Times New Roman
by Apex CoVantage, LLC

Contents

Figures

Tables

Contributors

Marco Calaresu earned a PhD in Political Science at Istituto Italiano di Scienze Umane–Scuola Normale Superiore (Florence-Pisa, Italy). He was a Visiting PhD Student (2009) and Visiting Scholar (2012) at New York University, Department of Sociology. He is currently a Postdoctoral Research Fellow at the University of Sassari. His research interests include urban and local security policies and the quality of democracy.

Anna Di Ronco is a PhD student in criminology at the Department of Criminology, Criminal Law and Social Law of the Faculty of Law, Ghent University (Belgium), and a member of the Institute for International Research on Criminal Policy (IRCP). She previously studied law at the University of Trento. Her research interests include the regulation, representation and enforcement of uncivil behaviour.

Manuel Maroto Calatayud is Assistant Professor of criminal law at the University of Castilla–La Mancha (Spain). He wrote his PhD thesis on corruption and the funding of political parties from a critical and comparative perspective. He is the author of several papers on the repression of political dissent and social media surveillance. He is also interested in methodologies of evaluation and reform of criminal justice policies. He has been a visiting scholar at the University of Pennsylvania and the University of Stockholm.

Nina Peršak holds a doctorate in law from the University of Ljubljana and an LL.M. (Law) and M.Phil. (Social and Developmental Psychology) from the University of Cambridge. She is a research professor at the Faculty of Law, Ghent University. Her research interests lie in the fields of criminology, criminal law, criminal legal philosophy (in particular criminalisation theory), human rights, victimology, sociology of law and social psychology. She is also a member of the European Commission's Expert Group on EU Criminal Policy.

Stefaan Pleysier is Associate Professor at the Faculty of Law of the KU Leuven, and coordinates (with Johan Put) the Research Line on Youth Criminology at the Leuven Institute of Criminology (LINC). He teaches youth criminology, juvenile justice and research methods both in the Bachelor and Master of Criminology. His research interests include youth crime, juvenile justice and the criminalisation of behaviour.

Léna Podoletz is an Assistant Lecturer at the Faculty of Law, Eötvös Loránd University (Budapest, Hungary). She has a background in criminology and law. Her research topics include the criminalisation of incivilities, prostitution and the regulation of urban space.

Joanne van der Leun is Professor of Criminology at Leiden Law School (the Netherlands) and Academic Director of the Institute for Criminal Law and Criminology. She has a background in sociology and has taught criminology since 2001. Her research interests lie in the field of crime, migration and policy. She is also a member of the independent Advisory Committee on Migration Affairs, which advises the Dutch government and Parliament on immigration law and policy.

Acknowledgements

First of all, I would like to thank all the contributors to the colloquium, organised at the Faculty of Law, Ghent University in July 2015, for a lively debate and discussion that led to the success of this event and ultimately to this book. Thank you also for your enthusiasm and cooperation later on in the process. It was a pleasure working with all of you. I am also indebted to the Ghent University Special Research Fund (BOF), whose funding enabled me to organise the mentioned colloquium and activities around it on the topic of incivilities. Next, I wish to thank the Center for the Study of Law and Society at Berkeley Law, UC Berkeley for the Visiting Scholarship in autumn 2015, which allowed me to have contact with a vibrant community of law, socio-legal and criminology scholars and carry out much of the editing work. I particularly wish to thank those who attended my talk, which included the presentation of some of the results from this project, at the CSLS on 6 November 2015 for the many helpful comments and overall interesting discussion. I am also grateful to Tom Sutton, Heidi Lee, Hannah Catterall and others at Routledge for their support and advice over the course of this project, along with three anonymous peer reviewers. For the continuous encouragement and support, I am greatly indebted to my family and friends, some of whom read significant portions of this book. Special thanks also to my colleagues and students at Ghent University, who keep providing me with vital food for thought.

1 The rude, the bad and the ugly

Penalising incivilities in Europe

Nina Peršak

Introduction

A reconfigured field of crime control, Garland wrote in 2001, introduced 'new practices of controlling behaviour and doing justice, revised conceptions of social order and social control, and altered ways of maintaining social cohesion and managing group relations' (Garland 2001: 6). The increasing regulation and social control of incivilities can be seen as a prime example of this shift in social control from the notion of crime towards broader notions of disorder and other sub-criminal behaviour. Disorder has become construed as a risk to future crime and as such to be managed, or better yet, criminalised. In a pre-crime society (Zedner 2009), risk has become the threshold that suffices for state punitive involvement. Although some petty offences, nuisance or anti-social behaviour (different names used for incivilities) may be harmful and thus legitimately proscribed (and have mostly already been criminalised in some way or another), many others represent only trivial and fleeting annoyance (a subjective feeling) to others or a simple violation of a rule, without causing any harm or objective setback to one's interests. It is the risk of incivilities or their assumed propensity to grow into more serious crime – a discourse inherited from the 'broken windows' theory (Wilson and Kelling 1982) – that often guides their criminalisation. Although they are often regulated through seemingly non-criminal measures (civil law in Britain, administrative law in Belgium, administrative-penal in Hungary, etc.), this may in some contexts have an even more negative and detrimental effect on the lives of those who are sanctioned and their families. Offenders who risk losing their homes, owing to their anti-social behaviour, often fear the Social Service agent much more than the police. Looking at the criminal law (and its amendments) therefore reveals only a partial picture of today's social control. As amendments to the 'semi-criminal' (Squires 2008) or 'infra-penal' law typically raises much less discussion among the scholars and general public; there are therefore many crucial aspects of punitive social control that remain hidden or under-explored.

Uncivil behaviour in question

Examining the types of conduct that are criminalised as incivilities, one could observe that the behaviour in question is often offensive, occasionally harmful and sometimes just a nuisance to the environment. In short, it is rude, bad or ugly. While no one has problems with criminalising 'bad', i.e. wrongfully harmful conduct, many scholars appropriately raise questions whether criminal law is the way to tackle merely offensive behaviour and behaviour that leads to unsightly outcomes (e.g. litter, graffiti, presence of certain elements or people in particular urban places). In the case of the latter, in particular, it is not immorality (wrongfulness) or harm – traditional criteria of criminalisation – but rather the aesthetics of the dominant majority that clearly dictate the norm and deviations from it as criminalisation-worthy.

However, uncivil behaviour is nothing new, neither is the concern with social order and attempts of authorities (national or local) to punitively control it. One can, for example, observe similarities with US vagrancy laws or with 'civilising' approaches on the European continent since the Middle Ages (Elias 2000, orig. 1939). In the UK, some observe many parallels with the regulation of immoral or inappropriate behaviour in Victorian times (Pickard 2014a). However, they notice that the label has changed: inappropriate behaviour in the UK is now called 'anti-social behaviour' (Pickard 2014b: xv). In some other European countries, what is new is the way old regulatory tools have been used to tackle new phenomena and social movements, the adoption of the new set of tools, designed in particular to fight incivilities, or the expansionist characteristic of this social control. What is distinctive about contemporary societies, according to Husak (2006: 92), is 'the readiness to demand legal solutions for such problems'.

At the same time, little is known about the actual prevalence or extent of incivilities (even in the countries we know best). Has uncivil behaviour been on the increase or are we only suffering from the good-old-days bias (selectively recalling only the good things that happened in the past, while forgetting the bad ones), forgetting that we have been up to many of the same things when we were young? Some claim that rudeness has indeed been on the increase. Stand-up comedians, for example, report an increase in various rude acts performed by their audience during their stand-up, including the ordering of a take-away by a man, sitting in the first row, who was, moreover, surprised that the comedian would take issue with his behaviour (Christie 2015). People may also hold perceptions that anti-social behaviour is on the increase, while in reality it is declining (Full Fact 2013, Office for National Statistics 2015). Many emphasise that it is difficult to measure the extent of anti-social behaviour because it is unclear what should be measured and because a variety of agencies, operating with their own definitions, deal with the range of behaviours covered by any definition (Carr and Cowan 2006). Moreover, rosy retrospection taints our beliefs and persuasions. Flint and Powell (2014: 45) observe, for example, the similarity between contemporary governmentalities and social observers from Victorian times in that '[i]n both eras, thresholds of decency were believed to have changed, linked to nostalgia for previous times of civility and the need for a polite ethos'. Some believe, moreover, that our concern with declining politeness is rather a reflection of our anxiety about our own isolation and alienation from others in today's asocial society (Waiton 2008).

Among explanations for such socially undesirable behaviour, we often hear factors such as bad parenting, unsuccessful socialisation and low education. Yet, according to a recent Berkeley study, it is upper-class individuals who are more likely to engage in unethical behaviour. In seven studies conducted, individuals of a higher social class were more likely to break the law while driving, exhibit unethical decision-making tendencies, take goods from others, lie in a negotiation, cheat to increase the chances of winning and endorse unethical behaviour at work. These unethical tendencies were partly explained by the upper-class individuals' more favourable attitudes towards greed (Piff et al. 2012). Although these studies did not directly involve 'classical' cases of incivilities (such as being offensive or polluting the environment through littering, urinating and the like), it can be argued that an important segment of the rude or insensitive behaviour comes from the same place, namely from prioritising self-interest over the welfare of others or the welfare of the community.

Responses to it

Some regulation against incivilities clearly responds to community concerns: there are always cases of some people engaging in a persistent unpleasant conduct, making the lives of many miserable, exhibiting blatant disregard of others. Some such behaviour is clearly harmful and for these one could easily find justification for criminalisation.

Although criminal law is not the only type of response to such behaviour, it is very commonly used. Punitive response – and therefore criminalisation in the broad sense of the word – can be, however, achieved also through other means and other types of law, such as civil law, administrative law or a lower-level type of penal law. This book reveals many laws and techniques with which European countries punitively address the issue of incivilities at the national as well as local level. The local, municipal government has particularly become an important actor in the social control of incivilities, not only executing but also legislating against them. This significant tool of power has raised, however, many new challenges.

Challenges lie not only in the application but also in the existence of a normative, legal basis for many a regulation of anti-social behaviour. Criminalisation of non-harmful uncivil behaviour raises many legal, human-rights and wider social concerns. When criminalisation is no longer the last resort of state intervention but a 'routine system for managing disorder', there is also, as Ashworth and Zedner (2008: 43) observe, 'little inhibition in employing it liberally to regulate minor forms of offence'.

Societal responses to incivilities, however, do not stop at the law. An increasing use of so-called defensive or hostile architecture, such as barrel-shaped bus stop benches, spiked walls, grounds and other surfaces, attests to human inventiveness when it comes to social control and to the employment of other disciplines as new, more pragmatic (perhaps even more insidious) tools of eliminating unwanted behaviour in the urban space, such as sleeping or lying down on a bench (Davis 1990, Peršak 2015). The management of incivilities through city planning, concretely through zoning or 'banishment' from specific zones (Beckett and Herbert 2009), and specific architecture announces a new dawn of urban social control and the moving of battlefields between the pro and anti camps into other areas of social life, which redefines the landscape of social control.

The background and aims of this book

My interest in incivilities was sparked in 1999 during my LL.M. studies in Cambridge. ASBOs (anti-social behaviour orders) had just come on the scene and there was a big discussion on what they meant and how they could be justified, if at all. The 'offence principle', which seemed to be useful to perhaps justify the sort of (two-step) criminalisation that was happening through ASBOs, yet very distinct from the security-based discourses on disorder (Peršak 2014), was then the topic of my master thesis and remained an interest I continue to share with my then professors, who, in 2006, published a wonderful edited volume on incivilities from a mostly Anglo-Saxon and criminal law philosophy perspective (von Hirsch and Simester 2006). The interest in what people see as anti-social and especially how they (and law) respond to it, however, stayed with me through my Ph.D. times on the criminalisation of harmful behaviour and my later studies in social psychology, where I studied the representations of the 'anti-social' in the British press. In 2012, my proposed research on incivilities received a grant from Ghent University, which also enabled one Ph.D. student to conduct her doctoral studies on this topic as well as to fund various activities around it, including the colloquium where drafts of contributions in this volume were presented.

In the meantime, several books on anti-social behaviour were published, although predominantly in, or tied to, Great Britain (e.g. Burney 2005, Squires and Stephen 2005, Flint 2006, Waiton 2008, Millie 2009, Donoghue 2010, Pickard 2014a), with some exceptions (e.g. chapters on France and Australia included in Flint 2006, one chapter on Austria [specifically Vienna], the Netherlands [Rotterdam] and Sweden in Burney 2005). While some presentations at the conferences of the European Society of Criminology touched upon the issue in other countries, nothing seems to have resulted in an English-language publication that would give us an insight into how the European continent regulates and controls incivilities. Are incivilities an issue in wider Europe? If yes, can its regulation be explained through the same (Western) culture-of-control and similar explanations or perhaps through something else? How do European states legally approach the issue? Are incivilities on the rise? What type? Is the regulation successful in tackling them? It seemed fair to assume that probably not everything can be explained by the phenomena observed in the UK or USA and that there may be local specifics we know almost nothing about. It is partly the aim of this book to help fill this gap and bring some of these nuances to the fore.

As, to date, there seem to be no criminological or socio-legal books published that would cover (either descriptively or normatively, or both) the growing social control of incivilities across different legal regimes in Europe, the main aim of this book is to make also some of these other parts of the 'incivilities picture' more visible. Concretely, the book's objectives are to expand and further the current criminological and socio-legal research on incivilities by: (i) exchanging ideas and experiences on how incivilities are conceptualised and regulated in different countries, comparatively and internationally; (ii) elucidating the variety of laws and measures (national, regional, municipal) used to tackle incivilities (including the reasons for selection of such approaches and their impact) and their effects; and (iii) explaining the nature of the behaviour in question and of the seemingly increasing punitive social control of incivilities through different perspectives (criminological, political, sociological, legal, descriptive as well as normative).

This book will hopefully provide some answers to these issues and quite possibly open many more new questions and avenues for further research. As mentioned, it builds on the papers that were first presented in July 2015 at a colloquium in Ghent, bringing together scholars from across disciplines and international borders in an opportunity to engage with international work being developed at the levels of theory, policy and practice. The contributors have been chosen for their expertise on the topics that the book addresses and for representing a variety of disciplines (criminology, law, sociology and political science), different criminological perspectives and a wide geographical landscape across Europe.

Structure of the book

The first part of the book addresses regulation of incivilities – from a legal, comparative, political science and criminology perspective. The examples are drawn from several European countries, such as Spain, Italy, Great Britain, Belgium, Slovenia and Hungary. Through examples we also look into how different legal systems (Anglo-Saxon, Romanist and Germanic) approach the issue of incivilities.

Chapter 2 inspects the criminalisation of incivilities through the formal and substantive lens. We examine some typical or common ways of punitive regulation of incivilities (i.e. types of laws used) and notice a trend of punitive regulation of human conduct using administrative or civil law, rather than criminal law proper – criminalisation 'through the back door'. The chapter also looks at the content of the conduct that is being prohibited as uncivil or offensive, drawing on examples of incivility regulation from several countries (Great Britain, Belgium, Slovenia). In the next step, we expose the most usual normative, social and psychological factors behind the regulation of incivilities as possible explanatory factors for (the rise of) such regulation, such as popular punitiveness (real or imagined, harvested by politicians), fear of crime, reduced social solidarity and mistrust, 'emotionalisation of law', policy transfer and local particularities. The chapter concludes with the discussion of the legal and societal consequences of prohibition of incivilities and with some future-looking considerations for the regulatory, necessarily normative, exercise against incivilities.

In Chapter 3, we move from justifications to effectiveness. Calaresu looks at the top-down instruments that Italian cities have used to fight 'borderline criminalities' and incivilities (as well as degradation, poor urban planning and the redevelopment of risk districts). Incivilities are here positioned as the issue of city governance and urban security. The chapter shows how the central government in Italy tried to obtain a new model of urban security governance and achieve a better decision-making capacity with the introduction, in 2007, of the so-called Security Pacts and local ordinances (administrative orders). The chapter aims to identify the factors that can explain the capacity of these two instruments to modify the previous model for governing crime and disorder and their capacity to effectively tackle incivilities. With data from semi-structured interviews with actors, relevant for the decision-making process in four Italian cities, Calaresu attempts to identify which variable may best explain the discrepancy in the efficacy of these two top-down instruments at regional and municipal levels in different areas of the country. The chapter concludes by discussing the general implications for the regulation or enforcement of incivilities when these top-down instruments are used by the central government to govern crime and disorder.

Maroto Calatayud in Chapter 4 demonstrates how political dissent and civil society mobilisation against austerity plans, dismantling welfare in Spain, have been progressively targeted through 'nuisance' ordinances, administrative sanctions and regulations – measures that, in his words, 'fly below the radar of constitutional controls'. Spain has one of the highest unemployment rates in Europe and has been particularly hit by the recent financial and economic crisis, pushing many people onto the streets, metaphorically as well as literally. Social protests have been met by a variety of approaches, from riot control and the introduction of harsher sanctions for public order offences in the Criminal Code to new judicial fees, which, according to the author, restrict access to justice. He focuses, however, on the 'soft repression' of nuisance regulations, which represent a move towards the repressive use of measures of minor weight in order to circumvent the classical criminal law safeguards and 'minimise the political cost of repression'.

Chapter 5 presents the situation in Hungary, where sweeping criminalisation of homelessness is taking place as a prime example of incivilities regulation. Podoletz asserts that we can learn a lot from studying the manner in which lawmakers approach incivilities: the way they address the conduct, described as public incivilities, shows how they think about differences and their place in the public space. After describing the steps leading up to the current criminalisation of the homeless and judicial attempts at limiting the expansive, repressive ways of the legislator, Podoletz dissects the reasons behind the concrete criminalisation and shows how fear of crime, the promise of safety, the concept of urban order, the importance of commercial attractiveness of urban spaces and the general trend of replacing social policy with criminal policy when tackling social problems have led to the exclusion and criminalisation of one of the most vulnerable groups in Hungarian society.

Part II focuses more criminologically on the social control and the representation of incivilities. In Chapter 6, Pleysier analyses Belgian social control of unwanted, undesirable behaviour in public space – 'public nuisance' – through its system of administrative sanctions as an example of a pro-active and pre-emptive intervention, typical of the 'pre-crime' society (Zedner 2009). He first describes the system of administrative sanctions in Belgium as a new emergent regulatory framework, which illustrates the trend of giving cities and communities new opportunities to tackle local safety and public nuisance 'in their own right'. He argues that this trend is in line with the observed transformation from a post-crime society to a pre-crime society, where crime control and public safety issues are no longer predicated on the breach of a (criminal) law, but rather aim to reduce and manage risk and govern 'the unknowable'. He then transfers the metaphor of the pre-crime society and the consequential logic of pro-active and pre-emptive interventions to the debate on the criminalisation, regulation and normalisation of nuisance in Belgium, and concludes by stressing the importance of researching the dynamics of localisation and hybridisation of safety policies and new regulatory tools on the ground.

Studying the way city-specific cultural values, including aesthetics, play out in the urban space increases our understanding of uncivil behaviour and of the social reaction thereto, as incivilities seem to be a distinctly 'urban' phenomenon, making urban space *the* locus in which mechanisms of social control work against incivilities. In Chapter 7, Di Ronco thus exposes the spatial and cultural dimensions of the regulation, representation and enforcement of incivilities by drawing on the cultural criminology literature and data from her two comparative studies. Based on the results of two recently conducted studies of two types of incivilities (street prostitution and public drunkenness) that inspected the regulation, representation and law enforcement of uncivil behaviour in different geographical locations (Birmingham, Brussels, Ghent, Milan and Trento), this chapter highlights how incivilities are socially constructed and tackled by the authorities through context-specific cultural and spatial elements, which shape the way powerful groups experience certain urban places and consequently their expectations – which ultimately determine the social, including legal, reaction to nuisance – regarding those spaces.

In Chapter 8, Peršak inspects media representations of incivilities in the British and Belgian-Flemish press. As the media influence or co-construct our social representations of a certain issue, take part in the shaping of the social 'problem' as well as play a crucial role in sensitisation of people to certain social phenomena, their role in generating fear, moral panic and pressure upon politicians to act in a certain way cannot be ignored. Drawing on three research studies, this chapter inspects the representations of what has been considered 'anti-social' in the British press (1996–2006) and media representations of regulated 'nuisance' (the Flemish term for anti-social behaviour) and of some nuisance-related issues in the Flemish press (1998–2014). Content analyses reveal, among others, what and who is considered a problem, which reasons are discussed and which solutions proposed, how the representations of nuisance and nuisance regulation have changed through time and the role of various actors in the incivilities media discourse.

Chapter 9 looks at the intersection between the enforcement of incivilities and migration control. Van der Leun observes that the irregular migration in the Netherlands has been tackled along the same lines as urban incivilities – selectively and with potential discriminatory outcomes, which can consequently affect police legitimacy and wider social peace in multi-ethnic neighbourhoods. The chapter inspects the justifications behind this approach and the impact of the (perceived) police selectivity regarding minority communities. Drawing on the research on surveillance of irregular migrants and street interviews with young adults in the Hague and Amsterdam and with police officers in the Hague, the chapter demonstrates the dynamics of social control that targets a mixture of incivilities, crime and migration.

Chapter 10 is the concluding chapter, in which an attempt is made to identify the themes that have emerged from this volume, consolidate key debates around various dimensions of incivilities and their social control, voice some common concerns regarding the legitimacy, effectiveness and negative repercussions of incivility regulation and share some suggestions for possible ways forward, including future research.

The social control of incivilities (and incivilities themselves) is, of course, a manifold and complex topic that is impossible to exhaustively cover in a single volume, and this has never been our goal. The purpose of this book is of more modest nature; it aims to contribute to the increasing discussion on the importance of a justified state intervention in the area of human conduct (particularly if the intervention is punitive), to question the notions of civility, tolerance, culture, aesthetics, space, victim, offender, offence and force us to think about them contextually, developmentally and historically, to look at law in terms of power and interests, not only as a set of (seemingly neutral) norms of generally accepted behaviour, as well as to situate the phenomenon in wider world trends and movements. It aims to shed light on the ways in which some so far understudied European countries approach the issue of anti-social behaviour and do so from multidisciplinary and comparative perspectives, thereby hopefully revealing a little more of the overall picture of incivilities and of the societal reaction to them in the twenty-first century.

References

Ashworth, A. and Zedner, L. (2008) ‘Defending the criminal law: Reflections on the changing character of crime, procedures, and sanctions’, *Criminal Law and Philosophy*, 2(1): 21–51.

Beckett, K. and Herbert, S. (2009) *Banished: The New Social Control in Urban America*, New York: Oxford University Press.

Burney, E. (2005) *Making People Behave: Anti-Social Behaviour, Politics and Policy*, Devon: Willan Publishing.

Carr, H. and Cowan, D. (2006) ‘Labelling: Constructing definitions of anti-social behaviour?’, in J. Flint (ed.) *Housing, Urban Governance and Anti-social Behaviour*, Bristol: The Policy Press.

Christie, B. (2015) ‘Bridget Christie: It’s a scientifically proven fact that wealth makes you obnoxious’, *The Guardian*, 22 August 2015. Online. Available at: www.theguardian.com/culture/2015/aug/22/wealth-makes-you-obnoxious-bridget-christie?CMP=share_btn_link (accessed 22 August 2015).

Davis, M. (1990) *City of Quartz: Excavating the Future in Los Angeles*, London, New York: Verso.

Donoghue, J. (2010) *Anti-Social Behaviour Orders: A Culture of Control?*, Basingstoke: Palgrave Macmillan.

Elias, N. (2000, orig. 1939) *The Civilizing Process*. Revised ed., Oxford, Malden: Blackwell Publishing.

Flint, J. (ed.) (2006) *Housing, Urban Governance and Anti-Social Behaviour*, Bristol: The Policy Press.

Flint, J. and Powell, R. (2014) 'Anti-social behaviour and "civilizing" regulation in the British city: Comparing Victorian and contemporary eras', in S. Pickard (ed.) *Anti-Social Behaviour in Britain*, Basingstoke: Palgrave Macmillan.

Full Fact (2013) 'Is anti-social behaviour on the rise?' Online. Available at: https://fullfact.org/crime/anti-social-behaviour-rise/ (accessed 1 January 2016).

Garland, D. (2001) *The Culture of Control: Crime and Social Order in Contemporary Society*, Oxford: Oxford University Press.

Hirsch, A. von and Simester, A.P. (eds.) (2006) *Incivilities: Regulating Offensive Behaviour*, Oxford: Hart Publishing.

Husak, D. (2006) 'Disgust: Metaphysical and empirical speculations', in A. von Hirsch and A. P. Simester (eds.) *Incivilities: Regulating Offensive Behaviour*, Oxford: Hart.

Millie, A. (2009) *Anti-Social Behaviour*, Maidenhead, New York: Open University Press.

Office for National Statistics (2015) 'Crime survey for England and Wales – report and data tables', 16 July 2015. Online. Available at: www.ons.gov.uk/ons/rel/crime-stats/crime-statistics/year-ending-march-2015/stb-crime-march-2015.html#tab-Anti-social-behaviour (accessed 5 January 2016).

Peršak, N. (2014) 'Using "quality of life" to legitimate criminal law intervention: Gauging gravity, defining disorder', in A. P. Simester, U. Neumann and A. du Bois-Pedain (eds.) *Liberal Criminal Theory: Essays for Andreas von Hirsch*, Oxford: Hart.

Peršak, N. (2015) 'Criminalising urban marginality: Homelessness, law, and defensive architecture', paper presented at the Annual European Society of Criminology Conference, Porto, September 2015.

Pickard, S. (ed.) (2014a) *Anti-Social Behaviour in Britain*, Basingstoke: Palgrave Macmillan.

Pickard, S. (2014b) 'Introduction', in S. Pickard (ed.) *Anti-Social Behaviour in Britain*, Basingstoke: Palgrave Macmillan.

Piff, P. K., Stancato, D. M., Coté, S., Mendoza-Denton, R. and Keltner, D. (2012) 'Higher social class predicts increased unethical behavior', *PNAS*, 109(11): 4086–4091.

Squires, P. (ed.) (2008) *ASBO Nation: The Criminalisation of Nuisance*, Bristol: The Policy Press.

Squires, P. and Stephen, D. E. (2005) *Rougher Justice: Anti-Social Behaviour and Young People*, Devon, Portland: Willan Publishing.

Waiton, S. (2008) *The Politics of Antisocial Behaviour*, London, New York: Routledge.

Wilson, J. Q. and Kelling, G. (1982) 'Broken windows: The police and neighbourhood safety', *The Atlantic Monthly*, 249(3): 29–38. Online. Available at: www.manhattan-institute.org/pdf/_atlantic_monthly-broken_windows.pdf (accessed 15 June 2015).

Zedner, L. (2009) *Security*, London: Routledge.

Part I

Regulation of disorder and uncivil behaviour

2 Criminalising through the back door

Normative grounds and social accounts of incivilities regulation

Nina Peršak

Introduction

The last decade has seen many scholars commenting on the shift of the criminological gaze towards wider socially undesirable behaviour, such as incivilities, that is not strictly considered as 'crime'. In 2005, one working group of the European Society of Criminology, for example, noted '[a] movement away from an exclusive concern with the narrow concept of "crime" towards notions of "disorder", "security" and "safety" that encompass other harms and incivilities that are "sub-criminal" but nonetheless are thought to threaten citizens quality of life and thus are legitimate objects of control' (Edwards and Hughes 2005: 2). This control often tends to be punitive, even if it resorts to using administrative or civil law, rather than criminal law proper.

On the one hand, this tendency can be construed as an expression of the 'civilising' of the law. Commenting on the evolution of law, Durkheim (1984, orig. 1893) claimed that with the development of society, penal laws would be progressively replaced with civil laws and more restorative (in place of retributive) laws. In his book *The Civilizing Process*, Elias (2000, orig. 1994) observed a growth in the refinement of manners and social constraints in Western societies since the Middle Ages. Spitting, for example, was then considered a healthy practice, a custom and a need; the only restraint placed on it was not to spit on or over the table (but under it). Later, certain restrictions and conditions were placed on spitting: e.g. one was to step on it, spit into the tissue, turn away when spitting and so forth. By 1774, the activity, including speaking about it, had become 'considerably more distasteful' (Elias 2000: 133). Yet, spitting remained acceptable throughout the nineteenth century: the so-called spittoons, some beautifully crafted, were placed in homes and public buildings to collect visitors' spit. In 1910, they evolved from prestige objects to private objects, and later started to wither away. Only relatively recently has spitting altogether become a sign of bad manners in most Western societies, sometimes even attracting censure of the criminal law.[1] This happened due to the increase of social pressure on people to restrain themselves or exert more self-control over their desires, wants and feelings, and the gradual internalisation of such restraints. In this light, the progressive societal penalisation of incivilities can be understood as a mere continuance of this civilising process or a 'civilising offensive' (*beschavingsoffensief*). This denotes a wide range of actions, mostly instigated by the powerful against the lower classes or other nations, serving as 'the attack on behaviour presumed to be immoral or uncivilised' (Mitzman 1987: 664–665), or a corrective treatment meant to steer people's conduct and 'civilisation' in a particular direction.[2]

On the other hand, the above-mentioned trend of using non-criminal laws to prohibit uncivil conduct and mould people's behaviour can also be seen as a way in which modern social control works. Rather than replacing punitive criminal law with other measures, incivilities are now effectively criminalised through other means, such as civil, administrative and lower-level penal law, which remain less scrutinised than criminal law proper. As the revisionist perspective of social control claims, new social control measures tend to be formally justified as more rational and more humane in comparison with the old ones, yet on closer inspection it is revealed that they coexist in addition to the old ones and are in fact more efficient and more penetrating than the old ones (Deflem 2008). In this light, tackling deviance through sub-penal measures can be seen as a particularly insidious way of reducing liberty, a way that needs to be closely monitored. The same applies to many new 'architectural' measures to address socially undesirable behaviour. The so-called defensive or hostile architecture observed in many urban settings (e.g. London, Verona, Savona, Bergamo, Tokyo, Brussels, Los Angeles) envisages, for example, ground spikes and wall spikes in places where homeless people might seek shelter, bars on benches to prevent people from lying down, slanted windowsills and narrow benches at bus stops (for the same purpose), 'pig's ears' on walls and benches against skateboarders and so forth.[3] Although primarily targeting the 'undesirables', it restricts the usage of certain spaces and things to narrowly defined 'acceptable' ways for all, making urban spaces less friendly and less humane.

In the Enlightenment-led model of liberal democracy, the norm so far has been to criminalise only the most common morally reprehensible and seriously harmful conduct,[4] while leaving the merely unpleasant, uncivil behaviour to be censured through informal social control. The traditional criminal-law principle of last resort (or *ultima ratio*) affirms the conviction that only the uttermost wrongful, harmful acts should be formally prohibited under the threat of punishment. A Continental jurist, taking this principle seriously, thus feels uncomfortable observing the criminalisation of behaviour that is located at the other side of the spectrum of serious wrongful harm and the general lowering of criminalisation criteria in order to catch and control more deviance – a phenomenon often referred to as the 'widening of the net' and the 'thinning of the mesh' of social control (Cohen 1985). In this perspective, no little fish should go free, as little fish tend to grow into big fish if left unattended – to rephrase the assumption behind the 'broken windows' theory in maritime terms.[5]

There are, of course, cases of uncivil behaviour that are not only obnoxious but harmful, either immediately or over longer stretches of time. Repetitive noise can have, for example, very concretely harmful consequences on the lives of neighbours (from hearing problems to problems of continuously interrupted sleep and consequent health issues, problems with concentration and so on). Many of these harmful acts have already been criminalised as crime proper (Burney 2005, Squires and Stephen 2005, Roberts 2006); however, the notion of anti-social behaviour encompasses also several other types of conduct that are only minor violations of the social norm, the criminalisation of which is therefore more difficult to justify. This concern translates into police resources, nicely summarised by Matthews (1992: 3), claiming that while the police ought to deal effectively with minor crimes, '[t]he issue is whether or not they should be encouraged to deal with that range of activities – which we will refer to as incivilities – that would not normally be considered as crimes, but which are a cause of social concern'.

In this chapter, we will examine some typical or common ways of punitive regulation of incivilities (i.e. types of laws and justifications used) and the content of the conduct that is being prohibited as uncivil or offensive, drawing on examples of incivility regulation from several countries. In the next step, the normative, sociological and psychological factors behind the regulation of incivilities will be exposed as possible explanations for (the rise of) such regulation. The chapter will conclude with the discussion of the legal and societal consequences of such prohibition and some future-looking considerations for the regulatory, necessarily normative, exercise against incivilities.

Legal techniques of social control: criminalising through the back door

In the area of black-letter law, the legal or formal trends in the widening of the net of social control through incivilities include or have included: (i) criminalisation through the civil law, where a violation of a civil-law order amounts to crime (as was the case in England and Wales until 2014) and (ii) criminalisation through a lower-level type of criminal law, such as a law of violations (as in Slovenia, Germany, Hungary) or administrative offences (as in Belgium and the Netherlands).[6]

The anti-social behaviour legislation in England and Wales has been described as a 'two-step criminalisation' (Simester and von Hirsch 2006) or 'hybrid procedure' (Ashworth 2000), because of its merging of criminal law with civil law. Anti-social behaviour orders (or ASBOs), introduced by the Crime and Disorder Act of 1998, are civil-law orders that have until recently[7] been used against individuals who act in improper, anti-social ways, which presumably negatively affect the quality of life in neighbourhoods (Budd and Sims 2001).[8] If or when these orders were breached, however, they obtained a criminal nature, as their violation could lead to conviction with a penalty of imprisonment of a maximum of five years.[9] This mixed character of the order blurs the boundaries between the civil and the criminal, which has repercussions affecting the scope of criminal law, as it bypasses certain principles of modern criminal law (e.g. *ultima ratio*). This can have very practical consequences when it comes, for example, to proceedings before the European Court of Human Rights, since if a matter is classified as 'criminal' in nature (according to the case law of Art. 6 of the European Convention on Human Rights), there are certain procedural guarantees (minimum rights) a member state must accord to the defendant.

The second type of criminalisation through the back door and the consequent widening of the net of social control is criminalisation through sub-criminal or infra-penal measures, such as violations, regulatory or administrative offences. In the Continental criminal legal system of Germanic legal circle, we distinguish two areas of law that both comprise the so-called penal law or criminal law in the broad sense: one is criminal law proper, or *stricto sensu*, and the other is the law of violations (*Ordnungswidrigkeiten*). Violations fall somewhere between criminal law and administrative law, and a lot has been written on which area befits violations best; in Slovenia, the majority seems to conclude that due to its penalties and similarities in procedure (subsidiary) it is a type of criminal law (Šelih 2003). While in Belgium the so-called administrative offences are being used to tackle incivilities or, literally, nuisance (*overlast*), they are similarly recognised by many Belgian scholars as essentially a criminal tool, and therefore as being part of the criminal law. Although violations are said to have historically grown out of regulatory offences, which were mere breaches of administrative provisions and as such considered 'ethically colourless' (Roxin 2005) and not breaching any legal value or 'legal good' (*Rechtsgut*), they now encompass many traffic violations, business violations, indecency offences, migration violations, etc., which – like criminal law in the strict sense – carry censure and may incur relatively high penalties (Peršak 2014a).

As they tend to be considered less serious, the amendments to this area of law are paid less attention by criminal lawyers. Whereas battles are fought regarding the Criminal Code, many changes to the law on violations remain below the radar. It may be argued, however, that in some respects violations may even be more dangerous as they tend to spread out (almost every new statute in Slovenia, for example, has a 'violations' part at the end) and become quite difficult to keep track of. This jeopardises legal certainty by reducing the chances of the public being aware of the (full) law. Legal certainty is additionally debatable when violations are published only in the local language in some municipal document (excluding access to tourists, foreigners) or when cities are composed of several municipalities (as in the case of Brussels), each of them having its own incivility regime (Peršak 2014b).

Since the law of violations usually involves greater ease of enactment with scholars and media paying less attention to it, prohibiting certain conduct as a violation (instead of as a 'criminal offence') can often mean taking a shortcut. The law on violations can be in this way easily abused in the sense that the conduct which should not be proscribed at all can more easily find its way into the criminal law through being enacted under the law of violations. A political compromise can thus be achieved with the opponents of the criminalisation winning by keeping the offence out of the Criminal Code and the proponents by making it, nevertheless, 'criminal' in the broader sense.

The contents of social control: protection from negative emotional experiences and moralisation

From the more formal or criminalisation point of view, then, the two mentioned trends of criminalisation through the back door, as it were, are criminalisation via the civil law and criminalisation via the lower-level administrative-penal law. If we look more substantively, however, at the contents of what is being criminalised in both of these cases, another feature of today's social control of incivilities reveals itself – namely the penetration of offence, moralism and paternalism as grounds for criminalisation, and the underlying emotionalism of law.

The uncivil conduct in the UK is termed 'anti-social behaviour'. Crime in itself is, of course (by definition), anti-social, so what separates this new anti-social conduct from existing crime is the fact that this group hosts a variety of breaches of social convention, a variety of socially undesirable conduct, some of which has already been criminalised in one way or another (Burney 2006), the other of which, however, comprises minor violations of social norms, which were until recently seen as a normal by-product of society – particularly urban, plural society. They were regarded as conduct admittedly not particularly pleasant for everybody, yet nevertheless merely offensive, rather than harmful and therefore not a legitimate subject matter of criminalisation (and consequently punishment) in a modern liberal society.

In England and Wales, the anti-social behaviour covered by ASBOs, parenting orders and various other orders and injunctions under the Anti-Social Behaviour Act of 2003, and since 2014 by a whole new set of powers, comprises various conduct including littering, shouting, spitting, rowdy behaviour, writing graffiti, begging, just hanging about, etc. – anything basically that causes or is likely to cause alarm, distress or harassment to others or is capable of causing a nuisance or annoyance related to housing or occupation of residential premises.[10] The vague definition itself is highly problematic from the legality principle and legal certainty point of view, to say nothing of its highly subjective nature, which makes criminalisation dependent upon irrational judgements (Hewitt 2007, Cornford 2012, Peršak 2014b). However, if we just look at the content and some real cases of ASBOs (issued to a farmer for his pigs running amok, suicide attempts and so forth [West 2005]), we see how the net of social control has extended to cover and formally censure all sorts of behaviour which some people may regard as unusual, a deviation from normality. By criminalising, society or the state is now conveying the message that such conduct is reprehensible, morally wrong and therefore deserving of punishment.

In Slovenia, uncivil conduct is regulated mostly through the law on violations, adopted by the Parliament, although municipal ordinances can and have also been used to fine place-specific undesirable issues (for example, to prohibit the feeding of animals in the municipal roads and green spaces, which is, since 2015, prohibited in Ljubljana under a fine of 100 EUR). Violations (*prekrški*) are – like the German *Ordnungswidrigkeiten* – minor offences that together with criminal offences proper, encompassed in the Criminal Code, form the so-called criminal law in the broad sense (*lato sensu*). They comprise a variety of offences, from more administrative breaches of some law to more substantive, censure-worthy violations (Peršak 2014a), and are spread out through various statutes. They are, however, considered part of the criminal law, rather than administrative law. The Public Order and Peace Act[11] criminalises a variety of offences, such as violent behaviour, indecent conduct, causing noise, intrusive or insulting begging in a public place, the usage of dangerous objects, graffiti, vandalism, incitement of intolerance and so on. Article 7 ('indecent conduct'), more concretely para. 3, of this Act criminalises indecent exposure, intrusive offering of sexual services or having sexual intercourse in a public place, insofar as this conduct 'disturbs people, causes alarm or indignation'.[12] Looking first at the form, one can here observe the similarity in phrasing with the English definition of anti-social behaviour from the Crime and Disorder Act of 1998 (on which more later on). Looking at the content, we can see that the object of prohibition here is the 'indecent' or 'obscene' behaviour in the public that upsets others.

When people are criminalised for obscene conduct, directly or indirectly (i.e. even if it is done with the help of a public-order tag of 'alarming other people'), we can talk of *legal moralism* (Feinberg 1988). As opposed to the 'old' legal moralism criminalising violations of conventional social mores, the new legal moralism often disguises itself through the 'harm' speak. Camouflaged as argumentation based on the harm principle, moralism and moralisation – which, despite the weakened influence of traditional morality, has not declined (Waiton 2008) – can often go unnoticed, exposed only when one examines more closely the 'harm' invoked.[13] On the other hand, where people are criminalised for harming themselves or attempting to harm themselves (e.g. the case of an ASBO issued to a person who had attempted to commit suicide), we talk of *legal paternalism* (Feinberg 1986). Both criminalisation principles are ordinarily not (or not anymore) considered legitimate grounds for criminalisation in modern liberal[14] societies (Peršak 2007, Simester and von Hirsch 2011, Wohlers 2014). In addition, the harm principle is being stretched through the inclusion of risks as objects of criminalisation. In this way, very remote harms that would normally be excluded from criminalisation, owing to an insufficient causal link or broken causality chain, can be and are criminalised. The risk society (Beck 1992) or pre-crime society (Zedner 2009) not only focuses on future harms but also systematically tackles hazards and insecurities through pre-emptive criminalisation based on mere risk rather than harm, progressively elevating many preparatory acts to the level of self-standing criminal offences.[15]

Underlying social factors explaining incivilities criminalisation

Punitiveness (real or imagined, harvested by politicians)

One of the explanations offered for the increased criminalisation impulse is the change in public or political attitudes, which increasingly lean toward punitiveness

(Bottoms 1995, Garland 2001, Pratt 2007). Appealing for (more) criminalisation may be, and often is, interpreted as a punitive stance, since criminalisation is a repressive state intervention imposing limits to the individual's freedom of conduct. However, it must be noted that some distinguish calls for criminalisation from appeals for harsher punishment.[16] Almond (2008: 465), for example, believes that whereas appeals for harsher punishment – as a sign of thirst for vengeance – are the proper indicator of popular punitiveness, appeals for criminalisation may have to do more with the 'legal control of underlying social risks', not vengeance as such.

Punitiveness may have to do with personal traits of individuals, their intolerance and so forth. Public appeals for criminalisation seen through the above perspective (question of control rather than vengeance), however, can also be understood as a sort of defence mechanism such as 'displacement', where an unacceptable feeling or thought about a person, place or object is redirected towards a target that is safer or easier to attack. A person may channel his or her everyday ontological insecurities, anxieties and fears (be they related to economic, personal, psychological or social causes) that have no single, clearly distinguishable object to target, into fear of crime and consequently, as a means of regaining control, into appeals for punishment of 'the other'. Such reaction may be further stimulated by the socioeconomic system. Criminalising and punishing the poor, one group of the usual 'others', may be the neoliberal way of dealing with social insecurities by channelling them into the punitive management of the unprivileged (Wacquant 2009).

An additional, facilitating factor is that such appeals for punishment are media reinforced (as topics relating to crime attract viewers and readers), and politicians encourage it too. For the latter, it is an easier solution, a quick fix, as they seem to 'have done their job' even though, in reality, they have not. Complex social issues are difficult to solve and impossible to solve overnight. They require in-depth studies and the implementation of specific measures with a holistic approach on several levels, all of which require time and coordination of various services. As politicians usually seek re-election, they want to be perceived as having done their job, being productive and thus warranting re-election. Time-consuming tasks can affect the perceived productivity of some politician, whereas quick actions, such as submitting legislative proposals to amend the Criminal Code, may increase it. Secondly, as Loughlin notices in the case of human rights and politicians, '[p]oliticians [. . .], having become fixated on their media images, lack the confidence to promote specific measures which protect the rights of unpopular minorities; enacting general principles enables responsibility for such action to pass from legislature to judiciary' (in Gearty 2006: 80, 81). Criminalising certain behaviour, instead of thinking about the specific measures to tackle the fear of crime and crime itself, thus throws the ball into the judiciary's court, shifts the responsibility onto someone else.

However, it may also be that public punitiveness is imagined or asserted in order to further the political agenda of politicians. Tham (2012: 3) has, for example, noted that 'the public sentiment' is claimed to be the 'central factor in shaping legislation and criminal policy' in the Swedish government and yet that the results of the project of the Scandinavian Research Council for Criminology on the general sense of justice in the Scandinavian countries have been 'exactly the opposite of what the government is pressing in the public', as the research made it evident that the public did not demand harsher but rather milder punishments than those imposed under current law and practice. The possible disparity between what the public really wants and what the government claims (or perceives) that the public wants should not be therefore ignored or their overlap simply assumed and left unquestioned.

Fear of victimisation

The 'broken windows' thesis (Wilson and Kelling 1982) asserts that minor incivilities will eventually lead to more serious crime if left unaddressed. This thesis of the 'inextricable link' between crime and incivilities has been tested many times with no conclusive evidence (Matthews 1992). Sampson and Raudenbush have found the association between disorder and predatory crime to be 'spurious' and that it is the structural disadvantage and attenuated collective efficacy,[17] rather than disorder, that present the 'active ingredients' in crime (Sampson and Raudenbush 1999: 627, 638). What incivilities do seem to generate is the 'fear of crime', the subjective feeling of residents that they might be victimised by crime – a feeling that may have no real support in the actual crime figures. Hope and Hough (1988), examining the broken windows thesis, have found that the 'rates of perceived incivilities are more strongly related to levels of fear of crime ($p<.05$) and neighbourhood satisfaction ($p<.01$) than the level of victimization itself'. Fear of crime or incivilities-related feelings of insecurity have also been used to explain the adoption of anti-incivilities legislation – for example, in Belgium (Di Ronco and Peršak 2014, Vander Beken and Vendeviver 2014).

The research on the experience of incivilities and fear of crime or of victimisations, however, also revealed that different types of incivilities may have differential impact on emotional upset or stress. Maxfield (1987: 33) observed that the belief that 'drunks and tramps on the street' were common was 'more consistently related to worry and anxiety about personal safety than were the other incivilities and, interestingly, that in general the more incivilities were widespread, the less people worried about them or were anxious about their own safety. This should also make us aware of the importance of distinguishing between different types of incivilities – particularly perhaps between the two groups, i.e. physical incivilities (litter, graffiti etc.) and social incivilities (offensive behaviour).[18] The prevalence of one type in a particular country or city (or perception of such a prevalence) may lead to different results in terms of social effects, psychological responses and legal solutions to it.

The fear of crime may, as already indicated above, hide other issues and feelings behind it. Maxfield (1984) observed that the fear of crime appeared to be a function of vulnerability, perceived risk and levels of tolerance. Low levels of tolerance need not, however, translate into any fear. In the case of prostitution in Ghent, Belgium, for example, the residents who have been reported to be increasingly bothered with the (otherwise legal) prostitution in their neighbourhood have not reported any particular increased feeling of insecurity (Maesschalck 2014). In this case the reduction of tolerance could perhaps be explained with the reduced social solidarity with the prostitutes, since the nationality of the prostitutes has been changing: previously predominant Belgian prostitutes have been declining in numbers, while foreign prostitutes (who reportedly do not speak Dutch) have been moving in. The lack of communication may have thus increased the mistrust and the negative attitude towards the 'outsiders'. In times of economic hardship, moreover, reduced tolerance can also emanate from heightened anxiety related to individual or collective socio-economic troubles.

Issues of solidarity and trust

The concept of anomie or normlessness and the lack of normative integration as well as diversity and confusion about social norms in complex and diverse urban societies are often invoked when explaining the moral and social predicament of today (Turner 2006). While Durkheim (1951) was among those paving the way, many subsequent empirical studies confirmed that social isolation and low social integration importantly contribute to poor health, delinquency, crime, and depression (Turner 2006). Sociologists emphasise that trust is an important measure of social solidarity, a 'social dimension that underpins social relations' (Turner 2006: 221), and that a decline in trust – a function of eroded social capital (Putnam 2000) – can explain public outrage and individual anxieties or fears about offensive behaviour.

The lack of social cohesion among residents (and consequently of collective efficacy) makes people more sensitive to 'outsiders' and influences their perception of disorder (Sampson and Raudenbush 1999). For example, older people distrust the youth, especially those wearing hooded tops and congregating, hence they feel 'alarmed' and seek an ASBO to prohibit the young from 'hanging about'. With social solidarity breaking down and rising social mistrust, many of the informal mechanisms of social control do not seem to work or are simply not applied, leaving the state to 'fix' the problem through the use of the stick – more aggressively and progressively.

The less we trust each other and institutions, the weaker the state, the more we rely on formal, written rules, contracts and laws to punish those who violate our trust (Durkheim 1973, Nietzsche 1887, Garland 1996, Sparks 2000). While social, interpersonal trust as well as public trust in institutions, such as governments and the judiciary (Turner 2006, Eurobarometer 2013), are in decline, the public seems to increasingly trust the law to solve societal troubles. Considering the fact that no matter how much we criminalise them, many of the most heinous crimes, such as murder and rape, continue to exist and happen, the expressed belief in deterrence or faith in criminalisation cannot therefore arise out of performance-based confidence in the law's deterrent powers, but probably from people's deep-seated belief in the necessity of strict criminal law or their more general views regarding the proper scope, values and functions of criminal law.[19] If law is aligned with our moral beliefs or shares similar values as we, we seem to trust it, regardless of its effectiveness. While criminologists may gather evidence of the law's ineffectiveness, many people also seem to believe that the proper function of criminal law is also to *declare* something as inappropriate, wrong and serious, and that this declaration demands punishment as its corollary.[20] They seem to put great emphasis on what Sunstein (1996) termed the 'expressive function of law' – on the function of law in 'making statements' or denouncing certain conduct as reprehensible and blameworthy. In this perspective, it is not about deterring anyone but about sending a particular message, which in itself justifies criminalisation. When analysing this trust in (criminal) law and the rationale for it, we cannot therefore disregard the importance of symbolism and of the communicative dimension of the criminal law, where criminalisation is seen as an expression or statement on the reprehensibleness of a certain conduct.

Perhaps a similar logic of justice or trust in law to perform its functions could be found behind the Belgian adoption of the system of municipal administrative sanctions (GAS). One of the main reasons given for adopting the so-called GAS legislation, aiming to tackle incivilities, was the fact that law enforcement and prosecutors could not keep up with the increasing rates of small delinquency and therefore many of such minor violations remained unprocessed (*geseponeerd*). No penal sanction ensued. 'The main objective of the law on incivilities was to provide a quick reaction (fine) towards persistent disorder, so that a warning to behave more properly could be given on a regular basis' (Devroe 2012: 505).[21] On some accounts, the law was therefore seen as having the mandate to issue warnings or notices to people when they misbehaved, and its failing to do so regularly was seen as a shortcoming that had to be rectified.

Emotionalisation of law and policy

Looking at the substance of many an incivility prohibition and definition, particularly in the UK, criminalisation seems to be aimed at protecting people from experiencing negative, unpleasant emotions, such as distress, alarm and indignation. One's freedom to behave as one wishes as long as one does not harm anyone, one's right to harmlessly non-conform, is in this way limited for the sake of protecting (some) other people's negative emotions or emotional reactions to one's conduct.

Scholars who have written on the phenomenon of the emotionalisation of law notice that it had globally spread during the last two decades and changed the law and criminal justice system in many ways. Feelings of anger, disgust, vengeance, shame, revulsion and remorse have become perceived as 'valuable barometers of social morality' (Bandes 1999: 4) and have been reintroduced into legal procedures (Bandes 1999, Karstedt 2002, Weisman 2014). This 'affective turn' (Cromby et al. 2010) and re-emotionalisation in the penal sphere was made possible by changes in the public sphere, including the emotionalisation of the public discourse on crime, and in the pattern of emotional culture in late modern societies (Karstedt 2002). This trend enabled the spread of various restorative justice initiatives, of legal institutes such as 'victim impact statements' and the success of victim-named legislation. Karmen (2009) traces the roots of this turn towards emotions to the reappearance of the crime victim in the 1980s. The crime victim was then 'rediscovered' by elected officials who realised that proposing a new law named after a victim who had suffered terribly in an event that received high media coverage (and 'if it bleeds, it leads') would not only assist them in building support for the new law but also that 'few officeholders would dare to argue against the bill, lest they be branded "anti-victim"' (Karmen 2009: 35). There are proponents of such a development who see in it a bigger recognition of the victim within the criminal justice system (and thus increased procedural justice or even legitimacy of the latter) as well as those who see such an evolution as a perverted or 'misguided justice' (Salas 2012). Some claim that we live in a 'therapy culture' that is obsessed with confessing and discussing personal stories, emotions and problems, often quite publicly (Furedi 2004); others stress that in this 'age of sentiment professing emotion is more important than feeling, let alone acting, on it' (Richardson 2015: n.p.).

This contemporary social psychological setting can also help explain the willingness and ease with which incivilities, when they are defined as causing negative emotions in the victim, are being criminalised. Before we move from the descriptive to the normative realm, however, some further questions need to be answered. Bringing emotions back involves profound problems that go beyond the mere instrumental use of emotions in criminal justice, or a restricted perspective of 'what works'. The crucial question is whether the protection of some elusive, subjective emotional sensitivities of people lies within the proper scope of law. Violations of our values (morality) do stimulate our feelings of discomfort, anger, sadness, pain and so forth. However, triggered emotional responses are not yet normative, moral principles upon which criminalisation should proceed. When criminalising on the basis of emotional responses rather than some established rational principles of criminalisation, it is worth considering whether what we 'feel' is (a) based on some moral principle/value, (b) shared by many, (c) reasonable and (d) worth upholding. If so, which emotions should be endorsed through criminal law and to what extent? Disgust or resentment may not be equally deserving of protection as, for example, fear (Bottoms 2006, Husak 2006, Peršak 2014b). Questions of responsibility – e.g. can the offender be aware of stimulating such emotions, is he intentionally doing so, could he be expected to desist? – would need to be considered. Furthermore, additional reasons for or against criminalisation should be taken into account on the legislative plane. Even if some negative emotional states or reactions are to be deemed legitimate grounds for criminalisation under certain conditions, there are other filters through which a proposed piece of legislation should pass before it truly qualifies for criminalisation (Schonsheck 1994), such as, for example, the likelihood of success in preventing such behaviour. If the likelihood is too small to pass through the filter, criminalisation is not justified.

Globalisation of criminal policy: policy transfer

In 1992, Matthews noted a certain 'Americanisation' of British social policy, which involves the 'developments of a "safety net" state and the widening of economic inequalities, together with the encouragement of competitive individualism and acquisitiveness', which was seen as a problem, since the two countries are not really comparable in their types of crime (Matthews 1992: 33). More recently, the then president of the European Society of Criminology (ESC) in his April introduction to the ESC Newsletter stated that we (referring to the European criminologists or ESC members) tend to draw a lot from American criminology: '[W]e cannot deny that most of our contemporary theories stem from US criminologists and most of the empirical tests of these theories are carried out by US criminologists using samples of US adolescents and published in US journals' (Bruinsma 2015: 4).

Is it possible that not only criminologists but also our legislators and policymakers similarly follow the trends they observe in other Western jurisdictions? Is it possible that the European legislator would adopt punitive laws, similar to those in the US or UK, even though the reality or prevalence of certain undesirable social conduct is not comparable to the situation in that Western jurisdiction from which the legal solution for it is copied? Can 'getting tough on crime', for example, be an appealing election strategy other politicians may copy, despite crime not being a topical issue or problem in their respective countries? In the area of criminological research, one can observe a proliferation of certain 'hot' criminological topics over the years, be it terrorism, the security vs. liberty debate or more recent concerns with procedural justice and with 'radicalisation'. Engaging with such issues may increase a researcher's visibility, publishability and chances of funding (especially in the international and EU context). It is not inconceivable, therefore, that politicians might fall prey to such external considerations as well, particularly when they reap positive results. Furthermore, the globalisation of criminal policy or of 'world threat politics' (Beck 2009) is fuelled by the idea that the whole world is at risk and the premise that no nation can cope with various problems alone (Beck 2009). Once we see the world as one global risk society with interwoven threats, the uncritical adoption or transplantation of 'solutions' to those risks becomes rather understandable – even more so if Tonry's (2015: 507) practical observation that 'most people assume that practices and institutions in their society are typical of those elsewhere' holds true.

Emulation may stem from a genuine belief on the part of policymakers that they are simply adopting 'best practices' as developed elsewhere, premised on the assumption (which on a closer inspection may or may not be correct) that the 'facts' or situation on the ground is in their case similar to the situation in the country whose practices they are adopting. The adoption of the wording in Article 7 of the Slovenian Public Order and Peace Act does not by accident resemble the English definition of anti-social behaviour, specifically its 'alarm, distress or harassment' element. Recent communication with the Ministry of Justice official who had been involved in amending the Act has revealed that he had intentionally looked at the phrasing of anti-social behaviour in order to incorporate it into Art. 7, para. 3, which now prohibits indecent exposure, intrusive offering of sexual services or having sexual intercourse in a public place, insofar as this conduct 'disturbs people, causes alarm or indignation'.[22]

Place- or context-specific explanations

Sometimes, however, the characteristics of incivility regulation or the differences between how one country (or one city) regulates incivilities compared with another can be explained by place-specific considerations. While risk society, culture of control, populist punitiveness and similar concepts are very ready-to-use and are quickly resorted to by those seeking to explain the increasing widening of the net of social control, including through the punitive regulation of incivilities, it may be the case that the main, or at least important partial, explanation for the particular national or local policy towards incivilities is driven rather by place-specific concerns. Local particularities, traditions, idiosyncrasies, the local political setting and policy, degree of commercialisation,[23] spatial distribution and pragmatic concerns, to name a few, can provide important contextual data for the development of a fuller picture (or theory) of incivility regulation. In the case of Belgium, as already mentioned above, the municipal legislation against incivilities grew also out of a pragmatic need to help tackle small delinquency that law enforcement and prosecutors just could not keep up with.

These place-specific or context-specific issues are often more difficult to detect, particularly from the outside. Those who do not live in a community whose laws and policies are being studied may be oblivious to many cultural factors and traditions. Insiders, however, may suffer from different blind spots and biases, such as the social desirability bias (fuelling the neglect of certain less flattering characteristics of the local policy and its proponents) or confirmation bias (driven by the desire to find the similarity or dissimilarity with the prevailing Western policy explanation models).

Conclusion: some consequences and considerations for the regulatory exercise

In the preceding text, I first tried to provide a picture of the most common forms and substance of laws dealing with incivilities. Next, I tried to flesh out some of the most important or most often mentioned explanations for the current 'civilising offensive', which tackles all sorts of socially unpleasant – harmful as well as harmless – conduct. Criminalisation, understood in the broad sense, seems to have become not the last resort but rather the first line of state intervention against those who deviate from what the mainstream deems 'acceptable' or 'normal'. However, treating the Criminal Code as an all-encompassing moral code, where everything deemed 'inappropriate' is considered valid material for criminalisation, comes with certain negative consequences.

Legal consequences of this often include the sacrifice of some fundamental criminal law principles, such as those of the last resort, of legality, of legal certainty and of harm (Peršak 2014b). The harm principle is weakened, as everything that offends some people (and almost anything can offend some people) – whether it is truly 'offensive' or not (Duff and Marshall 2006, Simester and von Hirsch 2006) – can be prohibited under the threat of punishment. *Societal* costs include diminished human rights, since the criminalising of any deviant behaviour (deviant as in deviating from the norm), albeit harmless,[24] also criminalises certain differences and diversity in society, which have been celebrated by Gearty (2006: 6) as the positive or 'upbeat' side of human rights. As people seem to be progressively offended even by styles of clothing – for example, many shopping centres across the UK have banned youngsters from wearing 'hoodies' – the space of individual autonomy and freedom is reduced. This erosion of the right to harmlessly non-conform can quash difference but also creativity – which is per definition a deviance from what is considered 'the norm'. In this respect, human rights themselves – particularly that part or those rights that promote 'human flourishing' – are being restricted. The same applies to children's right to play and, through play, engage in certain risks as part of growing up. When even such usual children's activities as throwing snowballs and climbing trees are prohibited,[25] a child's right to leisure, play and engagement in a wide range of recreational activities – as stipulated, for example, in Art. 31 of the Convention on the Rights of the Child – seems unjustifiably curtailed.

An additional, particularly worrying societal effect is that this sort of legislation often disproportionately targets the poor, young or ethnic minorities. Regulation against incivilities provides a new vent for all sorts of phobias and negative social isms. By labelling conduct of 'problematic' groups as 'anti-social', the powerful mainstream can legitimise their repressive actions towards them through a more politically correct overcoat.

Furthermore, not only is this trend socially and legally challenged, it may also be quite ineffective, even counterproductive. The reduction of the individual's area of freedom and the perceptions of illegitimate moralistic and paternalistic state interventions can breed resentment towards such a legal system. This in turn can lead to the reduction of trust in and respect for it and consequently to legal defiance. In this light the hegemonic pressure to conform is actually criminogenic – it can be considered as a structural 'strain' to which some may respond by rebelling, retreating or criminally innovating around the means to achieve the goals (Merton 1938).

Drawing on the above-discussed tentative explanations behind the criminalisation of incivilities, I wish to conclude with some possible considerations and suggestions for evidence-based policymaking and legislation. For an informed regulatory enterprise, which is necessarily normative, it would be, first, useful to evaluate and give proper weight to the most common explanatory factors. The ones mentioned above include punitiveness, fear of victimisation, (mis)trust, emotionalisation of criminal policy, global policy transfer and place-specific concerns, but there may be others. Not all of these factors probably deserve equal treatment or should be given equal weight. The weighing may vary from country to country, depending on the country's prevailing values, criminal law principles and policy goals; however, assuming that some baseline of rationality of lawmaking and policymaking exists everywhere, the differences might not be very big. In the next step, it might be useful to try to create an explanatory model that would include the mentioned (and perhaps some additional or more precise and statistically testable) variables, which could explain what percentage of a certain country or community attitude towards incivilities can be attributed to a particular variable. This model, or importance of various explanatory variables, could of course also vary from place to place, from community to community as well as through time. On the basis of this outcome, combined with the weights given to a particular factor (outcome of the first exercise),[26] legislators or policymakers (be they national, local or supranational) would be in a better position to decide whether they should do something about the issue or not in terms of adopting or modifying laws and regulations. If, for example, fear of victimisation through incivilities features prominently in the explanatory model, but – when broken down – turns out to be driven mostly by negative attitudes, such as intolerance or xenophobia, the legislator would be right to ignore it (give it a lower or zero weight) and not criminalise the conduct that upsets the residents on this basis.

In a wider social and policy sense, however, such a finding should never be ignored. Intolerance, racism, xenophobia and similar concerns are important social issues, with known damaging consequences, that policy should confront and tackle head on. Even if the legislator would be right not to legislate on the basis of the illegitimacy of claims for criminalisation, the illegitimacy of such claims should still act as a wake-up call for the government, NGOs and civil society to raise their awareness campaigns and address this issue. On the other hand, what is equally important is to be aware that cultural norms and personal sensibilities or notions of civility differ in place and time and that clamping down on any type of minor 'disorder' can do more harm than good. What Stein stressed more than half a century ago still (or even more so) holds today: 'The price of maintaining a society that encourages cultural differentiation and experimentation is unquestionably the acceptance of a certain amount of disorganisation on both the individual and social level' (Stein 1960: 19).

Notes

1 Burney (2006), for example, mentions the case of a Glaswegian who was convicted of assault by spitting and several football players who were severely fined or even issued a police warning for spitting at others.
2 Powell (2013) notes that the concept has been recently used in the UK as an attempt to understand contemporary government attempts at modifying the behaviour of particular problematic parts of the population.
3 Such interventions, however, differ in the audience they (primarily) target and in the degree of hostility. Although many can be considered inhumane, some situational solutions can also be quite harmless and even humorous. The city of Hamburg, for example, decided to paint some façades in the busy St. Pauli nightclub district with a special, hydrophobic paint that resists water and even deflects it. The buildings, if urinated on, would thus 'take revenge' by deflecting the urine right back onto the shoes of the uncivil passerby (Noack 2015).
4 This explains why the 'harm principle' is the most widely accepted principle of criminalisation (see e.g. Mill 1849, Feinberg 1984, Peršak 2007, Simester and von Hirsch 2011).

5 The 'broken windows theory' (Wilson and Kelling 1982) links disorder and incivilities with more serious crime by asserting that small crimes such as vandalism, public drinking, litter and so on can attract bigger or more severe crimes if they are not checked and quickly eliminated. Serious crime is thus seen as emanating from disorder.

6 See Chapters 3 (on the regulation of incivilities in Italy), 5 (on Hungary), 6 (on Belgium) and 9 (on the Netherlands) in this volume.

7 The new Anti-Social Behaviour, Crime and Policing Act of 2014 replaced the ASBO with an injunction (a civil offence) and a criminal behaviour order.

8 The procedure to obtain an ASBO could be initiated by the police or by the local authority, who had to prove to the civil standard (a balance of probabilities), which is lower than the criminal standard (the 2002 House of Lords judgement *McCann*, however, raised the required standard of proof in the ASBO cases to that required in the criminal procedure), that the defendant had acted 'in a manner that caused or was likely to cause harassment, alarm or distress to one or more persons not of the same household as himself'. This very broad and vague definition encapsulates everything from hanging about to littering, graffiti and noisy neighbours. An ASBO prohibited a person from 'doing anything described in the order', usually from accessing certain places or certain behaviour, for a minimum of two years. There was, however, no maximum: these orders could last indefinitely. If the offender breached the order without reasonable excuse, he or she was liable to conviction of an offence for which the maximum penalty was five years' imprisonment (Ashworth 2000). The order could be issued to a child of at least 10 years of age. See more in Burney (2002), Campbell (2002), West (2005). Although the basic concept of an ASBO was the same across the Great Britain, there were some notable differences among jurisdictions. In Scotland, local authorities were the lead agencies in seeking ASBOs while the police played more of a supportive role. Until October 2004, ASBOs against young people could not be sought in Scotland, only in England and Wales. There was also a difference in terms of the ASBO application process and the consequences of an ASBO breach for 12- to 15-year-olds, and other nuances in the application (DTZ and Heriot-Watt University 2007). The new Anti-Social Behaviour, Crime and Policing Act of 2014 grants further powers to tackle ASB, such as criminal behaviour orders, police dispersal powers, community protection notices, public spaces protection orders, closure powers and absolute ground for possession (Police.UK 2014).

9 In addition to civil ASBOs, the jurisdiction has also known CRASBOs (or criminal ASBOs), i.e. anti-social behaviour orders on conviction. Owing to its clearer double nature or mixed character, we shall henceforth focus solely on ASBOs.

10 This catch-all concept of 'harassment, alarm or distress' was first introduced in the Public Order Act of 1986 (Burney 2006: 201). The new Anti-Social Behaviour, Crime and Policing Act of 2014, however, widens the definition by describing anti-social behaviour in Part I, Section 2, para. 1, as '(a) conduct that has caused, or is likely to cause, harassment, alarm or distress to any person, (b) conduct capable of causing nuisance or annoyance to a person in relation to that person's occupation of residential premises, or (c) conduct capable of causing housing-related nuisance or annoyance to any person'. The previous definition in the Crime and Disorder Act of 1998 included only the conduct that is now encompassed under (a) and was limited only to conduct that was directed towards 'one or more persons not part of the same household', while the current definition extends it to 'any person'.

11 Zakon o varstvu javnega reda in miru (ZJRM-1), Official Journal of the Republic of Slovenia, no. 70/2006; in force since 21 July 2007.

12 *'v kolikor slednje koga moti, povzroči vznemirjenje ali zgražanje ljudi'*. For such conduct, which clearly depends on the subjective perception and emotional experience of passersby, a fine of 50,000 to 100,000 (then) tolars, which amounts to approximately 200 to 400 EUR, is envisaged. All these acts are considered types of 'indecent

behaviour', which is statutorily defined as 'individual or group behaviour which causes alarm, agitation or threatens other individuals or a group, or when with insulting words harms the reputation of an individual or a group or an official in their official business' (*s katerim povzroči vznemirjenje ali razburjenje ali ogrožanje posameznika ali skupine ali kadar z žaljivimi besedami in dejanji škoduje ugledu posameznika ali skupine ali uradne osebe pri uradnem poslovanju*) (Art. 2, point 5 of ZJRM-1).

13 An example of such deconstruction in the case of prostitution can be found in Peršak (2014c: 208–212).

14 'Liberal' here is meant in the classic, Mill's sense; liberal as in valuing the individual's freedom and self-determination.

15 A recent criminal law conference especially stressed this phenomenon in the area of information and communications technology and cyberspace interests (Tosza 2014).

16 'In this sense, the underlying dynamics of public attitudes are more proactive than populist punitive accounts usually allow for; they may reflect an "appetite for blame" (Baldwin 2004: 382), but this blame translates into something other than a demand for vengeance' (Almond 2008: 465).

17 They defined collective efficacy as 'the fusion of social cohesion with shared expectations for the active control of public space' (Sampson and Raudenbush 1999: 637).

18 A similar distinction is drawn by Sampson and Raudenbush (1999), who distinguish between social disorder (threatening behaviour by mostly strangers) and physical disorder (deterioration of urban landscapes). The London Metropolitan Police makes further distinction within social disorder, splitting anti-social behaviour into three groups: personal (targeting the individual or a group), nuisance (targeting the community) and environmental (targeting the wider environment, public spaces, buildings) (Metropolitan Police 2015).

19 Some conceptually distinguish between trust and confidence. Trust is said to be based on value similarity (trust is founded upon the perception that salient values are held in common), whereas confidence is based on performance (Siegrist et al. in Breakwell 2007).

20 When a group of third-year university students (of the Faculty of Criminal Justice and Security, University of Maribor, Slovenia in 2009; $n = 65$) were asked, for example, whether the criminalisation (specifically of hate speech) was justified or not, the content analysis of their arguments revealed that they expected the law to punish those who deserved it (69.6 per cent out of those who argued for criminalisation and provided arguments for it), to prevent crime (36.3 per cent), but also to (merely or primarily) declaratorily condemn certain conduct (12.3 per cent). The latter group reasoned that the law ought to punish the perpetrators of such conduct because this conveyed an authoritative message on the part of society that such acts were not acceptable and would not be tolerated.

21 This also leads Devroe to conclude that one cannot speak of the 'swelling culture of control' (as suggested by Garland in the case of the UK) in Belgium. And yet, this seemingly pragmatic motivation for the inception of the Belgian regulation on incivilities does not seem that far from the official justification for the British expansion of anti-ASB powers. In an interview in 2006, the Home Secretary, Charles Clarke, explained that the reason for a lot of new powers was the lack of confidence in court procedures, especially their slowness: 'going through the regular court procedures [. . .] was actually happening seven or eight months later. So there was actually no impact. [. . .] [P]eople gave up referring things to the courts, the police themselves gave up. [. . .] But [now] the courts can solve this by taking their decisions quickly' (in Crawford 2013: 184).

22 Personal communication with the ministry official, who also revealed that their intention or goal behind this 'transfer' was to find a way to narrow the scope of the prohibition, so that not all indecent public sexual behaviour was to be criminalised.

23 Neoliberalism or market demands and economic considerations may be a place-specific issue; however, in view of their impact on many (or most) of today's cities or local communities, they may perhaps deserve a separate entry – as a self-standing factor.

24 Harmless in the sense of not satisfying the conditions for criminalisation under the harm principle.

25 These are real cases of some prohibited incivilities in Belgium. For example, in Sint-Niklaas one is only allowed to climb trees in children-friendly public spaces, while throwing snowballs has been penalised in Antwerp (De Redactie 2013, De Standaard 2014).

26 The steps could probably just as well be reversed with the descriptive exercise coming first, followed by the normative evaluation of the factors or explanations, resulting from the first exercise. However, having the normative evaluation first probably diminishes the risk of a biased weighing exercise, which might happen quite inadvertently once the legislator or policymaker has the knowledge on the main reasons in support of the criminalisation of incivilities.

References

Almond, P. (2008) 'Public perceptions of work-related fatality cases: Reaching the outer limits of "populist punitiveness" ', *British Journal of Criminology*, 48: 448–467.

Ashworth, A. (2000) 'Is the criminal law a lost cause?', *Law Quarterly Review*, 16: 252–253.

Baldwin, R. (2004) 'The New Punitive Regulation', *Modern Law Review*, 67(3): 351–383.

Bandes, S. A. (1999) 'Introduction', in S. Bandes (ed.) *The Passions of Law*, New York: New York University Press.

Beck, U. (1992) *Risk Society: Towards a New Modernity*, London: Sage.

Beck, U. (2009) *World at Risk*, Cambridge, Malden: Polity Press.

Bottoms, A. (1995) 'The philosophy and politics of punishment and sentencing', in C.M.V. Clarkson and R. Morgan (eds.) *The Politics of Sentencing Reform*, Oxford: Clarendon Press.

Bottoms, A. (2006) 'Incivilities, offence and social order in residential communities', in A. von Hirsch and A. P. Simester (eds.) *Incivilities: Regulating Offensive Behaviour*, Oxford: Hart Publishing.

Breakwell, G. M. (2007) *The Psychology of Risk*, Cambridge: Cambridge University Press.

Bruinsma, G. (2015) 'Epistemological questions in criminology we cannot ignore', *Criminology in Europe (ESC Newsletter)*, 14(1): 2–4.

Budd, T. and Sims, L. (2001) *Antisocial Behaviour and Disorder: Findings from the 2000 British Crime Survey* (Home Office Research Findings No 145), London: Home Office.

Burney, E. (2002) 'Talking tough, acting coy: What happened to the anti-social behaviour order?', *The Howard Journal of Crime and Justice*, 41(5): 469–484.

Burney, E. (2005) *Making People Behave: Anti-Social Behaviour, Politics and Policy*, Devon: Willan Publishing.

Burney, E. (2006) ' "No spitting": Regulation of offensive behaviour in England and Wales', in A. von Hirsch and A. P. Simester (eds.) *Incivilities: Regulating Offensive Behaviour*, Oxford: Hart Publishing.

Campbell, S. (2002) *Implementing Anti-Social Behaviour Orders: Message for Practitioners (Findings 160)*, London: Home Office.

Cohen, S. (1985) *Visions of Social Control*, Cambridge: Polity Press.

Cornford, A. (2012) 'Criminalising anti-social behavior', *Criminal Law and Philosophy*, 6(1): 1–19.

Crawford, A. (2013) '"Sticks and carrots . . . and sermons": Some thoughts on compliance and legitimacy in the regulation of youth anti-social behaviour', in A. Crawford and A. Hucklesby (eds.) *Legitimacy and Compliance in Criminal Justice*, New York, London: Routledge.

Cromby, J., Brown, S. D., Gross, H., Locke, A. and Patterson, A. E. (2010) 'Constructing crime, enacting morality: Emotion, crime and anti-social behaviour in an inner-city community', *British Journal of Criminology*, 50(5): 873–895.

Deflem, M. (2008) *Sociology of Law: Visions of a Scholarly Tradition*, Cambridge: Cambridge University Press.

De Redactie (2013) 'Sneeuwballengevecht tegen GAS-boetes Antwerpen', *DeRedactie.be*, 26 January 2013. Online. Available at: http://deredactie.be/cm/vrtnieuws/regio/antwerpen/1.1534164 (accessed 10 September 2015).

De Standaard (2014) 'Satirische website steekt de draak met GAS-boetes', *De Standaard*, 10 May 2014. Online. Available at: www.standaard.be/cnt/dmf20140510_008 (accessed 10 September 2015).

Devroe, E. (2012) *A Swelling Culture of Control? De genese en toepassing van de wet op de gemeenteljike administratieve sancties in België*, Antwerp, Apeldoorn: Maklu.

Di Ronco, A. and Peršak, N. (2014) 'Regulation of incivilities in the UK, Italy and Belgium: Courts as potential safeguards against legislative vagueness and excessive use of penalising powers?', *International Journal of Law, Crime and Justice*, 42(4): 340–365.

DTZ and Heriot-Watt University (2007) *Use of Antisocial Behaviour Orders in Scotland*, Edinburgh: Scottish Government Social Research. Online. Available at: www.gov.scot/Resource/Doc/198276/0053019.pdf (accessed 20 August 2015).

Duff, R. A. and Marshall, S. E. (2006) 'How offensive can you get?', in A. von Hirsch and A. P. Simester (eds.) *Incivilities: Regulating Offensive Behaviour*, Oxford: Hart Publishing.

Durkheim, E. (1951) *Suicide. A Study in Sociology*, Glencoe, IL: Free Press.

Durkheim, E. (1973) *Moral Education*, New York: Free Press.

Durkheim, E. (1984, orig. 1893) *The Division of Labour in Society*, Basingstoke: Palgrave Macmillan.

Edwards, A. and Hughes, G. (2005) 'The governance of safety in Europe: Special issue of the journal Theoretical Criminology'. Online. Available at: www.esc-eurocrim.org/files/governance_of_safety_in_europe.doc (accessed 25 May 2010).

Elias, N. (2000, orig. 1994) *The Civilizing Process*. Revised ed., Oxford, Malden: Blackwell Publishing.

Eurobarometer (2013) *Flash Eurobarometer 385: Justice in the EU*, Nov. 2013. Online. Available at: http://ec.europa.eu/public_opinion/flash/fl_385_en.pdf (accessed 6 June 2015).

Feinberg, J. (1984) *Harm to Others – The Moral Limits of the Criminal Law*, New York, Oxford: Oxford University Press.

Feinberg, J. (1986) *Harm to Self – The Moral Limits of the Criminal Law*, New York, Oxford: Oxford University Press.

Feinberg, J. (1988) *Harmless Wrongdoing – The Moral Limits of the Criminal Law*, New York, Oxford: Oxford University Press.

Furedi, F. (2004) *Therapy Culture: Cultivating Vulnerability in an Uncertain Age*, London, New York: Routledge.

Garland, D. (1996) 'The limits of the sovereign state: Strategies of crime control in contemporary society', *British Journal of Criminology*, 36(4): 445–471.

Garland, D. (2001) *The Culture of Control: Crime and Social Order in Contemporary Society*, Oxford: Oxford University Press.

Gearty, C. (2006) *Can Human Rights Survive?*, Cambridge: Cambridge University Press.
Hewitt, D. (2007) 'Bovvered? A legal perspective on the ASBO', *Journal of Forensic and Legal Medicine*, 14(6): 355–363.
Hope, T. and Hough, M. (1988) 'Area crime and incivility: A profile from the British Crime Survey', in T. Hope and M. Shaw (eds.) *Communities and Crime Reduction*, London: HMSO.
Husak, D. (2006) 'Disgust: Metaphysical and empirical speculations', in A. von Hirsch and A. P. Simester (eds.) *Incivilities: Regulating Offensive Behaviour*, Oxford: Hart Publishing.
Karmen, A. (2009) *Crime Victims: Introduction to Victimology*, Belmont, CA: Wadsworth Cengage Learning.
Karstedt, S. (2002) Emotions and criminal justice, *Theoretical Criminology*, 6(3): 299–317.
Maesschalck, S. (2014) 'Overlast in de prostitutuebuurt Gent 'Zuid': Een beleids – en buurtperspectief', master thesis, Ghent University.
Matthews, R. (1992) 'Replacing "broken windows": Crime, incivilities and urban change', in R. Matthews and J. Young (eds.) *Issues in Realist Criminology*, London: Sage Publications. Online. Available at: http://rogermatthews.net/images/papers/replacing_broken_windows.pdf (accessed 14 August 2015).
Maxfield, M. (1987) *Explaining Fear of Crime: Evidence from the 1984 British Crime Survey*, London: Home Office Research and Planning Unit.
Merton, R. K. (1938) 'Social structure and anomie', *American Sociological Review*, 3(5): 672–682.
Metropolitan Police (2015) 'What is anti-social behaviour?' Online. Available at: http://content.met.police.uk/Article/What-is-antisocial-behaviour/1400022084553/1400022084553 (accessed 5 September 2015).
Mill, J. S. (1991, orig. 1849) *On Liberty and Other Essays*, Oxford: Oxford University Press.
Mitzman, A. (1987) 'The civilizing offensive: Mentalities, high culture and individual psyches', *Journal of Social History*, 20(4): 663–687.
Nietzsche, F. (2006, orig. 1887) *On the Genealogy of Morality*, Cambridge: Cambridge University Press.
Noack, R. (2015) 'When peeing in public in this German city, beware walls that pee back', *Washington Post*, 12 March 2015. Online. Available at: www.washingtonpost.com/news/worldviews/wp/2015/03/12/when-peeing.in-public-in-tis-german-city-beware-walls-that-pee-back (accessed 20 September 2015).
Peršak, N. (2007) *Criminalising Harmful Conduct: Harm Principle, Its Limits and Continental Counterparts*, New York: Springer.
Peršak, N. (2014a) 'Paternalistic interventions through the law on violations', in M. Ulväng and I. Cameron (eds.) *Essays on Criminalisation & Sanctions*, Uppsala: Iustus Forlag.
Peršak, N. (2014b) 'Norms, harms and disorder at the border: The legitimacy of criminal law intervention through the lens of criminalisation theory', in N. Peršak (ed.) *Legitimacy and Trust in Criminal Law, Policy and Justice: Norms, Procedures, Outcomes*, Farnham, Burlington: Ashgate.
Peršak, N. (2014c) 'The framing of prostitution and victimhood and violence for criminalisation purposes', in N. Peršak and G. Vermeulen (eds.) *Reframing Prostitution: From Discourse to Description, from Moralisation to Normalisation?*, Antwerp, Apeldoorn, Portland: Maklu.

Police.UK (2014) 'New anti-social behaviour powers came into effect'. Online. Available at: www.police.uk/news/new-anti-social-behaviour-powers-come-effect/ (accessed 10 June 2015).

Powell, R. (2013) 'The theoretical concept of the "Civilising Offensive" (Beschavingsoffensief): Notes on its origins and uses', *Human Figurations*, 2(2). Online. Available at: http://hdl.handle.net/2027/spo.11217607.0002.203 (accessed 5 March 2015).

Putnam, R. D. (2000) *Bowling Alone. The Collapse and Revival of American Community*, New York: Simon & Schuster.

Pratt, J. (2007) *Penal Populism*, London: Routledge.

Richardson, J. (2015) 'Hi . . . hey . . . hello . . . Dear reader, how do you start an email?', *The Guardian*, 24 August 2015. Online. Available at: www.theguardian.com/media/mind-your-language/2015/24/hi-hey-hello-dear-reader-how-do-you-start-an-email?CMP=share_btn_link (accessed 24 August 2015).

Roberts, P. (2006) 'Penal offence in question: Some reference points for interdisciplinary conversation', in A. von Hirsch and A. P. Simester (eds.) *Incivilities: Regulating Offensive Behaviour*, Oxford: Hart Publishing.

Roxin, C. (2005) *Strafrecht. Allgemeiner Teil, Band I. Grundlagen*, München: Beck.

Salas, D. (2012) *La Justice dévoyée. Critique des utopies sécuritaires*, Paris: Les Arènes.

Sampson, R. J. and Raudenbush, S. W. (1999) 'Systematic social observation of public spaces: A new look at disorder in urban neighborhoods', *American Journal of Sociology*, 105(3): 603–651.

Schonsheck, J. (1994) *On Criminalization: An Essay in the Philosophy of the Criminal Law*, Dordrecht, Boston, London: Kluwer.

Simester, A. P. and von Hirsch, A. (2006) 'Penalising offensive behaviour: Constitutive and mediating principles', in A. von Hirsch and A. P. Simester (eds.) *Incivilities: Regulating Offensive Behaviour*, Oxford: Hart Publishing.

Simester, A. P. and von Hirsch, A. (2011) *Crimes, Harms, and Wrongs: On the Principles of Criminalisation*, Oxford: Hart Publishing.

Sparks, R. (2000) 'Perspectives on risk and penal politics', in T. Hope and R. Sparks (eds.) *Crime, Risk and Insecurity*, London: Routledge.

Squires, P. and Stephen, D. E. (2005) *Rougher Justice: Anti-Social Behaviour and Young People*, Devon, Portland: Willan Publishing.

Stein, M. R. (1960) *The Eclipse of Community: An Interpretation of American Studies*, Princeton, NJ: Princeton University Press.

Sunstein, C. R. (1996) 'On the expressive function of law', *University of Pennsylvania Law Review*, 144(5): 2021–2053.

Šelih, A. (2003) 'Ustavnost prekrškov', in *IX. dnevi javnega* prava (Portorož, 18–20 June 2003), Ljubljana: Inštitut za javno upravo.

Tham, H. (2012) 'The arrogance of power – a Swedish example', *Criminology in Europe (ESC newsletter)*, 13(1): 2–3.

Tonry, M. (2015) 'Is cross-national and comparative research on the criminal justice system useful?', *European Journal of Criminology*, 12(4): 505–516.

Tosza, S. (2014) 'Minutes of the XIX. congress of AIDP (Information society and penal law) – Section I', *La Revue Internationale de Droit Pénal*, 85(3–4): 565–580.

Turner, B. S. (2006) 'Social capital, trust and offensive behaviour', in A. von Hirsch and A. P. Simester (eds.) *Incivilities: Regulating Offensive Behaviour*, Oxford: Hart Publishing.

Vander Beken, T. and Vendeviver, Ch. (2014) 'When things get serious: Reflections on the legitimacy of local administrative sanctions in Belgium', in N. Peršak (ed.) *Legitimacy and Trust in Criminal Law, Policy and Justice: Norms, Procedures, Outcomes*, Farnham, Burlington: Ashgate.

Wacquant, L. (2009) *Punishing the Poor: The Neoliberal Government of Social Insecurity*, Durham, NC: Duke University Press.

Waiton, S. (2008) *The Politics of Antisocial Behaviour*, London, New York: Routledge.

Weisman, R. (2014) *Showing Remorse*, Farnham, Burlington: Ashgate.

West, E. (2005) *A Little Book of ASBOs: Asbolent Behaviour from Around the Country*, Cheam, Surrey: Crombie Jardine.

Wilson, J. Q. and Kelling, G. (1982) 'Broken windows: The police and neighbourhood safety', *Atlantic Monthly*, 249(3): 29–38. Online. Available at: www.manhattan-institute.org/pdf/_atlantic_monthly-broken_windows.pdf (accessed 15 June 2015).

Wohlers, W. (2014) 'Criminal liability for offensive behaviour in public spaces', in A. P. Simester, A. du Bois-Pedain and U. Neumann (eds.) *Liberal Criminal Theory: Essays for Andreas von Hirsch*, Oxford: Hart Publishing.

Zedner, L. (2009) *Security*, London: Routledge.

3 The top-down instruments for governing crime and disorder

What lessons can be drawn from the Italian experience (2007–2011)?

Marco Calaresu

Introduction

The literature generally describes 'incivilities' as a deterioration of the shared rules of civil harmony, the violation of standards of care and maintenance of urban environments and shared public urban spaces (Wilson 1968), the neglect of the territory (Taylor 2002) or a series of anti-social behaviours (ASBs) or signs that bear witness to urban disorder (Skogan 1990). Nevertheless, as Di Ronco and Peršak (2014: 341) stated, defining incivilities is 'very problematic' and 'controversial'. For what is defined as anti-social or uncivilised can change over time and in space, depending on both social and individual 'aesthetic expectations' (Millie 2008), and is often self-bestowed by majorities (Millie 2011). From time to time, then, the reference to the regulation and social control of incivilities may come under the label of policies fighting crime and micro-criminality, 'soft crimes' or 'borderline criminalities' (Molotch and McClain 2003), such as begging, youth gangs, windscreen washing, illegal street vending, prostitution, vandalism, improper use of public space, vagrancy, modest use of drugs and being drunk and disorderly. In Italy, the typical incivilities targeted by instruments for governing crime and disorder (such as security pacts and administrative orders) include consumption of alcoholic beverages, prostitution, vandalism, damage to property, serving of food and drink, dumping of rubbish, begging, noise, etc. (see more below).

Whatever the definition referred to on the various occasions, many researchers agree that incivilities are capable of stirring feelings of 'insecurity' and 'fear of crime' in citizens (Burney 2005), regardless of the true data on the perpetration of crimes and victimisation (Lagrange 1993, Selmini 2003). As a matter of fact, when we speak of security in the late modern society, what the democratic state is required to protect is no longer just the 'social contract' of Hobbesian fame – by which it guaranteed the civil harmony as well as its source of primary legitimisation – but a series of existential challenges carried forward by groups undermining state authority, which citizens interpret as an attack against their survival. From this viewpoint, we may define urban security as an 'extended political guarantee' (Calaresu 2013: 34), ensuring the protection of citizens, prevention and sanctioning of crime and a reduction of real and perceived insecurity – the latter referring as well to phenomena different from punishable crimes – or possibly as restitution of the integrity and legitimate fruition of ownership of their personal assets, anticipating the effective assertion of the exercise of rights and freedoms envisaged by the Constitution.

But who are the political actors – and at what level of the government – who can (and must) ensure to the citizen that this extended political guarantee is (correctly) exercised? If, on the one hand, the central level – referring to the government-parliament circuit – still retains control over the legitimate monopoly of violence and is thus the competent entity for public order and security, the local level, on the other hand, especially the city, appears to have become the privileged place for the production of policies regarding the regulation and control of incivilities. This phenomenon is well known among scholars (Garland 1996, 2001) and can be read – in a diachronic perspective – as a changing dynamic of centralisation/decentralisation of powers.

From the first half of the 1990s, the democratic state tried, in the wake of a crisis of power and legitimacy (Castells 1997), to decentralise an important part of its responsibilities towards peripheral units. The political costs of the shift of responsibility from the centre in this way would be paid, first and foremost, with a high degree of heterogeneousness of the public policies carried out by local governments (Donolo 2002). Plans and courses of action were based on security models often extremely divergent and with very different effects from each other, in terms both of governance and of inequality in the application of administrative (and sometimes penal) sanctions against citizens belonging to different territories within the same national context (Crawford 1999, Johnston and Shearing 2003, Edwards and Hughes 2012). In the second place, the costs of relieving the centre of the responsibility would lead to uncontrolled development – in quality and quantity – of the use of restrictive and/or punitive powers by local authorities, anxious to respond to their citizens' growing feelings of insecurity and fear (Taylor 1999). In the third and final place, scholars have highlighted how the governance model of urban security generated after the shift of responsibility from the state would prove incapable of guaranteeing an adequate level of decision-making capacity (Calaresu 2012).

In answer to these phenomena, the central levels of power of many European countries attempted in the last decade to reassert their monopoly of production and management of the security asset by reintroducing a rigid formal-legal separation of competencies in the field of security and public order. In other cases, governments tried instead, in a manner not mutually exclusive, to follow the path of making the peripheral organisations 'responsible from above' in the production of public policies, using new forms of exercising power (Garland 1996), often by means of contracts (Lascoumes and Le Galès 2004, Wacquant 2009), partnerships and multi-agency coordination (Selmini 2016).

Italy is not an exception as regards the experiences described above, with some peculiarities that deserve to be taken into account. For this reason, this chapter is organised as follows: in the first part (Background), by means of a diachronic analysis based on the secondary literature, the evolution is reconstructed of urban security policy in Italy before (1994–2007) and after (2007–2011) the introduction of security pacts and administrative orders as top-down instruments for governing crime and disorder. In the second part (Questions, hypotheses and methods), questions and research hypotheses are put forward. In the third part of the chapter (Results and discussion), we will present results, based on empirical data (obtained through semi-structured interviews with actors committed within the decision-making process in four Italian cities), which were used to identify the variable that may best explain the variance in the efficacy (intended as the capacity or power to produce a desired effect and results) of these two top-down instruments at a regional and municipal level. The fifth and last part (Conclusions) will discuss the general implications for the regulation or enforcement of incivilities when top-down instruments, among a variety of laws and measures, are used by the central government to deal with crime and disorder, and in particular to tackle incivilities.

Background

The 'original' model of urban security in Italy (1994–2007)

Compared with more experienced governments, Italy suffered a delay in terms of the institutional initiatives and practices of the so-called urban security policy. Until the 1990s, Italian policymakers (as well as researchers) showed no or little interest in the reactions of citizens to petty crime and urban disorder, concentrating their attention instead on policies to fight crime and on organised crime (Triventi 2008: 90). Such delay, in view of the French and British contexts, is but one peculiar feature in the Italian experience. For the latter – in the 1980s – the input to develop new strategies on the matter came from the central government, while in the first case it was the result – in the 1970s – of a synergy between the municipalities and the governmental will to reform. In Italy, instead, the drive to tackle urban security problems is generated within the relationship between socio-criminological research, epistemic communities, the civil society and, last but not least, the local governments. Indeed, the Italian experience began in 1994 with the *Città Sicure* project in the Emilia-Romagna regional context. The development process for the Italian case (1994–2007) could be then divided into three different stages:

In the first stage – between the launch of *Città Sicure* (in 1994) and the introduction of the protocol on urban security in the city of Modena (in 1998) – the security issue began to be included as part of the local policies. A significant development of local actions related to urban security and policing occurred with a self-responsibilisation of cities (Selmini 2016). Each and every medium/large-sized town – in the North and the Centre – boasted its own security policy (Pavarini 2006: 13), with the borders of state intervention indirectly redefined by the actions taken by the local governments. They dealt with incivilities by embracing non-mutually exclusive two-fold approaches. On the one hand, they did so by trying to use the skills honed during years of activity in the fields of social services, mobility and town planning, as well as administrative and municipal law enforcement.[1] On the other hand, this was done by submitting the requests put forward by citizens to the attention of the central government, which believed to be lacking the formal or substantial powers that would have enabled them to deal with urban security issues (Selmini 2005). Meanwhile, the central government could not, or would not, play a pivotal role in the field by institutionalising the different experiments at the local level. It did not even decide to start the reforms needed (Pavarini 2006).

At the end of this phase, the Italian state – not differently from other European countries – decided to use the contractualisation of the policy in an attempt to institutionalise and centralise the model of governance. The Inter-ministerial Committee for Economic Planning – resolution of 21 March 1997 – granted the possibility to draw up territorial agreements to achieve and strengthen 'integrated security'. One year later, on 9 February 1998 (with Romano Prodi as the Italian prime minister), the 'first season' of contractualisation on security started with the signing of the agreement between the *sindaco* and the *prefetto*[2] of Modena in Emilia-Romagna. It is hard to make generalisations about this experiment. Nevertheless, it can be noticed that the protocols did not manage to go beyond a procedural setting, or prompt any joint action or operational projects (Giovannetti 2009: 131) able to last over time to 'really test new forms of cooperation between local administrations and the State' (Braccesi 2005: 30). Moreover, this first attempt at contractualisation was characterised by a ritualistic and bureaucratic involvement by the national government representatives (Selmini 2016).

The second stage – between 1998 and 2001, the last year of Giuliano Amato as prime minister – was characterised by a further effort of institutionalisation of the network carried out by the central level through the issuing of the Leg. D. N° 112/1998 and the Leg. D. N° 279/1999. With these laws, the mayor of the capital of the province, together with the president of the province, could join the *Comitato Provinciale per l'Ordine e la Sicurezza* (County Committee on Public Safety and Public Order) as a full member and submit proposals for its agenda. At the same time, the law (Decree of the President of the Council of Ministers of 12 September 2000, Art. 7, para. 1) started to recognise the importance of collaboration in the field of security between the state and the peripheral levels of government.

It is worth mentioning in this phase the presence of a large number of 'agreements' among local authorities, police forces, the judiciary and several other parties, stipulated at the request of the prefect, mayor or public prosecutor, co-funded by local institutions and the central government. All these agreements, inspired by the French experience of *Contrats Locaux de Sécurité* and the British 'contract culture' (Le Galès 1997: 444), aimed at the implementation of video surveillance systems and participative security tools and at creating partnerships for the coordinated, integrated and permanent management of the urban security issue. Those attempts, as happened in the first stage of development of the policy, did not seem sufficient to ensure an increase in the level of network institutionalisation. Local administrators were indirectly entrusted with large discretionary power: they continued, at this stage, to enjoy great freedom in defining what constituted (or not) an incivility within their community; they were also crucial actors in the definition of the agenda and in the evaluation of which decisions should or should not be effectively implemented (Selmini 2005: 48–9).

The third stage of development – from 2001 to 2007, the latter being the year of the introduction of the security pacts – was defined as 'the stage of the failed agreement' (Braccesi 2005: 29). The main actors involved in this failed agreement were the municipalities and the central government, which at that time was chaired by Silvio Berlusconi (2001–2006). Compared with the previous stage, the government started a lively lawmaking activity, although almost entirely focused on the exacerbation of criminal laws, such as the first 'security package' (Law N° 128/2001) and the 'high impact' operations for the recovery, control and redevelopment of local areas.

At the same time, the municipalities were not granted the financial and regulatory powers which were needed (Garland 1996) to carry out their activities in a consistent way. In this scenario, another peculiar feature emerges, making Italy so different from France and the UK: the regions played a crucial role in the compensation of the absence (or passive role) of the government and the parliament. With the provisions of Law N° 59/1997 and the Constitutional Law N° 3/2001, the regions were given exclusive jurisdiction on the management of local and municipal police forces[3] and have had to carry out prevention or suppression actions that did not fall within the scope of action of the central government. In this framework, in Italy regions performed activities, which were in other countries attached to national governments (Selmini 2005), often providing regulatory instruments to municipalities (Braccesi 2005: 33),[4] the latter being unable to pass laws regulating incivilities themselves (Calaresu 2013).

Moreover, the local and municipal police forces exercised a substitute function. This does not mean that national police stopped being responsible for crime at the city level.[5] It means, however, that in Italy the local and municipal police forces, even without formal competencies related to public order and security (Pavarini 2006), acquired a substitute function in tackling street-level crime such as petty theft, muggings, burglaries and drug dealing (Selmini 2016).

The redefining of the model through top-down instruments (2007–2011)

The years between 2007 and 2011 can be seen as years of 'remarkable change' in the strategy of the central actors, that is, the government (Selmini 2016). With respect to the French and the British contexts, the Italian urban security policy network has been until this moment characterised by a weak structure: not only did peripheral political and administrative institutions prevail over the central authority (high level of decentralisation), social stakeholders and institutions have done the same, as they were capable of exercising pressure on the governmental institutions (owing to the low level of institutionalisation).

At least in terms of the will for changes in the national government, the 2007–2008 biennium may be seen as a turning point with the introduction of new top-down instruments. The previous model of urban security governance was then questioned by the attempt to increase the level of institutionalisation and the level of centralisation of the policy network. As Mosconi (2010) stated, in this period of time the national government, using top-down instruments – such as security pacts and administrative orders – for tackling incivilities, clearly turned toward a 'tough', punitive and exclusionary approach to crime and disorder.[6]

The security pacts were introduced on 20 March 2007 with the Law N° 296/2006, Art. 1, para. 439. This 'second season' of contractualisation was expected to start 'a new operational model capable of promoting cooperation between the parties, with the strategic, shared definition of synergic lines of action' (Italian Government – Ministry of Home Affairs 2007). Ratified on 13 September 2008 with an agreement between the *Associazione Nazionale Piccoli Comuni* and the Ministry of Home Affairs (Law N° 125/2008), the Decree by Law N° 92 extended the power of implementation of coordinated surveillance territorial plans and of the strengthening of the logistic, instrumental and financial collaboration between the government and the local authorities to the small to medium-sized municipalities and to unions of municipalities (Italian Government – Ministry of Home Affairs 2008).

Two years after their introduction, fifty-one security pacts were signed in Italy, involving 11,652,444 inhabitants, distributed in 241 municipalities (Calaresu 2013: 73),[7] mostly in the North West (39.22 per cent) and North East (23.53 per cent) of Italy; overall, the Northern part of Italy (62.75 per cent) had the highest score compared both with the Centre (19.61 per cent) and with the South plus the Islands (17.64 per cent) (Calaresu and Tebaldi 2015: 2).[8] The prefecture (a territorial agency managed by the Ministry of Home Affairs) is the only actor that is always involved, signing from time to time the pacts with the municipalities, the provinces and the regions (or a combination of such actors) with different institutional configurations and distributions over the territory.[9] Security pacts, regardless of their configuration, usually contained an indication of the incivilities that the signing administrations had to deal with throughout the duration of their contract. According to some research (Calaresu 2013: 107) over 40 per cent of the thirty-seven pacts[10] considered 'illegal itinerant trade and counterfeiting of goods' to be the main problem; 24 per cent reported the 'recovery of degraded urban areas'; 21 per cent 'social conflict and disruption', while almost 20 per cent extended the security issue to 'bullying, juvenile delinquency, truancy, drug dealing and abuse of drugs and alcohol'. Ten per cent of pacts were instead split between a general need to 'combat and prevent criminal acts', 'crime' and 'lack of security'. As far as it concerned the places indicated as the object of interest, in addition to the protection of the areas of 'major concern in terms of crime, degradation and unlawfulness' (reported in about 55 per cent of the cases), pacts explicitly referred to 'schools' (35.2 per cent), 'popular gathering places', such as 'nightclubs' and 'shopping malls' (27.4 per cent), 'old town centres' (23.5 per cent), 'community spaces' and 'green and protected natural areas' (17.6 per cent), 'buses', 'public means of transport and their stops' (11.7 per cent), 'public car parking', 'peripheral urban areas, suburbs or isolated areas' (9.8 per cent), 'squares' and 'inter-municipal areas' (7.8 per cent). More generally, about 80 per cent of security pacts addressed issues affecting 'municipal areas' or 'territory'. Due to the frequent participation of the provinces in the agreements (Calaresu and Tebaldi 2015: 7), more than 50 per cent of the documents made also a clear reference to the 'provincial' area. On the other hand, no reference to the regional level has ever been made (Calaresu and Padovano 2011: 114). As regards their duration, almost 60 per cent of the pacts provided for a two-year term, while the share of agreements that did not specify an explicit duration is quite high: over 20 per cent of the total amount (Calaresu 2013: 96).

In the same years, the city mayors in their official, governmental capacities[11] were also allowed by the Legislative Decree N° 267/2000, Art. 54 (as amended by Decree-Law N° 92/2008 and converted into Law N° 125/2008), to address a wide range of urban security issues using the administrative orders on the premise of four principal factors: urgency and necessity, contingency, temporariness and proportionality. In addition to this, the ministerial decree of 5 August 2008 was the legislative tool by which the government tried for the first time to provide an 'authentic interpretation' of the scope of the actions envisaged within the field of urban security. By means of the above-mentioned decree, the minister described security as the 'physical integrity of the population' and urban security as the 'public good to be protected through the defence activities undertaken within local communities, in compliance with the rules governing civil life, in order to improve living conditions in urban centres, civil coexistence and social cohesion'.[12] It is important to note that with the legislation introduced in 2008, the ordinances assumed 'new functions and characteristics' (Moroni and Chiodelli 2014: 2). Firstly, due to the fact that the concept of urban security was defined 'very vaguely' (Recasens et al. 2013: 371), the areas in which orders might be employed significantly increased. Secondly, as Moroni and Chiodelli (2014: 2) stated, an ordinance can be applied after that 'in a manner no longer determined by contingent and urgent factors', with the 'requisite limited timescale also disappeared'. According to some scholars, these modifications transformed a traditional mayoral practice into 'semi-criminal measures' (Selmini 2016), with municipal police becoming heavily involved in the empowerment of such ordinances (Ruga Riva 2010, Selmini 2013). As Di Ronco and Peršak (2014: 344–345) also underlined, 'any breach of such orders was, moreover, considered a contravention (criminal offence *lato sensu*) and led to a criminal proceeding potentially resulting in the imposition of criminal sanctions'.

A survey carried out by Cittalia – Fondazione ANCI Ricerche (Chiodini and Milano 2009: 18) documented[13] a number of 788 administrative orders issued by 445 municipalities in Italy (5.5 per cent of the 8100 Italian municipalities). More than 65 per cent of the ordinances were issued in the North West and the North East of Italy, while the South registered about 20 per cent of the total. Even adding the latter share with the percentages obtained from the Centre of the peninsula (about 12 per cent), the percentage of ordinances in the South turns out to be slightly lower than half of the total of the northern regions (Calaresu and Padovano 2011: 100).[14] The 68 per cent of the orders applied to the entire population, while 17 per cent addressed private and specific 'subjects' and 15 per cent focused on shop-owners (Chiodini and Milano 2009: 23). As regards the most common type of incivilities tackled by the ordinances (Chiodini and Milano 2009: 27–9, Moroni and Chiodelli 2014: 3) the percentages are allocated as follows: 'consumption of alcoholic beverages' (13.6 per cent), 'prostitution' (13 per cent), 'vandalism or damage to public or private property' (9.4 per cent), 'serving food and/or beverages' (8.3 per cent), 'rubbish dumping' (7.6 per cent), 'begging' (7.4 per cent), 'noise' (6.8 per cent), 'decency of the city' (6.3 per cent), 'camping' (6 per cent). Considering the types of places considered by the orders, the order applied in the vast majority of cases to the entire city jurisdiction (60 per cent), while the remaining part (40 per cent) was split between 'generic types of spaces' (such as green areas and bus stations) and 'specific neighbourhoods', 'roads' or 'squares'. As concerns the period of validity of the orders, as high as 87 per cent did not set an explicit deadline. In other cases, the duration of the provisions is roughly three months. Less frequently, the ordinances were limited to a short or very short period of time, usually in the case of celebrations, concerts or public events (Chiodini and Milano 2009: 24).

At the end of this stage, on 7 April 2011, the Italian Constitutional Court declared with judgement N° 115 that administrative orders issued by the mayors in the area of urban security were partly unconstitutional, owing to their use outside of situations of necessity and urgency. It remains unclear whether this court decision has really prevented the city mayors from using their power to use ordinances outside of situations of necessity and urgency[15] or whether the court decision has somehow limited the area of application of the ordinances at least from the point of view of their content.

Some empirical evidence (Calaresu 2013, Selmini 2013, Calaresu and Tebaldi 2015) pointed out that these top-down instruments seem to have been able – at least formally – to improve the level of institutionalisation and centralisation of the policy network by colliding with the original model of governance (1994–2007). After years of substantial control by the local authorities, the state would be able with the ordinances to re-establish its sovereign role in governing crime and disorder at the local level. Moreover, with the security pacts and their legitimisation of a given organisational set-up with deep symbolic relevance, the central government would be able to impose a list of (new) activities and duties on the peripheral actors, who must also support most of the costs of this 'new form of governing at a distance' (Garland 1996: 454).

Questions, hypotheses and methods

It is fair to wonder, therefore, whether the formal institutionalisation and centralisation of the model on a national level – obtained during the fourth phase (2007–2011) by the central government through the aforementioned top-down instruments – was for the same years followed (and if so, on what conditions) by an improvement in the efficacy of urban security policy (intended as the capacity or power to produce a desired effect and desired results) at a local level in Italy, with particular reference to their capacity to tackle incivilities.

For this purpose we need to start with what was obtained from the empirical analysis of policymaking so as to reconstruct the decision-making and implementation processes of public policies at the local level. The empirical analysis of policymaking has the advantage of emphasising the role of local governments in understanding successes and failures of policies. Concrete models of development of local policies are no longer considered in ancillary, executive terms compared with national policy, but as a part of the network of politically important institutions, groups, movements and subjects of which the governance of each public policy is composed.

In this perspective, our thesis asserts that the introduction of top-down instruments for governing crime and disorder at the national level may have produced different effects at the local level in terms of efficacy of the policy. To explain the variance at regional and municipal levels in the efficacy of urban security policy following the introduction of pacts and ordinances, we therefore formulate the following hypothesis: the introduction of top-down instruments did actually succeed in improving the capacity to tackle incivilities (our *explanandum*) in the local contexts that showed – before the introduction of those instruments – a high degree of predictability and low degree of complexity of interaction between local actors (our *explanans*). Whereas, on the contrary, a low degree of predictability and high degree of complexity of interaction at a local level – recorded before the introduction of pacts and ordinances – led to poor capacity to tackle incivilities, even following the introduction of the top-down instruments.

The degree of predictability and the degree of complexity of interaction between local actors has been measured through a synthetic indicator such as the level of institutionalisation of the local context. The term 'institutionalisation' refers here to the processes which give public policies an inter-organisational form and stability due to the fact that dominant or hegemonic coalitions consisting of public stakeholders, or imbued with public responsibilities, are able to generate coherent and consistent inter-organisational networks both in the relations among them and with third parties (Tebaldi 2010a). Therefore, the highest level of institutionalisation is acknowledged whenever we find policy networks with a controlled access to the decision-making arenas and based on the centrality of the relationship among public political-administrative institutions, weakly influenced by private and partisan interests. The policy organisational field (Powell and Di Maggio 1991) is also provided with one or more governance bodies. The field is imbued with legal, economic, and organisational capability, making the mentioned bodies self-sufficient, with a self-referential validation and internalisation acceptance despite the criticism against the very same structures. That means that such core actors may generate autonomous decision-making processes and equally independent implementation processes, regardless of the decisions taken by national bodies in a specific policy area or of the opinions voiced by non-institutional bodies belonging to the policy network (Tebaldi 2010b). If this is not the case or the results expected are limited in scope, the level of institutionalisation will be regarded as low or null.

The method chosen to empirically test the hypothesis was the 'positional' method (Dahl 1961), by which a panel was set up that included 31 selected actors, engaged in the decision-making process under analysis (2007–2011) in a small number of sample cities in four different Italian regions, namely Bologna in Emilia-Romagna, Cagliari in Sardinia, Catania in Sicily, and Genoa in Liguria.

These cities were selected on the basis of the following criteria:

(a) The presence of a large number of contiguous municipalities in the selected area, an extensive periphery legally recognised[16] as a 'metropolitan area'.[17]
(b) Their participation in both the first (1998–2005) and the second (2007–2011) season of contractualisation on security by signing both contracts and security pacts.
(c) The temporal proximity of the signing of the security pacts in the second season of contractualisation (Cagliari: 11 June 2007; Bologna: 19 June 2007; Catania: 11 July 2007; Genoa: 14 July 2007).
(d) Their use of the ordinances in the area of urban security and particularly in order to tackle incivilities within the indicated period (2008–2011).
(e) A balanced geographical distribution on the peninsula, consistent with the above-mentioned criteria (Centre/North: Bologna in Emilia-Romagna, Genoa in Liguria – South/Islands: Cagliari in Sardinia, Catania in Sicily).[18]

Each of the thirty-one interviewees was selected according to his or her function or position of power (politico-administrative and technical-operative component) during the considered period:

(a) Mayor or deputy mayor of the municipality or member of the city council (councillor).
(b) Councillor of the opposition or former member of the city council with a different political orientation (councillor).
(c) Executive or officer of the municipal and/or provincial, regional public administration.
(d) Chief, deputy chief or executive of the local or municipal police force.
(e) Prefect or vice-prefect of the city or state police force executive.

The actors thus chosen underwent an in-depth personal interview (also performed when necessary by telephone or Skype) lasting approximately an hour, based on a semi-structured outline and an analytical grid as benchmark.

Results and discussion

Bearing in mind the difficulty of finding a univocal definition among scholars of what incivilities are, the questions devised concerning the regulation and control of anti-social behaviour gave the interviewees the freedom to form their own concepts of ASBs, not use pre-defined ones. Apart from the existing differences between the politico-administrative and the technical-operative actors listed in our panel, and those between the contexts with a high and a low level of institutionalisation – that will be taken into account in the following paragraphs – the most common types or conceptions of incivilities given by the actors were the following (sorted by the number of citations): 'drug-dealing' (120); 'consumption of alcohol and drugs' (100), 'alcohol-related violence' and 'behaviour' (97); 'street prostitution' (90); 'vexatious begging' (75) which 'insults public decency' (70); 'damage' and 'vandalism' to public and private property (54); 'illegal occupation of properties' (20); 'illegal trade' (15) and 'illegal street vendors' (12); 'illegal occupation of public ground' (8); and in general all 'behaviour' that 'seriously disturbs the use of public spaces' (8).

The reader is advised that in the next two sections of this work, all the quotes listed (unless the source is mentioned next to them) will contain words and expressions directly taken from the respondents.

Degree of predictability and complexity of interaction among local actors: contexts with a high level of institutionalisation

In the cases of the cities of Genoa (Liguria) and Bologna (Emilia-Romagna), the empirical evidence collected shows that better results in terms of capacity to tackle incivilities had been achieved, first and foremost, thanks to the 'strong interest' in urban security issues, implemented 'over the years' (also prior to the introduction of top-down instruments by the central government) through 'negotiations' and 'personal relations' between the mayor and the prefect of the city. Starting with this iron pair, the local network in these contexts appears to be founded, as we will see, upon public institutions of a politico-administrative type, within a coherent system and with a good level of stability and cohesion of the dominant coalition.

In the second place, the actors interviewed considered that the network responsible for 'taking charge' of the problems of urban security was able to obtain, during the course of the different development phases of the policy (1994–2011), a good level of functional specialisation (the who does what), especially concerning the creation of 'committees', 'offices', 'institutes' and dedicated 'work-groups'. This resulted in the 'clear picture' – for the actors engaged in the process – of the hierarchical sub-division of roles and functions in an institutional system, composed of a limited number of actors and of maps of interdependence on the subject of urban security and the battle against ASBs (the who does what, in relation to whom). The Emilia-Romagna and Liguria regional boards, in particular, seem to have played a strategic role by, on the one hand, 'pointing out priorities and limits' in the planning phase of actions connected with handling incivilities (e.g. how to define incivilities, which of these incivilities are part of the political agenda and which are not), while, on the other hand, 'coordinating the choices' of the municipal boards in the implementation phase (e.g. by what sort of approach and with which policy instruments urban security problems should be tackled), guaranteeing them the 'technical support' (financial, logistic, normative and organisational resources). As far as the committees set up at a municipal level were concerned, they proved to be an important 'reference point' for the various municipal departments engaged in the urban security issue, defined alternately in terms of 'liveability', 'quality of life', 'urban redevelopment' and 'struggle against anti-social behaviour'.

Thirdly, both in the case of Genoa and that of Bologna, better results seem to have been achieved in terms of opposing incivilities thanks to the 'sharing of contents', the 'alliances' and the 'institutional cooperation' that developed over time around a 'well-outlined' policy idea between the actors that decide (policy and decision makers) and those that have to put into practice the decisions (administrative roles, law enforcement agencies and municipal police). As an example, the interviewees pointed out how setting up the *Comitato Provinciale per l'Ordine e la Sicurezza* (the introduction of which dates back to the early years of the twenty-first century) enabled informal relations to be created, not just between administrations but also between the heads of the security and police agencies, and between these and local government. All these actors collaborated by 'facing together' issues like: illegal occupation of peripheral areas, illegal and itinerant trading, the control of commercial premises and food adulteration, the control of alcohol and drug administration, prostitution, redevelopment of peripheral districts considered at risk, and safety and security on public transport and at public stations.

In the attempt to move the test forward on the hypothesis proposed, we point out that the interviewees agreed on indicating the two-year period 2005–2007 as the moment of change in creating 'consultation practices' and 'facilities' at a local level that enabled the consolidation of inter-institutional loyalty and the achievement of common goals on the subject of urban security. At the moment of introduction of the new top-down instruments by the central government (2007–2008), these conditions would then lead to further improvement in the capacity to counter ASB in the cities examined.

As regards the use of the two top-down instruments under analysis at a municipal level, we can state that, on the one hand, the ties and procedural relations developed in these contexts during the years 2005–2007 enabled the ordinance – by definition an emergency and contingent instrument at the mayor's disposal – to be turned into a 'consultation channel' aimed at 'thematic and institutional cooperation' between the actors involved. The said ties and relations also allowed recourse to be made to the ordinance just in a 'sporadic', 'targeted' way. The use of the ordinance – by the mayor in collaboration with the prefect – actually proved almost always to be part of government action centred on instruments, plans and courses of action tending towards prevention rather than reaction, possibly even in contrast with the guidelines and national laws on the subject.

On the other hand, the organic provision of *ad hoc* consultation practices and facilities, with (inter)sectorial coordination and planning (such as the combined forces technical table, working-groups and control rooms, apart from the already mentioned *Comitato Provinciale per l'Ordine e la Sicurezza Pubblica*), as well as the facilities aimed at studying and analysing criminal and deviant phenomena that preceded the introduction of the security pacts (2005–2007), enabled the pacts to be considered more a 'technical-operative' instrument than a 'symbolic' one. An instrument with its mechanism developed on the basis of non-generic commitments provided for the expense items to be accurately defined for each single plan and/or initiative on the agenda, and assessable *ex post* by the signatory parties. This would enable 'greater efficacy' of the instrument in its function of regulation and struggle against incivilities, at the moment of its implementation. The selected actors agreed, in short, in acknowledging that the introduction of pacts and ordinances on the national level improved the efficacy of urban security policy at a local level, since the said top-down instruments became a part of 'multi-annual plans', basically 'coherent' and 'not reversible', already under way at a local level at the moment they were introduced.

In conclusion, the empirical results obtained by means of the in-depth interviews seem to show that in contexts with a high institutionalisation level, the introduction of the top-down instruments did manage to improve – at least in the perception of the actors involved – the capacity to tackle incivilities.

Degree of predictability and complexity of interaction among local actors: contexts with a low level of institutionalisation

A counterfactual confirmation of the test of our hypothesis is provided by reconstructing the decision-making and implementation processes of the same policy in the cities of Cagliari (Sardinia) and Catania (Sicily), for the same time-span previously considered.

The two cases under examination seem to show the incapability of institutional actors to achieve – after the introduction of the top-down instruments – a satisfactory degree of efficacy of the urban security policy, as a result of several factors connected with the low degree of interaction predictability and the high complexity of the organisational context. First and foremost, even if interest in the issues of urban security over the years increased also in these cities thanks to the leadership of the mayor and prefect, the institutional system did not prove to be stable and cohesive as in the cases previously analysed. Regions of Sardinia and Sicily fail, in all phases of the policy, in the role of broker and in gatekeeping (ability to dispense logistic, normative and organisational resources, but above all financial ones); the role of broker elsewhere carried out precisely by this level of government in support of the cities. It should be noted that for the two regions examined, the situation appears to be, rather than a 'political' type of choice or one of 'political orientation' of the majority, the consequence of 'structural inadequacy' and 'poor' transversal 'administrative culture' of the two groups on the right-left axis. Contrary to what happened in Emilia-Romagna and Liguria, the regional bodies are thus placed at the edges of the network, not wanting or not being able to cover a strategic role, or both.

Secondly, in contrast with what happened in Genoa and Bologna, the interviewees did not seem to feel they were able – each for his own sphere of action – to 'take charge' of citizens' security problems (real or perceived). This was mainly due to the lack of, or only partial, distribution of the economic/financial resources in their favour, the lack of real powers and the absence of management offices and municipal departments specifically dedicated to the regulation and struggle against ASB at a regional level. The setting up of consultation and comparison tables (also with the participation of citizens' associations or other local bodies that might be interested) in both cities did not seem to be enough – in the eyes of the actors involved – to overcome the difficulties following the lack of, or delayed, acknowledgement or adaptation of the normative instruments by the regional organisations in question, or both. The absence of the region in the policymaking process meant that the hierarchical subdivision of roles and functions (the who does what) and the clarification of maps of interdependence (the who does what, in relation to whom) in the urban security policy proved inevitably less precise and mandatory compared with the cases previously examined.

Thirdly, if for Genoa and Bologna, as we have seen, better results were achieved in terms of countering ASB, owing to the 'cooperation' and 'reciprocal trust' between institutions, in Cagliari and Catania, in contrast, the 'lack of sharing' of 'ideas' and 'results' was complained of, as well as an excessive 'generic nature' of the commitments undertaken by the actors involved, aggravated by high 'opacity' in defining the funds to be dedicated to realising them.

In this situation, not even the provincial government board seemed to be able to exercise a 'cover function' with respect to the regions, which might ensure the promotion and creation of truly integrated systems of security on the territory in terms of coordination and linking up the administrations and different security agencies (as the prefecture, the state and the municipal police). None of the subjects interviewed seemed to have had the necessary sufficient resources available (legal, economic, human, organisational, legitimising, functional and symbolic) to control the salient moments of the decision-making process. In particular, it was noted that the local actors were incapable of adequately managing the police resource to control ASB 'in the field', 'in the street' and 'in daily work'. Mayors and public security executives in both contexts actually complained of the inadequacy of staff in the municipal police force, not just numerically but in connection with levels of professionalism. The police resource is the main instrument at the disposal of the municipal board to carry out the mayor's ordinances; to patrol; to control road conditions, traffic and road accidents; and to support, as regards security pacts, law enforcement agencies (above all the *Polizia di Stato* and *Arma dei Carabinieri*).

Finally, the absence of coordination by a superordinate level of government meant that the municipalities did not manage to set up stable, structured institutional organs on the territory in the different phases of development of the policy (1994–2007). At the moment of the introduction of the new top-down instruments by the central government (2007–2008), therefore, in contrast with what arose in Genoa and Bologna, we observed a lack of consultation practices and structures at a local level able to ensure that cooperative objectives were achieved. Consequently, the instruments of pacts and ordinances did not seem to be able – at least in the perception of the actors involved – to improve the capacity to tackle incivilities under the local administrations examined. On one hand, the ordinance was managed as an 'emergency' and 'contingent' instrument, which from simple intervention of an administrative nature often tended to turn into a kind of 'semi-penal intervention' against citizens, in particular, the minorities. Even though the ordinance seemed in these contexts to be an instrument able to guarantee the mayors 'greater perception of power', paradoxically it seemed at the same time to put the safety of the agents who had to have it implemented at risk. On the other hand, in these contexts the security pacts boil down to 'symbolic statements' between the parties, or at least appear to be subject – in the phase of implementation – to uncontrollable exogenous factors of disturbance (e.g. a financial crisis at a regional and/or municipal level or the arrival of a new, more urgent security problem imposed by current events on the agenda). Even if we suppose that there exists the will and politico-administrative capacity on the part of the subjects involved in planning the instruments, necessary to control ASB within the model designed by the pacts, it seems that in the contexts examined a further step is missing – a step from planning to concrete realisation of the planned interventions – aimed at changing the impact on the social target in question.

To sum up, the empirical results show that the top-down instruments for governing crime and disorder were not actually successful in improving the efficacy of the urban security policy, with particular reference to tackling incivilities, in the contexts with low institutionalisation such as Cagliari and Catania.

Conclusions: what lessons can be drawn from the Italian experience?

In conclusion, let us look at some general implications for the regulation or enforcement of incivilities when the central government uses top-down instruments, among a variety of other laws and measures, for governing crime and disorder.

Three lessons can be drawn from the Italian experience for both scholars and policymakers. As a first lesson, we can point out how the top-down instruments for governing crime and disorder are meant by the governments as a 'shortcut' to strengthen the policies related to urban security. Empirical evidence shows how the central government is able to create through this shortcut – even in a relatively short period of time – a model of governance based on a high level of institutionalisation and centralisation of the policy network, despite the inertial force of the original and previous model of the policy (and its sub-optimal effects).

But this top-down institutionalisation shortcut does not come without some relevant political costs, and this brings us to the second lesson. These particular kinds of instruments seem to be associated, in practice, with a de-legitimisation of the peripheral levels of government, together with a reduction in central government expenditure that could affect, directly and indirectly, the local governments and their capacity to tackle incivilities. Also, they seem to be related to the adoption of laws, decrees and measures at a national level, oriented towards a more punitive and exclusionary approach to crime and disorder (instead of a proactive and inclusionary one) that is likely to target marginal social groups.

Finally, as a third and more important lesson, it can be said that the institutional shortcut, if not supported by adequate preconditions at the local level, is likely to end up as a *cul-de-sac*. In fact, if on the one hand the top-down instruments could encourage formally homogeneous and consistent administrative behaviour through peripheral administrations (every city that we analysed has decided to adopt security pacts and ordinances after their introduction by the central government), this is, on the other hand, not sufficient to align the results of local policymaking in terms of efficacy of the policy. Our research shows that a remarkable variance is to be expected in the capacity of these two top-down instruments in tackling incivilities at regional and municipal levels, depending on the (high) degree of interaction predictability and the (low) complexity of the organisational context, (already) present on the specific local context implementing the top-down shortcut. In a nutshell: the strength and institutional capacity gained in the past at the local level reinforce or inhibit adaptive inclination.

According to the promoters of the bottom-up approach (e.g. Hjern and Hull 1982), the aforementioned strength and institutional capacity are crucial in order to understand the achievements or failures of public policies. From this perspective, the implementation of top-down instruments for governing crime and disorder in contexts that do not enjoy suitable institutionalisation seems to be a big gamble with no payoff, despite the formal benefits generated at the national level by the top-down shortcut. Decision makers have then to consider that the expected results of urban security reform policy, carried out with top-down instruments, may be overrated if they are not properly contextualised, based on the experience – in terms of institutionalisation – gained in the past at the local level. Indeed, when top-down instruments, among a variety of other laws and measures, are used by the central government for governing crime and disorder, it could be said that the effects of an innovative institutional form are curbed by the institutional medium they are set in.

Notes

1 With reference to the latter, as Selmini (2016) stated, that new form of policing at the local level was admitted and sometimes even ignored by the central government.
2 A prefect (*prefetto*) in Italy is the representative of the central state authority in a province for public safety and for enforcing the law.
3 Except for the management of the 'calls for competition'.
4 Regions also review both the submitted and the implemented projects aimed at tackling incivilities (Selmini 2016).
5 They still are better equipped in any sense to deal with organised or mafia-type crime, white collar crime and corruption, to say nothing of the protection of the state from terrorism.
6 Alongside some important pieces of legislation, which were contemporary to or immediately followed the introduction of the top-down instruments, such as, for example, Law N° 125/2008, which provided for the deployment of military and police forces in the cities, for collaboration between municipal and state police in case of need, the introduction of illegal immigration as an aggravating circumstance of the crime, the aggravation of some penalties for predatory crimes such as false certification or declaration of identity to a public officer.

7 Including subscriptions in the period between 18 May 2007 (date of the signing of the first agreement) and 31 December 2009.
8 For a detailed analysis of the diffusion of security pacts by regions, geographical area and demographic size, see Calaresu and Tebaldi (2015).
9 For further discussion about this topic, see Calaresu and Tebaldi (2015).
10 Out of fifty-one security pacts that enclosed a clear statement of the topics to be handled (Calaresu 2013: 107).
11 Chiodini and Milano (2009: 55), among others, clearly show the critical aspects of this approach, claiming: 'The consideration of the Mayor, albeit legitimised by direct suffrage, in his capacity as a governmental officer rather than a representative of the local community, is in fact particularly significant, showing that the attribution of powers to deal with security-related issues within the city takes place within a perspective that is mainly State-related, with respect to which the procedures entrusted to the mayor must necessarily be part of a relationship that still seems to be characterised by a hierarchical State administration-mayor approach, mostly with the Prefect as a mediator'.
12 More specifically, the Decree regulates the scope of the first four paragraphs of the amended Art. 54 of Leg. D. N° 267/2000, contained in Art. 6 of Conversion Law N° 125/2008 of Decree-Law N° 92/2008.
13 Covering administrative orders issued between August 2008 and August 2009.
14 For more information about the diffusion of the ordinances, see Calaresu and Padovano (2011) and Pizzetti (2012).
15 As Di Ronco and Peršak stated (2014: 345): 'Recent judgments of courts, overturning mayors' decisions to issue administrative orders on the basis of the Constitutional Court's ruling, show a slightly reduced but still present trend to expand the traditional ambit of the public order mandate to counter daily (often, harmless) uncivil and disorderly behaviour'.
16 Even before the introduction of Law N° 142/1990 and of the Leg. D. N° 267/2000.
17 Respectively: for the area of Catania by Regional Law N° 9/1986, for the Bologna area by Regional Law N° 33/1995, for the Genoa area by Regional Law N° 12/1991 (supplemented by Regional Law N° 7/1997), for the Cagliari area by Regional Law N° 4/1997. More recently – as of 1 January 2015 – Catania, Bologna, Genoa and Cagliari, among others, have achieved the status of *città metropolitane* (metropolitan cities), completely replacing the administrative functions of their provinces, as provided by Law N° 56/2014.
18 Despite all the above-mentioned similarity criteria, our sample cities differ from a political, social and economic point of view, basically reflecting the differences between the North and the South of the country (Donolo 2002: 91, Donolo 2005: 43–4). For example, it is worth mentioning that the cities of Bologna, Genoa, Cagliari and Catania (and their provinces) occupy very different positions in the Il Sole 24 Ore (2014) annual ranking for 'Quality of Life' among the 107 Italian provinces. The ranking is composed of thirty-six statistical indicators, grouped into six distinct categories: 'standard of living', 'services and environment', 'business and jobs', 'public order', 'population', 'free time'. While the Bologna province is among the top ten Italian cities in this special ranking (7th), and the Genoa province ranks in one of the top thirty positions (24th), Cagliari occupies an intermediate ranking (63rd), whereas Catania scored as one of the last ten provinces in the ranking (99th).

References

Braccesi, C. (2005) 'Le politiche di sicurezza urbana in Italia', in C. Braccesi and R. Selmini (eds.), *Sicurezza urbana e ruolo della polizia locale*, Sant'Arcangelo di Romagna: Maggioli.

Burney, E. (2005) *Making People Behave: Anti-Social Behaviour, Politics and Policy*, Cullompton: Routledge.

Calaresu, M. (2012) 'La politica di sicurezza urbana in Italia. L'esperienza dei "patti per la sicurezza" nel triennio 2007–2009', *Rivista Italiana di Politiche Pubbliche*, 3(7): 387–418.

Calaresu, M. (2013) *La politica di sicurezza urbana. Il caso italiano (1994–2009)*, Milano: Franco Angeli.

Calaresu, M. and Padovano, S. (2011) 'Gli strumenti top-down nel governo della sicurezza: l'esperienza pattizia e delle ordinanze sindacali nel triennio 2007–2009', in S. Padovano (ed.), *La Questione Sicurezza. Genesi e sviluppo di un concetto equivoco*, Soveria Mannelli: Rubettino.

Calaresu, M. and Tebaldi, M. (2015) 'Local security policies and the protection of territory: An analysis of the Italian experience (2007–2009)', *City, Territory and Architecture*, 2(1): doi 10.1186/s40410–014–0017-y.

Castells, M. (1997) *The Power of Identity*, vol. II of *The Information Age: Economy, Society and Culture*, Oxford: Blackwell.

Chiodini, L. and Milano, R. (2009) 'Il potere "ordinario" dei sindaci di ordinanze extra ordinem', in CITTALIA – Fondazione ANCI Ricerche (ed.), *Oltre le ordinanze: i sindaci e la sicurezza urbana*, Roma: Fondazione IFEL.

Crawford, A. (1999) *The Local Governance of Crime: Appeals to Community and Partnerships*, Oxford: Clarendon Press.

Dahl, R. (1961) *Who Governs? Democracy and Power in an American City*, New Haven, CT: Yale University Press.

Di Ronco, A. and Peršak, N. (2014) 'Regulation of incivilities in the UK, Italy and Belgium: Courts as potential safeguards against legislative vagueness and excessive use of penalising powers?', *International Journal of Law, Crime and Justice*, 42(4): 340–365.

Donolo, C. (2002) 'Politiche integrate come contesto dell'apprendimento istituzionale', in F. Battistelli (ed.) *La cultura delle amministrazioni fra retorica e innovazione*, Milano: Franco Angeli.

Donolo, C. (2005) 'Dalle politiche pubbliche alle pratiche sociali nella produzione di beni pubblici? Osservazioni su una nuova generazione di policies', *Stato e Mercato*, 73(April): 34–65.

Edwards, A. and Hughes, G. (2012) 'Public safety regimes: Negotiated orders and political analysis in criminology', *Criminology and Criminal Justice*, 12(4): 433–458.

Garland, D. (1996) 'The limits of the sovereign state: Strategies of crime control in contemporary society', *British Journal of Criminology*, 36(4): 445–471.

Garland, D. (2001) *The Culture of Control: Crime and Social Order in Contemporary Society*, Oxford: Oxford University Press.

Giovannetti, M. (2009) 'Le politiche di sicurezza e prevenzione della criminalità in Italia', in CITTALIA – Fondazione ANCI Ricerche (ed.), *Oltre le ordinanze: i sindaci e la sicurezza urbana*, Roma: Fondazione IFEL.

Hjern, B. and Hull, C. (1982) 'Implementation research as empirical constitutionalism', *European Journal of Political Research*, 10(2): 105–115.

Il Sole 24 Ore (2014) *Qualità della Vita 2014*. Online. Available at: www.ilsole24ore.com/temi-ed-eventi/qdv2014/ (accessed 20 September 2015).

Italian Government – Ministry of Home Affairs (2007) *Patto per la sicurezza delle città metropolitane con ANCI*. Online. Available at: www.interno.gov.it/ (accessed 20 September 2015).

Italian Government – Ministry of Home Affairs (2008) *Patto per la Sicurezza dei piccoli comuni con ANPCI*. Online. Available at: www.interno.gov.it/ (accessed 20

September 2015).Johnston, L. and Shearing, C. (2003) *Governing Security. Explorations in Policing and Justice*, London: Routledge.

Lagrange, H. (1993) 'La peur a la recherche du crime', *Déviance et Société*, 17(4): 385–417.

Lascoumes, P. and Le Galès, P. (eds.) (2004) *Gouverner par les instruments*, Paris: Presses de Sciences Po.

Le Galès, P. (1997) 'Relazioni centro-periferia e politiche pubbliche in Francia. Flessibilità e complessità senza federalismo', in B. Dente (ed.), *Governare con il federalismo*, Torino: Fondazione Agnelli.

Millie, A. (2008) 'Anti-social behaviour, behavioural expectations and an urban aesthetic', *British Journal of Criminology*, 48(3): 379–394.

Millie, A. (2011) 'Value judgments and criminalization', *British Journal of Criminology*, 51(2): 278–295.

Molotch, H. and McClain, N. (2003) 'Dealing with urban terror: Heritages of control, varieties of intervention, strategies of research', *International Journal of Urban and Regional Research*, 27(3): 679–698.

Moroni, S. and Chiodelli, F. (2014) 'Municipal regulations and the use of public space: Local ordinances in Italy', *City, Territory and Architecture*, 1(11): doi: 10.1186/2195–2701–1–11.

Mosconi, G. (2010) 'La sicurezza dell'insicurezza. Retoriche e torsioni della legislazione italiana', *Studi sulla Questione Criminale*, 5(2): 75–99.

Pavarini, M. (2006) 'L'aria delle città rende (ancora), liberi? Dieci anni di politiche locali di sicurezza', in M. Pavarini (ed.), *L'amministrazione locale della paura. Ricerche tematiche sulle politiche di sicurezza urbana in Italia*, Roma: Carocci.

Pizzetti, F. (2012) 'Conclusioni. Sicurezza urbana e ordinanze sindacali tra diritto e realtà', in A. Galdi and F. Pizzetti (eds.) *I sindaci e la sicurezza urbana, Le ordinanze sindacali e i loro effetti*, Roma: Donzelli.

Powell, W. and Di Maggio, P. (1991) *The New Institutionalism in Organizational Analysis*, Chicago: University of Chicago Press.

Recasens, A., Cardoso, C., Castro, J. and Nobili, G. G. (2013) 'Urban security in Southern Europe', *European Journal of Criminology*, 10(3): 368–382.

Ruga Riva, C. (2010) 'Diritto penale e ordinanze sindacali. Più sanzioni per tutti, anche penali?', *Le Regioni*, 1–2: 385–396.

Selmini, R. (2003) 'Paura, rischio e insicurezza tra domanda sociale e culture politiche: Torino, Bologna e Napoli', in G. Amendola (ed.), *Il governo della città sicura. Politiche, esperienze e luoghi comuni*, Napoli: Liguori.

Selmini, R. (2005) 'Le politiche di sicurezza urbana in Europa', in C. Braccesi and R. Selmini (eds.) *Sicurezza urbana e ruolo della polizia locale*, Sant'Arcangelo di Romagna: Maggioli.

Selmini, R. (2013) 'Le ordinanze sindacali in materia di sicurezza: una storia lunga, e non solo italiana', in S. Benvenuti, P. Di Fonzo, N. Gallo and T. F. Giupponi (eds.) *Sicurezza pubblica e sicurezza urbana. Il limite dei poteri di ordinanza dei sindaci stabilito dalla Corte Costituzionale*, Milano: Franco Angeli.

Selmini, R. (2016) 'Urban policing in Italy: Some reflections in a comparative perspective', in A. Edwards, E. Devroe and P. Ponsaers (eds.) *Policing European Metropolises*, London: Routledge.

Skogan, W. G. (1990) *Disorder and Decline: Crime and the Spiral of Decay in American Cities*, New York: Free Press.

Taylor, R. B. (1999) 'The Incivilities thesis: Theory, measurement, and policy', in R. L. Langworthy (ed.), *Measuring What Matters: Proceedings from the Police Research*

Institute Meetings, Washington, DC: National Institute of Justice and Office of Community Oriented Policing Service.
Taylor, R. B. (2002) *The Incivilities or "Broken Windows" Thesis*, Philadelphia: Temple University.
Tebaldi, M. (2010a) 'Le politiche di trasporto locale in prospettiva comparata: idealtipi e modelli di governance in Italia, Francia e Regno Unito', in M. Tebaldi (ed.), *La governance della mobilità locale*, Bologna: Il Mulino.
Tebaldi, M. (2010b) 'La governance della mobilità locale in Italia. Criticità e (possibili) soluzioni', in M. Tebaldi (ed.), *La governance della mobilità locale*, Bologna: Il Mulino.
Triventi, M. (2008) 'Segni di inciviltà sul territorio e paura del crimine. Un'analisi dei dati dell'Indagine sulla sicurezza dei cittadini', *Quaderni di Sociologia*, 48(3): 73–102.
Wacquant, L. (2009) *Prisons of Poverty*, Minneapolis: University of Minnesota Press.
Wilson, J. Q. (1968) 'The urban unease: Community versus the city', *The Public Interest*, 12: 25–39.

4 Punitive decriminalisation?

The repression of political dissent through administrative law and nuisance ordinances in Spain

Manuel Maroto Calatayud

Introduction

The authoritarian past of Spain, ruled from 1939 to 1977 by a military dictatorship that founded its legitimacy on victory in a civil war, bequeathed a political legacy that still resonates into the present. Attitudes rooted in the past appear to endure in relation to the regulation of 'public order' and 'anti-social behaviour', the two main formulas with which a broad range of control techniques beyond the reach of the criminal justice system have been applied. Especially affecting politically and economically marginalised groups, these measures regulate many aspects of daily life and activities. The focus here is on the exercise of (peaceful) political dissent and protest. Although control over such activities might not be the main function of these regulations (more clearly oriented towards the control of economically excluded sectors of the population), it is one of the aspects more often perceived as problematic and openly criticised in both the media and academia.

Incivilities and the municipalisation of public order in Spain

Incivilities in Spain are regulated today through administrative rules of a diverse nature and normative rank (from national legislation on public order to city ordinances on nuisances). Administrative and criminal law have substantially different legal regimes and implications: while administrative law cannot constitutionally imply sanctions that entail the deprivation of liberty (so the most commonly applied administrative sanctions are fines), the system of procedural safeguards in criminal proceedings is far more strict (administrative sanctions are, in fact, imposed through a non-judicial process). This predominantly administrative approach to incivilities is relatively new: before the coming of democracy, a draconian administrative regulation with broad-ranging criminal law misdemeanours (*faltas*) against 'the general interest and the order of cities' coexisted in Spain. Although this group of misdemeanours was repealed with the Criminal Code in 1989, public order misdemeanours were kept. In 2015, the category of criminal misdemeanour (*falta*) was completely removed from the Criminal Code, favouring the administrative handling of minor infractions. Minor infractions such as incivilities are not legally supposed to be relevant enough to constitute criminal offences (*delitos*), but both expansive interpretations of the elements of the crime and charges of disobedience to authorities occasionally allow for the escalation from petty transgressions to criminal acts. Even in these cases, the greater procedural safeguards of criminal proceedings might result in non-criminal sanctions being more punitive than criminal sanctions themselves.

Two central areas in the regulation of anti-social behaviour will be analysed in this chapter:

(a) The first is the administrative legislation on 'public order' and 'social dangerousness', which played a central role in the exercise of power during Franco's dictatorship, with an explicit legal tradition in Spain that dates back at least to the nineteenth century in the former case, and to the first half of the twentieth century in the latter. Reliance on these administrative technologies of control has recently been revived with the entry into force in July 2015 of a new *Law on the Protection of Citizen Security*, which is clearly designed to frustrate some of the most widespread practices that protesters employed during the last cycle of demonstrations against the austerity measures (2011–14).

(b) The second central area is the abrupt emergence, since the beginning of the twenty-first century, of local ordinances and municipal nuisance regulations that further extend the long arm of public authorities in controlling, particularly through fines, the use of public spaces and behaviour that is considered contrary to 'civility'. Although the centuries-old tradition of city regulations in Spain can be traced back to the period leading up to the formation of the liberal state, such intensive recourse to these kinds of regulations, which attempt to legitimise ambitious bouts of hyperactive state interventionism (Crawford 2009), is also a feature of other democracies. However conveniently the historical peculiarities of Spain might explain these regulations, they appear to respond more to the logic of a 'culture of control' (Garland 2001) and their expansion, strongly associated with neoliberalism and the punitive turn in the UK and the US, seemingly founded on criminological theories such as the 'broken windows' paradigm.

Over the past few years, both approaches in the policing of anti-austerity protests (see also Blay 2013) have complemented each other. This complementary relationship can more or less be summed up as follows: where the application of criminal law and particularly of offences against public order entered into an open conflict with the established principles of criminal justice and constitutional rights, national administrative legislation on public order (now rebranded as 'citizen security') can circumvent such conflict. It can do so insofar as it invests the police with broad executive powers to impose fines and to ban activities related to political demonstrations in public spaces and other activities such as recreational drug use, prostitution and so forth. Where the citizen security law would not apply, because the activities were not considered to harm security or public order, the vast network of thousands of local ordinances on 'civility', 'noise', 'public cleansing', 'mobility' and similar would still give local police bodies the power to fine and prohibit almost any 'unconventional' or 'undesired' use of public space. These measures constitute a closely knit punitive system, in which breaching an irrelevant rule in an obscure local ordinance can very easily escalate to the equivalent of a criminal offence.

A refusal to cooperate in any way with a law enforcement agent usually results in the filing of criminal charges for disobeying a police officer (Larrauri Pijoan 2007: 18). However, there are no equivalent 'escalation' systems in terms of procedural guarantees and constitutional controls: local ordinances often 'fly below the radar' of judicial review, and on the few occasions when they were declared illegal or unconstitutional, it was often after a long process and a succession of legal appeals.

Policing the protests against austerity

From 2011 to 2013–14, Spanish politics underwent important transformations, driven by intense social mobilisation against austerity and corruption. In May 2011, a new cycle of political protest began with the emergence of the *Indignados* or *15M* (May Fifteen, *15 de Mayo*) movement, inspired by the Arab Spring revolts, which in turn inspired other similar initiatives such as the Occupy Wall Street protests in the US. One of the most significant of them all was the occupation of the *Puerta del Sol* Square in the heart of Madrid, by thousands of protesters for almost a month. This enormously symbolic political action was possible due to the strong reaction to the previous arrest of nineteen peaceful protesters, who tried to camp out in the square on the night of 16 May. The images of heavy-handed police coercion against this small group of people were disseminated through social media, which mobilised tens of thousands to occupy the square – a protesting multitude since Spain's transition to democracy, who established a public space for political socialisation over the following weeks. The success, even if temporary, of the 'take the square' protests in Madrid, Barcelona and many other cities in the country was followed by a significant increase in the number of protests (Martín García 2014: 303; see also Figure 4.1). In 2012, there were twice as many demonstrations as in 2011 and four times as many as in 2004. A total of 2,732 protests were held in Madrid between January and September 2012 alone.

The spectacle of repressive policing of peaceful political protesters triggered a successive cycle of mobilisation. This realignment provoked by the use of excessive force against protesters, which was also perceived as illegal, immediately obliged the authorities to reconsider the political costs of conventional policing and legal measures to stifle protests. Since the start of the 2011 protests, the authorities engaged in the intensive use of 'administrative sanctions' of various kinds, including fines, prohibitions and restriction orders, provided for in the laws on public order and local ordinances to prevent nuisance. The group of lawyers supporting the Madrid camp in the *Puerta del Sol* (*Comisión Legal Sol*) refers to almost 1,000 fines from March 2011 to December 2012, amounting to around 300,000 euros (see Table 4.1). This set of sanctioning mechanisms is non-criminal and more politically neutral in nature, less easily associated with traditional forms of political repression and far less open to judicial control and review than criminal sanctions. They have proved themselves to be an effective dissuasive tactic against social mobilisation that has hardly attracted as much media attention as police violence and criminal arrests. As the Spanish Constitution prohibits the imposition of custodial sanctions through non-criminal procedures, this softer form of repressing dissent fundamentally turned to the imposition of administrative fines

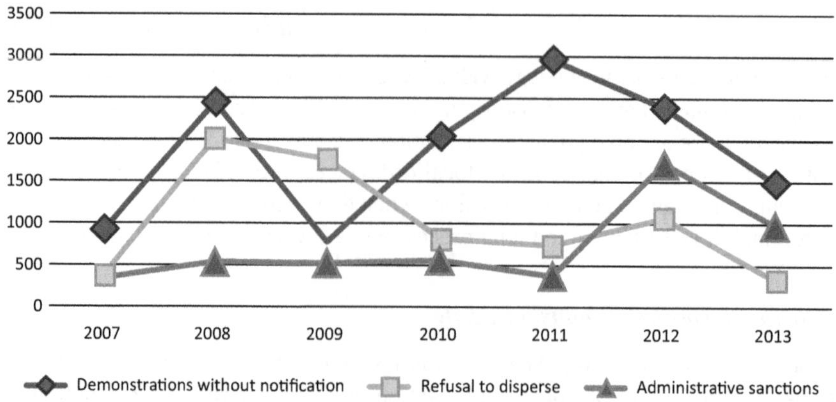

Figure 4.1 Demonstrations without prior notification, refusal to disperse and administrative sanctions (2007–2013).

Source: Based on data from the Statistical Yearbook 2013, Ministry of Home Affairs (Ministerio del Interior 2014). The figure includes only data on sanctions imposed related to the exercise of the freedom of assembly based on the Law on Citizen Security, and not on other provisions such as local ordinances, etc.

Table 4.1 Bureaucratic repression of the Madrid 15M protests (2011–2012)

Date	*Motive (M) or Location (L) of the Demonstration*	*Category of Administrative Infraction*	*Number of Sanctions*
May 15–20, 2011	In *Puerta del Sol* (L)	Organising an unreported gathering	29
June–September 2011	In front of the parliament (L)	Disturbing the peace	9
	Catholic *World Youth Day* (M)	Disturbing the peace and disobedience	21
	In front of the Parliament (L)	Organising an unauthorised protest	12
	In front of the Madrid Stock Exchange building (L)	Disturbing the peace and disobedience	21
January–April 2012	Higher public transport prices (M)	Disobedience and resistance	89
	Labour reform (M)	Disobedience and disturbing the peace	87
	Discussion meetings in *Puerta del Sol* (L)	Disobedience	2
	Police raid in the *Lavapiés* neighbourhood of Madrid (L)	Disturbing the peace	5
	Struggle for Housing (M)	Disobedience	75
	Neighbourhood meetings (M)	Use of megaphones, signs, etc. in violation of several city ordinances	6
	Arrests during protest against higher public transport prices (M)	Disobedience	73

12–15 May 2012	*15M* anniversary (M)	Disobedience and disturbing the peace	314
June–December 2012	Meeting which crossed the path of a religious procession (L)	Disturbing the peace	6
	Eviction (M)	Disobedience	3
	Miners demonstration (M)	Disobedience	3
	In front of the headquarters of the two major parties (L)	Disobedience and disturbing the peace	3
	Demonstration of civil servants (M)	Disobedience	56
	Visit of Angela Merkel (M)	Disobedience and disturbing the peace	3
	On 25 September in front of the Parliament, and on 4 October in solidarity with those arrested on 25-S (L-M)	Disobedience	5
	In front of the Ministry of Foreign Relations (L)	Disobedience	4
	Debt Audit (M)	Disturbing the peace	2
	Press conference of the 25-S coordinating committee (M)	Disturbing the peace	1
	In front of the parliament during debate on the budget (L)	Disobedience and disturbing the peace	62
	General strike (M)	Disturbing the peace	26
	Against a *Golden Dawn* event (M)	Disturbing the peace	2
	In front of the Parliament of Madrid against health service privatisation (L)	Disobedience	2
	Against the minister of health of the regional government (M)	Disturbing the peace	8
	Total number of administrative sanctions: 929		

Breakdown of the 956 administrative sanctions registered by the legal committee of the Puerta del Sol Camp

Sanctions	*Amount of each fine (€)*	*Total amount (€)*
896	300	268,800
52	500	26,000
8	600	4,800
		Total amount (€): 299,600

Source: Data provided by the *Legal Committee Sol (Comisión Legal Sol)*. Adapted from Oliver Olmo and Urda Lozano (2015a)

and the obstruction of the exercise of fundamental rights by bureaucratic means (such as a restrictive interpretation of the Constitution, consisting of making mandatory the prior notification of the intention to organise a demonstration).

Note that these measures are not a univocal, top-down decision made by the authorities to circumvent criminal justice so as to control dissent quietly. On the contrary, the number of people accused by the police of committing public disorder offences significantly increased over the same period. However, if we focus on the number of judicial convictions for the same crimes, we see that it remained almost stable over the same period (see Figure 4.2). An explanation

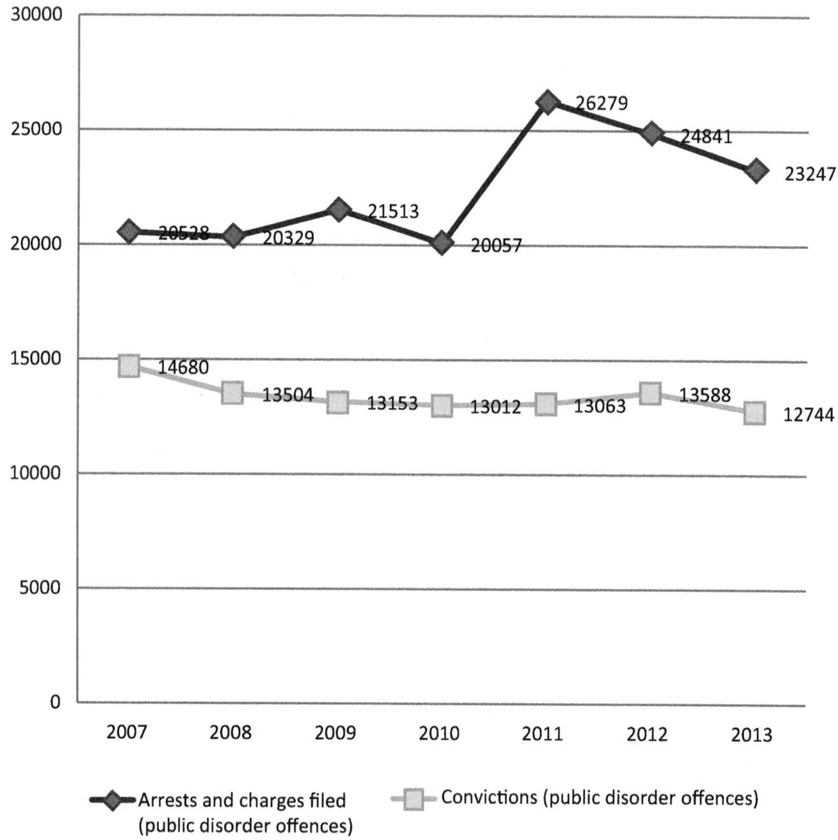

Figure 4.2 Public disorder offences: arrests and charges filed vs. convictions (2007–2013).

Source: Based on data from the Statistical Yearbook 2013, Ministry of Home Affairs (arrests and charges filed) (Ministerio del Interior 2014) and National Institute of Statistics. Note that the figure represents only offences committed by adults and excludes criminal misdemeanours (*faltas*) (in 2012, 906 minors were convicted of public disorder offences and 346 of public disorder misdemeanors). Other crimes less commonly associated with protests are excluded, but are nevertheless frequent, such as those considered 'crimes against the Constitution'.

for this divergence is that the Spanish courts have commonly considered these demonstrations as the legitimate exercise of the fundamental right to assembly and, even in protests not fully covered by constitutional precepts, as insufficient grounds for criminal prosecution (on the basis, among others, of the 'chilling effect' that criminal punishment could have on the fully legitimate exercise of rights). Certain decisions issued by a number of higher courts in Spain have corroborated this position, some of which even made explicit criticism of the political motives for such prosecutions. The discontent of some high-ranking members of the executive branch with this judicial reluctance to convict has also been explicitly declared on some occasions.

The shift from criminal to administrative sanctions therefore appears to be an adaptive response to two main obstacles: (a) judicial reluctance to convict peaceful protesters for activities that are either clearly or potentially protected by constitutional provisions; and (b) the more considerable social reaction provoked by criminal convictions and by the use of direct police coercion, compared with that provoked by the imposition of fines or non-criminal prohibitions.

Producing the anti-social subject: the problem of 'non-suitable enemies'

The reluctance of criminal courts to convict probably has to do not only with legal and constitutional concerns, but also with the fact that the targets of these sanctions were not necessarily the traditional 'suitable enemies' of the criminal justice system (Christie 1986, Wacquant 1999), but social actors capable of mobilising very significant political and media sympathies. Studies on the social composition of these protests (Calvo 2012) show that the typical activist was a young university-educated person, with an average economic status (which in Spain implies, especially for young people, a very high risk of unemployment). Rather than an already impoverished sector of the population that had to be contained and isolated, they represented the next rung up the ladder and had considerable means at their disposal to resist transformations that might imply a loss in status. It is hardly by chance that one of the current rallying points for social activists in Spain is the protest against evictions due to non-payment of mortgages: thousands of families who were previously able to afford a mortgage have been evicted from their homes, still owing what remains of their mortgage to the banks, regardless of whether the bank is eventually able to sell the property. However, the conservative media has, from the outset, attempted without success to portray these protests as driven by stigmatised social sectors. The stereotype most commonly used was *perroflauta*, a pejorative composition of the word *perro* (dog) and *flauta* (flute) (as these are considered the typical 'tools' homeless persons use) coined to associate protesters with poverty, begging and low standards of hygiene). Recourse to local ordinances on incivilities and public order legislation may also be considered an attempt to redefine protest and alternative uses of the public space through symbolic terms such as 'disorderly', 'dirty' and 'uncivil' behaviour, unrelated to the exercise of political rights – in short, merely a 'public nuisance', disturbing the peace and the rights of well-behaved citizens.

Repression of protest and administrative punitivism: the legal basis

A typology of political repression: classical-legal, dirty, soft

As we have seen, repression of protest through bureaucratic and less politically charged means has its political rationale. By repression I mean broadly those actions by public authorities that in the words of Davenport (2007: 2) 'violate First Amendment–type rights, due process in the enforcement and adjudication of law, and personal integrity or security'. It is therefore a normative, rights-based approach that takes it for granted that democracies need to integrate and to allow a fair amount of political dissent and disobedience, if they seek to be considered as such. While there are very different approaches on how to categorise different practices and strategies of repression (Fernandez 2008, Earl 2011), Oliver Olmo (2011) proposes a distinction between legal repression, 'dirty' repression and soft repression (*bureau repression*).

Legal repression, somehow the 'classical' type of repression, mainly refers to (a) police practices of riot control and (b) criminal offences regarding public order and refusal to cooperate with law enforcement bodies. Although widely used against protesters over recent years, activists have to some extent avoided the worst consequences of classical repression and have even turned them into a mobilising opportunity, as was evident in the first days of the protest in the *Puerta del Sol*. Socially excluded and legally alienated ethnic and social groups (e.g. migrants) face much greater difficulties in their efforts to resist legal repression, despite the effectiveness of strategies that involve non-excluded participants (Brigadas Vecinales de Observacion de Derechos Humanos 2014). The best example of the diversification of these social control mechanisms is the administrative detention of migrants in special detention centres (*CIE*, *Centros de Internamiento de Extranjeros*), which circumvents the unconstitutionality of detention dictated by civil authorities and is not officially a punishment.

Dirty repression would include practices such as the use of 'agent provocateurs', police infiltration of social movements, physical and psychological abuse by the police, etc. We have also seen this in the reactions to the protests: especially interesting was the unusually transparent picture of violent-looking infiltrators at some demonstrations, who even had to defend themselves from the police. These practices pose a serious risk of demobilisation by forcing movements and organisations to adopt a defensive, securitarian, if not semi-clandestine, attitude and by polarising their opinions towards non-violent tactics. However, they usually entail a high risk of undermining the legitimacy of the authorities in cases where the practices are revealed and successfully exposed, as has happened over the recent years.

Bureaucratic repression, or *soft repression*, would include a range of more subtle repressive tools. As mentioned earlier, administrative fines seem to have been the most widely used tool over the last years, together with other dissuasive practices such as strict rules on prior notification of the demonstration and arbitrary 'stop-and-search' procedures. These measures have increased more than any other over the recent years. Bureaucratic repression appears to be particularly effective against mobilisation in that it generates a much lower key political reaction from the general public and the politically active community: fines and bureaucratic obstacles will never trigger counter-mobilisations in quite the same way. They exist at an 'infra-political' level that hardly incites indignation and 'moral outrage' against police repression.

As previously mentioned, there are two fundamental legal bases through which the Spanish legal order provides for the use of administrative sanctioning power to repress political dissent: on the one side we have the *Law on Citizen Security Protection*; on the other, we find thousands of different local ordinances regulating 'incivilities', 'nuisance' or annoying behaviour of any kind, that have since the beginning of the century proliferated in Spain. Of course, these laws are not manifestly for the purpose of repressing dissent, but that is quite plainly the function they so often fulfil; so much so that it may no longer be considered a latent function. In general, the more these administrative regulations have encroached upon the exercise of fundamental rights and liberties (and they have done so, for example, to the point of banning the use of the Islamic veil or abolishing the right to public assembly through public ordinances), the more their repressive functions become politically charged rather than latent.

The Law on Citizen Security Protection

The first *Law on Citizen Security Protection* dates back to 1992. At that time, due to its 'flexibility' in terms of basic safeguards associated with the power to sanction, the law was very controversial and was even declared partially unconstitutional by the Spanish Constitutional Court. The measure was justified by the then socio-liberal government as a way to tackle drug-related problems and as a necessary update to the legislation on public order, still rooted in pre-constitutional laws. However, concerns surrounding the potential for political protest over very high-profile international events such as the 1992 Olympic Games in Barcelona and the World Fair in Sevilla were clearly reasons for its introduction (Arana and Germán 2008: 3).

Let us highlight some of the main contributions of the original *Law on Citizen Security Protection* that enabled the authorities to repress political dissent:

(a) The recognition of sweeping powers, to be used at the discretion of the police, to request an identity card from any member of the public and to detain those unwilling to present it, for the purposes of their identification. These stop-and-search practices constitute a clearly threatening measure especially among people not used to being the subject of police interest. Refusal to provide identification can also result in an escalation of sanctions, as it can constitute an administrative or even a criminal offence of failure to cooperate with a law enforcement agency.

(b) The provision of severe sanctions (up to 30,000 euros) for those who convoke public demonstrations without previous notification. That provision actually reversed the meaning and spirit of the Spanish Constitution, Article 21 of which firstly sets out the right to 'peaceful unarmed assembly' and secondly, although it requires prior notification to be given to the authorities, contemplates bans only 'when there are well-founded grounds to expect a breach of public order, involving danger to persons or property'. An extremely restrictive interpretation of the second provision of this article, interpreting such notification as mandatory for 'informative purposes', has passed into law with obvious chilling effects on the exercise of these rights: those personally 'communicating' the call for a demonstration will be held responsible for any infraction committed during the event. Even worse, *Legal Sol*, the main legal support group of the 15M Movement, has on numerous occasions reiterated that the imposition of fines not only continued but became more frequent, when prior notification of the demonstration had been given (Legal Sol 2013).

(c) Setting disproportionate sanctions for different conducts involving 'disorderly behaviour', 'public order administrative offences' and 'refusal to cooperate with the authorities' (fines up to 30,000 euros per person); a tendency that is even plainer in the most recent reform of the law, of March 2015, that provides for fines of up to 600,000 euros per person for non-communicated demonstrations near key public infrastructures (El País 2013a)

(d) Legalising the absence of some procedural safeguards surrounding the power to sanction, lending greater weight to police testimony in the course of a sanctioning process, and placing limitations on the role of judicial review, in favour of a system based on police and executive discretion. This relaxation of safeguards has to be added to the general lack of a system of guarantees in the regulation of administrative sanctioning equivalent to those used in criminal procedures.

In March 2015, the government amended the law, in order to introduce harsher sanctions and new definitions of infractions, in a reform that ran into heavy criticism from key institutions such as the Council of State, a consultative legislative body that published a report on the proposal contesting the constitutionality of its provisions (Consejo de Estado 2013). The introduction of the new law, which entered into force in July 2015 and is already under review in the Constitutional Court at the time of writing of this chapter, is noteworthy in at least three different ways:

(a) The new law was only introduced once the cycle of protests, which started in 2011, had already come to an end. The year 2014–5 appears to have marked the start of a new political phase, in which electoral and institutional participation has substituted street protests and extra-institutional mobilisation. In one remarkable example, the new mayor of Barcelona, elected in May 2015, had previously led the anti-eviction movement, a role that resulted in her arrest on several occasions. Among the measures that the new municipal government envisages in the short term is the repeal of the Barcelona ordinance of incivilities (*Ordenanza de Convivencia de Barcelona*), a good example of a local nuisance regulation that inspired the expansion of this kind of municipal hyper-interventionism all over the country. Rather than being an isolated case, the electoral success of anti-austerity activists was one of the features of the 2015 municipal elections in Spain.

(b) The reform took place at the same time as the introduction of a new Criminal Code in which penalties for offences against public order and others related to protests were also considerably aggravated (Oliver Olmo and Urda Lozano 2015b). Given the aforementioned role played by the judiciary in containing anti-protest punitivism, there is one substantial change in the Criminal Code that deserves even more attention: the complete elimination of the section on 'criminal misdemeanours' (*faltas*), i.e. minor criminal offences that merited fines rather than prison sentences but which were nevertheless protected by procedural safeguards that were similar to those associated with *regular* offences (*delitos*), in particular full judicial control of the sentencing process. The government formally presented the elimination of criminal misdemeanours, with a long tradition in the Spanish criminal justice system, as a benevolent measure aimed at decriminalising relatively irrelevant infractions. However, it seems evident that this reform is, on the contrary, punitive in nature: most of the old criminal misdemeanours are transformed into administrative infractions included either in the *Law on Citizen Security Protection* or in local ordinances on incivilities (Faraldo 2014). This critical analysis is coherent with the larger picture of punitivism that is present in most aspects of the reform of the Criminal Code. It appears to respond to the obvious fact that administrative sanctions were much easier to impose than misdemeanours, as they provided almost complete executive control of the process. They are also ultimately more difficult to challenge in the courts, not only because judges only intervene at a later stage in the process, but also because in administrative courts citizens have to pay a (recently introduced) fee to access the justice system, and because of the evidentiary privileges of police statements. This trend towards 'punitive decriminalisation' (Vieira Velloso 2013: 182) is far from being exclusive to Spain (see Ashworth and Zedner 2010, Natapoff 2015 on the USA, Zedner 2015) and certainly appears to be at the core of an international trend towards the emergence of nuisance regulation as a powerful tool for social control.

(c) As Table 4.2 illustrates, this reform of the law introduces a new list of administrative infractions that plainly fits some of the most common protest activities in the anti-austerity repertoire of collective action.

Table 4.2 Administrative infractions in the new *Law on Citizen Security Protection* in relation to collective protests

Description of the Infraction	*Fines*
Organising or promoting unnotified or prohibited demonstrations or rallies Possessing dangerous objects for the purposes of intimidation, when not a crime or a serious administrative infringement Violating the rules on pedestrian circulation or the planned itinerary for the demonstration that causes minor problems Showing disrespect towards a law enforcement officer, when not constituting a crime offence Occupying or entering any building against the will of its owners, when not constituting a crime offence. Occupying a street in contravention of the law or an administrative decision Not carrying a personal ID card or failing to report its loss More than three losses of the ID card in one year Harming public or private property or buildings in the public space, when not a crime Climbing on buildings or monuments in such a way as to risk causing harm to persons or property Removing fences or other devices set up by the security forces, when not a crime	100–600 €
Disturbing the security of public events, spectacles or religious celebrations Seriously disturbing security in demonstrations near the Congress, Senate and regional legislative assemblies, even if vacant, when not constituting a crime offence Disorderly conduct in the streets, public spaces or buildings that seriously affects security when blocking the street with vehicles, trash cans, tires or other objects Obstructing the activities of public officials in the exercise of their functions, when not constituting a criminal offence Refusal to cooperate with the authorities or law enforcement agents, when not constituting a criminal offence. Failure to produce identification or purposefully giving incorrect personal details Refusal to disperse at meetings or demonstrations in public spaces when they are illegal or have led to public disorder Disturbing the course of a legal meeting or demonstration, when not constituting a criminal offence Entering infrastructures that provide basic services, including overflying them, when seeking to interfere in their operation Lack of collaboration with law enforcement agencies in the investigation or prevention of a crime Unauthorised use of images or personal or professional data of authorities or security forces that poses a risk to their personal or family security or the success of an operation	601–30,000 €
Meetings or demonstrations, for which no prior notification has been given or that have been banned, close to infrastructures that provide basic services, including overflying them, when they pose a risk to people	30,001–600,000 €

Source: Adapted from Ávila Cantos et al. (2015)

The local ordinances on 'incivilities' and nuisance

Where the reach of the new *Law for Citizen Security Protection* ends, local ordinances enter the scene. As previously stated, they regulate an extremely broad range of incivilities, nuisances or merely annoying behaviour and are the second grand legal basis for the administrative repression of political dissent in Spain. Their importance has exponentially grown over the last decade, especially since the legal recognition in 2003 of municipal powers to create infractions and to impose sanctions when they are not respected. The first so-called 'ordinance of civility' to have a real impact on urban discipline was the Barcelona ordinance of 2005 (*Ordenanza de medidas para fomentar y garantizar la convivencia ciudadana en el espacio público de Barcelona*), now expected to be repealed by the new progressive city government elected in 2015. The Barcelona ordinance was in fact the model followed by most middle-sized and large cities in the country that copied and pasted (in many cases literally) the dispositions of the former into their own city regulations. It regulated a wide set of matters affecting constitutional rights, some of them as controversial as the legality of prostitution-related activities.

Let us not forget that local ordinances have the lowest standing among legal norms in the Spanish legal system: they are not in any way supposed to restrict fundamental rights or liberties recognised by the Constitution or the law. However, these ordinances have been used to regulate such controversial issues as prostitution, the wearing of Islamic veils, treatment of the homeless and the political use of streets, and in general to heavily discipline the use of public space. Even if according to the Spanish Constitution (Art. 149) only the central state, and not regions or municipalities, can legislate on public safety, and more importantly even though fundamental rights are not supposed to be regulated by anything other than legislation passed in the parliament (Art. 81 of the Constitution), by disguising 'public safety' and 'public order' issues as problems of 'civility', 'mobility', 'hygiene', 'noise standards' and so forth, municipalities in Spain are now powerful authorities in the exercise of social control over 'deviant' behaviour. The following are some common examples of the use of nuisance ordinances in relation to political protests:

(a) Protesters distributing leaflets in the streets to inform the public of a coming demonstration were stopped by the police and sanctioned in two ways: first, in application of a street cleaning ordinance, as if they were merely littering the street; secondly, following their refusal to stop distribution of the leaflets, they were charged with a criminal misdemeanour of refusal to cooperate with the police.
(b) Protesters using megaphones during a demonstration were sanctioned by the police for breaching the provisions of a local ordinance on noise and likewise for failing to keep to municipal by-laws when asked to do so.
(c) Protesters camping out in a public space were sanctioned by the police for breaching the provisions of local ordinances on street cleaning, parks and gardens, etc., with similar results for failing to follow municipal by-laws when asked to do so (see also Graeber 2013: xi–xiii; 2015).

(d) Protesters setting up stands in the street for the purpose of collecting signatures to petition municipal authorities were required to pay a fee or were sanctioned by the police for breaching the provisions of a local ordinance on street commerce, street performances and unauthorised artistic activities.
(e) Local ordinances on 'public mobility' and 'civility' were used to ban gatherings in public spaces that had not been authorised, openly contradicting the provisions of the Constitution (El País 2013b).
(f) Other attempts to curtail political protest through administrative rules have involved, for example, the use of rules on the protection of historic heritage, in an attempt to prevent demonstrations from passing through the historic centres of major cities in which touristic and commercial activities predominate (El País 2014).

Taking only the first of these examples, the use of these 'infra-legal' devices clearly leads to a 'symbolic downgrading' of these activities: by distributing leaflets, and ignoring constitutional requirements and even the jurisprudence of the European Court of Human Rights (Voorhoof 2010: 8), protesters are not considered to be exercising any right or protected freedom, but just engaging in littering and anti-social behaviour. The logic of soft repression frequently implies confusing the exercise of political rights with simple annoying, 'uncivil', apolitical behaviour, failing to acknowledge the rights and entitlements of the participants and therefore contributing to their 'legal alienation'.

Even if these ordinances contain provisions that are obviously unconstitutional, normative decentralisation via municipalisation and their discursive framework presents them as instruments that are unrelated to fundamental rights, which has made it difficult to challenge their validity in the court. In some cases, however, judges have declared some of these ordinances illegal. This is the case of the town Lleida's local ordinance on civism, which prohibited the use of the Muslim 'burka' in public on the grounds of public security concerns. In 2013, the Spanish Supreme Court ruled that the ordinance regulated the exercise of the constitutional right to religious freedom, which is an exclusive competence of the national parliament, and therefore declared it illegal. The ordinance on civility and anti-social behaviour of Valladolid was also considered illegal by a higher court, which held that it violated several principles related to the imposition of sanctions and that it curtailed legitimate protests in public spaces (Vecinosvalladolid.org 2013). The consequences of the end of the change in the political cycle and the various judicial decisions that have invalidated disproportionate ordinances are still being felt.

Conclusions: criminal vs. non-criminal approaches to social control

Several significant differences between criminal sanctions and administrative sanctions have been highlighted in this paper as tools for policing political dissent and social mobilisation. They may be summed up as follows.

The challenge of punitive decriminalisation

Circumventing social scrutiny

Politically motivated criminal sanctions can easily provoke strong negative public reactions, which can even reinforce public sympathy for social mobilisation. There are of course exceptions, such as those cases of criminal sanctions associated with politically motivated terrorist offences, where a process of stigmatisation creates a favourable climate of punitive exceptionalism. But with the exception of those areas where 'suitable enemies' have been constructed, even conservative legal thinkers and the mainstream media tend to consider that criminal law should refrain from the prosecution and the punishment of political acts in the public arena that neither damage property nor involve the risk of physical harm. Administrative sanctions, however, operate at a different level: they are less politically charged, the legal order considers them less stigmatising and intrusive, and the public reaction is never quite the same. In addition, legal action against a national authority or a national law is usually easier to organise than against hundreds of individual local ordinances that usually fly under the radar of media and legal attention.

Circumventing procedural safeguards

Institutional safeguards in criminal and administrative procedures are significantly different:

(a) One of the major differences is the delay in completing a judicial review of administrative sanctions: only after the sanctions have been imposed by the administration and any administrative appeals have been exhausted can the party liable to pay the fine apply for a judicial review of the administrative proceedings. In the vast majority of cases, the administration will not take into account the objections of the party that has been fined during the administrative phase. According to the 2014 official statistics, 1226 administrative appeals against sanctions for public disorder were dismissed, and only 236 were accepted (Ministerio de Interior 2015: 772). Criminal offences, even criminal misdemeanours, require court action from the outset, which involves substantially greater safeguards of the rights of each party than in the administrative process.

(b) That striking difference in access to judicial review and judicial safeguards brings us to a further difference: the discretionary prosecutorial powers of administrative authorities, which allow them to decide whether to sanction in each case. In contrast, criminal procedures are not ruled by this 'opportunistic' principle and the court has a duty to investigate each case regardless of the circumstances. This discretionary power promotes paternalistic attitudes in authorities, which have been known to forgo sanctions in an attempt at appeasement, to calm critical public responses or as a form of tokenism before initiating negotiations with activists and demonstrators over their plans for future actions.

(c) Other procedural aspects make administrative sanctions potentially more advantageous for authorities bent on sterner repressive measures. In addition to the aforementioned privileged evidentiary value of police testimony, unlike the courts, administrative authorities have no legal obligation to take account of the economic circumstances of the party liable to pay the fine (since a fixed-fine model and not 'day-fines' is applied). That situation also means that authorities may issue notifications of the start of a sanctioning procedure that refers to potential sanctions that may range, for a common example, 'from 300 to 30,000 euros'. Moreover, the most recent system of judicial fees in Spain means that anybody contesting an administrative sanction through the courts will have to pay a tax that in very many cases will be in excess of the fine for which that person is liable. These kinds of monetary sanctions and barriers to accessing the justice system can have a significant chilling effect on the future exercise of rights, especially when it affects politically inexperienced activists.

An international phenomenon

The problems arising from these tactics of social control are therefore similar to those posed by civil sanctions and civil orders well known in other countries, such as the British anti-social behaviour order (ASBO). In other words, 'regulatory ideas are being used to circumvent and to erode established criminal justice principles, notably those of due process, proportionality and special protection traditionally extended to young people' (Crawford 2009: 810). As Ashworth (2008: 99) remarked, an extreme approach of this kind would lead to the conclusion that since an order such as an ASBO is not formally considered a penalty, it is not covered by the same human rights law that limits criminal proceedings but only by more broad rights such as the respect for private life (Art. 8 of the European Convention on Human Rights).

Strategies of legal resistance

Given these alarming trends, a reasonable question would be whether critical legal scholars will defend the formal, legal 'criminalisation' of public disorder behaviours as a means of upholding constitutional guarantees on the exercise of fundamental rights and liberties (Ashworth and Zedner 2008). Such a move may advance serious arguments against the neoliberal tendency towards the 'decriminalisation' of some areas of formal social control. The recent developments in Spanish criminal and administrative legislation make this discussion even more urgent: the concept of criminal misdemeanour has been taken out of the Criminal Code, and the acts previously falling under that category now become either 'full offences' or 'administrative infractions'. While matters such as petty theft have become criminal offences (the poor will be punished), peaceful protest and civil disobedience, misrepresented as 'public disorders', will be administratively managed and curtailed (the soon-to-be-poor will be policed).

Legal scholars have not paid enough attention to the re-emergence of statutes, ordinances, and law enforcement measures aimed at disorderly or uncivil public conduct and, more broadly, at 'the quality of life in public spaces' (Livingston 1997). To be fair, there is some considerable attention being paid by Spanish administrative and criminal law scholars to the topic of safeguards in administrative sanctioning processes, and most of them express the need to apply the constitutional guarantees of criminal procedure in administrative proceedings. Any such change is unlikely to happen, although the 'equalise the safeguards' approach to administrative sanctions has gained greater relevance over recent years.

Among other resistance practices (Legal Sol 2014, González Sánchez 2014), some well-known formulas founded on constitutional grounds appear especially appropriate to challenge some of the problems raised in this paper. An interesting example is the 'chilling effect' doctrine, described by the US Supreme Court and then adopted in other national and international legal systems (Bailone 2010, Maqueda Abreu 2015), including Spain and the case law of the European Court of Human Rights. The idea that the potential discouragement of the legitimate exercise of rights by the threat of legal sanction should be a motivation to consider this threat of legal sanction itself unconstitutional opens the door to a legal doctrine of limitation of coercion explicitly based on the concrete democratic necessity of integrating dissent and disobedience.

Even if there seems to be a new trend towards punitive decriminalisation, it has to be historically contextualised. Arthur Kinoy, civil rights attorney and one of the founders of the US Center for Constitutional Law, was directly involved in some of the cases (especially *Dombrowski v. Pfister*) that led to the chilling effect doctrine. His memoirs (Kinoy 1984), illustrate that it was through local ordinances and civil injunctions that black people were formally controlled and segregated, and consequently deprived of their most basic political rights. When Rosa Parks refused to give up her seat on a bus in Alabama, she was in violation of a city ordinance on transportation that segregated black citizens from white citizens. As we know, neoliberal methods of punishment appear to value this kind of decentralised, diversified punitive control very highly. A rights-based, legal democratic theory capable of guiding strategic political action constitutes, perhaps more than ever before, a much-needed project to counter these emergent forms of punitive control.

References

Arana, X. and Germán, I. (2008) 'Análisis de la aplicación de la Ley Orgánica 1/1992, de 21 de febrero, sobre protección de la seguridad ciudadana en relación con el fenómeno social de las drogas', *Eguzkilore: Cuaderno del Instituto Vasco de Criminología*, (22): 5–51.

Ashworth, A. (2008) 'Criminal law, human rights and preventative justice', in B. McSherry, A. Norrie and S. Bronitt (eds.) *Regulating Deviance: The Redirection of Criminalisation and the Futures of Criminal Law*, Oxford: Bloomsbury Publishing.

Ashworth, A. and Zedner, L. (2008) 'Defending the criminal law: Reflections on the changing character of crime, procedure, and sanctions', *Criminal Law and Philosophy*, 2(1): 21–51.

Ashworth, A. and Zedner, L. (2010) 'Preventive orders: A problem of under-criminalization?' in A. Duff, L. Farmer, S. Marshall, M. Renzo and V. Tadros (eds.) *The Boundaries of the Criminal Law*, Oxford: Oxford University Press.

Ávila Cantos, D., Domínguez Sánchez, A., García García, S., Maroto Calatayud, M., Martín García, O. and Oliver Olmo, P. (2015) 'La burrorrepresión de la protesta y de la pobreza', in D. Bondia, F. Daza and A. Sánchez (eds.) *Defender a quien defiende. Leyes mordaza y criminalización de la protesta en el Estado español*, Barcelona: Icaria.

Bailone, M. (2010) 'El antiterrorismo como paradigma de desaliento de la participación ciudadana', in L. Diez Picazo and A. Nieto Martín (eds.) *Derechos fundamentales en el Derecho penal europeo*, Pamplona: Civitas.

Blay, E. (2013) 'El control policial de las protestas en España', *Indret: Revista para el Análisis del Derecho*, 4: 2–32.

Brigadas Vecinales de Observación de Derechos Humanos (2014) *3° Informe sobre los Controles de Identidad Racistas en Madrid.* Online. Available at: http://brigadasvecinales.org/wp-content/uploads/2015/05/Tercer-informe-BVODH.pdf (accessed 20 September 2015).

Calvo, K. (2012) 'El 15-M ¿Quiénes son?'. Online. Available at: http://blogs.elpais.com/alternativas/2012/05/el-15m-quienes-son.html (accessed 20 September 2015).

Christie, N. (1986) 'Suitable enemies', in H. Bianchi and R. van Swaaningen (eds.) *Abolitionism: Towards a Non-Repressive Approach to Crime*, Amsterdam: Free University Press.

Consejo de Estado (2013) *Dictamen sobre el Anteproyecto de ley orgánica de protección de la seguridad ciudadana.* Online. Available at: www.boe.es/buscar/doc.php?id=CE-D-2014–557 (accessed 20 September 2015).

Crawford, A. (2009) 'Governing through anti-social behaviour. Regulatory challenges to criminal justice', *British Journal of Criminology*, 46(9): 810–831.

Davenport, C. (2007) 'State repression and political order', *Annual Review of Political Science*, 10: 1–23.

Earl, J. (2011) 'Political repression: Iron fists, velvet gloves, and diffuse control', *Annual Review of Sociology*, 37, 261–284.

El País (2013a) 'Council of Europe slams PP bill that hikes fines for protestors at public rallies'. Online. Available at: http://elpais.com/elpais/2013/12/03/inenglish/1386099589_255306.html (accessed 20 September 2015).

El País (2013b) 'Guadalix de la Sierra prohíbe las acampadas y las asambleas'. Online. Available at: http://elpais.com/elpais/2011/08/30/actualidad/1314692228_850215.html (accessed 20 September 2015).

El País (2014) 'La Abogacía del Estado rechaza cerrar a las protestas el centro de las ciudades'. Online. Available at: http://politica.elpais.com/politica/2014/03/27/actualidad/1395949651_719312.html (accessed 20 September 2015).

Faraldo, P. (2014) 'La despenalización de las faltas: entre la agravación de las penas y el aumento de la represión administrativa', *Indret: Revista para el Análisis del Derecho*, 3: 1–32.

Fernandez, L. (2008) *Policing Dissent: Social Control and the Anti-Globalization Movement*, New Brunswick, NJ and London: Rutgers University Press.

Garland, D. (2001) *The Culture of Control*, Oxford: Oxford University Press.

González Sánchez, I. (2014) *La penalidad neoliberal: aumento de presos y reconfiguración del Estado en Espan~a* (1975–2008), Unpublished thesis, Universidad Nacional de Educación a Distancia.

Graeber, D. (2013) *The Democracy Project: A History, a Crisis, a Movement*, New York: Spiegel & Grau.

Graeber, D. (2015) 'David Graeber: Ferguson and the criminalization of American life'. Online. Available at: http://anarchistnews.org/content/david-graeber-ferguson-and-criminalization-american-life (accessed 20 September 2015).

Kinoy, A. (1984) *Rights on Trial: The Odyssey of a People's Lawyer*, Cambridge, MA: Harvard University Press.

Larrauri Pijoan, E. (2007) 'Ayuntamientos de izquierdas y control del delito', *Indret: Revista para el Análisis del Derecho*, 3: 1–23.

Legal Sol (2013) 'Reabriendo el debate sobre el ejercicio del derecho fundamental de reunión'. Online. Available at: https://legal15m.wordpress.com/2013/04/07/reabriendo-el-debate-sobre-el-ejercicio-del-derecho-fundamental-de-reunion/ (accessed 20 September 2015).

Legal Sol (2014) 'Burorresistiendo. Manual de emergencia y autodefensa contra las multas'. Online. Available at: http://delirante.nodo50.info/legal/MANUAL%20BURORRESISTIENDO.pdf (accessed 10 February 2016).

Livingston, D. (1997) 'Police discretion and the quality of life in public places: Courts, communities, and the new policing, *Columbia Law Review*, 57(3): 551–672.

Maqueda Abreu, M. L. (2015) 'La criminalización del espacio público. El imparable ascenso de las "clases peligrosas"', *Revista Electrónica de Ciencia Penal y Criminología*, 17–12. Online. Available at: http://criminet.ugr.es/recpc/17/recpc17-12.pdf (accessed 15 January 2016).

Martín García, O. J. (2014) 'Soft repression and the current wave of social mobilisations in Spain', *Social Movement Studies*, 13(2): 303–308.

Ministerio del Interior (2014) 'Anuario Estadístico 2013'. Online. Available at: www.interior.gob.es/web/archivos-y-documentacion/anuario-estadistico-2013 (accessed 20 September 2015).

Ministerio del Interior (2015) 'Anuario Estadístico 2014'. Online. Available at: www.interior.gob.es/web/archivos-y-documentacion/anuario-estadistico-de-2014 (accessed 20 September 2015).

Natapoff, A. (2015) 'Misdemeanor decriminalization', *Vanderbilt Law Review*, 68(4): 1055–1116.

Oliver Olmo, P. (2011) 'Represión sucia contra el 15M', *Diagonal*. Online. Available at: www.diagonalperiodico.net/la-plaza/represion-sucia-contra-15m.html (accessed 20 September 2015).

Oliver Olmo, P. and Urda Lozano, J. C. (2015a) 'Bureau-repression: Administrative sanction and social control in modern Spain', *Oñati Socio-Legal Series*. Online. Available at: https://papers.ssrn.com/sol3/papers.cfm?abstract_id=2574670 (accessed 20 September 2015).

Oliver Olmo, P. and Urda Lozano, J. C. (2015b) *Protesta democrática y democracia antiprotesta. Los movimientos sociales ante la represión policial y las leyes mordaza*, Navarra: Pamiela.

Vecinosvalladolid.org (2013) 'Sentencia del TSJ anulando parcialmente la "ordenanza antisocial" por contener preceptos inconstitucionales y nulos de pleno derecho'. Online. Available at: www.vecinosvalladolid.org/spip.php?article7841 (accessed 20 September 2015).

Vieira Velloso, J. G. (2013) 'Beyond criminocentric dogmatism: Mapping institutional forms of punishment in contemporary societies', *Punishment & Society*, 15(2): 166–186.

Voorhoof, D. (2010) 'Legal opinion on the aspects of freedom of expression and on the right to distribute leaflets and impart information and ideas, in the case of Mr. Katsuhisa Fujita'. Online. Available at: http://wind.ap.teacup.com/people/html/20100430voorhoof.fuijta.legalopinion.doc (accessed 20 September 2015).

Wacquant, L. (1999) '"Suitable enemies": Foreigners and immigrants in the prisons of Europe', *Punishment & Society*, 1(2): 215–222.

Zedner, L. (2015) 'Penal subversions: When is a punishment not punishment, who decides and on what grounds?', *Theoretical Criminology*. Online. Available at: http://tcr.sagepub.com/content/early/2015/08/13/1362480615598830.abstract (accessed 20 September 2015).

5 Tackling homelessness through criminalisation

The case of Hungary

Léna Podoletz

Introduction

In this chapter I would like to describe an issue that has been widely discussed in Hungary by academics, politicians, police officers and police chiefs, social workers, local governments, the Constitutional Court of Hungary and by the members of the public, during the course of the last few years, namely the criminalisation of homelessness in Hungary. This topic has generated a very intense debate among the aforementioned groups, in which all the sides presented very different and strong opinions. I believe it also serves as a perfect illustration of the trend of addressing incivilities through the blurring of the boundaries between criminal and civil/administrative law that seems to be an increasing tendency across Europe. Millie (2008: 380) noted the blurring of the boundaries between criminal and anti-social behaviour. Attempting to handle something that is exclusively a social problem with the tools offered by the criminal law leads, moreover, to the blurring of the boundaries between criminal and social policy law. The policing of homelessness is a very striking example. As pointed out by Stuart (2014), the study of such policing can be a very important source for understanding the changes in urban governance and social control. Examining the trends and tools of regulating visible poverty as a form of public incivility can tell us a lot about tolerance and concern for the vulnerable members of a specific society, and homelessness lies at the intersection of these two phenomena. How the lawmakers react to visible poverty can inform us about their standpoints on the uses of social policy and about the responsibility of the state – and the society, in general – for its members who happen to be in need. The way lawmakers address the conduct or the phenomenon we refer to as public incivilities shows us the way they think about differences (whether these be cultural or lifestyle differences) and their place in public spaces, in other words whether lawmakers think it is tolerable to use public spaces in many different ways, not all of which may be considered usual by the standards of mainstream society. This chapter discusses the criminalisation of homelessness in Hungary, the events that led up to the infamous change of the Constitution ('Fundamental Law of Hungary') and the current legislative background regarding this issue. It also highlights some of the possible underlying reasons and consequences of such changes.

The ambiguity of the Hungarian category of infractions

Many authors have discussed the re-emergence of regulations criminalising the poor in many different Western countries and some of these works have pointed to the increasing trend of punishing the homeless (see, for example, DeVerteuil, May and von Mahs 2009: 650; von Mahs 2005: 944; Livingstone 1997: 556–557; May 2015, Stuart 2014, Beckett and Murakawa 2012: 231; Herbert 2008, Amster 2008).These trends would appear to be the exact opposite of the phenomenon Garland calls 'defining deviance down' (Garland 2002: 117–119). Of course, the literature talks about less hostile examples as well when describing state-level or local policies aimed at homeless people (see DeVerteuil, May and von Mahs 2009: 651 or Stuart 2014: 1909). However, it seems like the latter cases appear to be becoming less common at the beginning of the twenty-first century. By 'criminalisation' we usually mean the inclusion of an act in the Criminal Code (or criminal law) or in the Code of Infractions or the criminal regulations created by local authorities. However, homelessness is not regulated only within the realm of criminal law. Sometimes the tools come from the toolbox of civil or administrative law, especially at the local level, and sometimes they blend criminal and civil measures together to create legally hybrid techniques, as Beckett and Murakawa (2012: 231–232) have pointed out. The techniques used to criminalise homelessness in Hungary are of this hybrid nature, as is the whole phenomenon of so-called petty offences or administrative offences (violations). Before describing the steps of the criminalisation of homelessness, it is therefore necessary to give a brief introduction to the legal system of Hungary and to the nature of the law that regulates infractions.

In Hungary, all crimes are included in the Criminal Code (currently Act C of 2012 in the Code) and no other acts but the ones described in that act are 'crimes'. This means that only those offenders who committed these offences can be subjected to a criminal procedure. However, the Criminal Code is not the only act defining offences. Some minor offences are defined by the Code of Infractions (currently Act II of 2012 on Infractions, Infractions Procedure and the Infractions Database). The nature of infractions has been debated in the Hungarian legal literature for some time, because even though the acts listed there are petty offences, the procedure is very different from the one described in the Criminal Code. If we take a quick look at the issue from a historical perspective, we can see that it has been introduced as a procedure to deal with petty offences (which are, of course, of a criminal nature). The sanctions listed in the Act also suggest that we are dealing with the procedure for 'petty offences' and therefore, at least technically, with a criminal procedure of some kind. But contrary to the regular criminal procedure (applicable in the cases of criminal offences from the Criminal Code), where punishment can only be imposed by courts, here some sanctions can be imposed also, for example, by the patrolling police officers. The new Code of Infractions seemingly put an end to this discussion when it declared in its introductory section that these offences were indeed offences of a 'criminal nature', yet the ones that are not dangerous enough to be included in the Criminal Code. So the 'criminal nature' becomes the central element of infractions, while the offences included in the Code of Infractions are very clearly of a mixed nature (Nagy 2012: 220). In Hungary, the conduct to which the academic literature usually refers as incivilities or anti-social behaviour is mostly regulated by the Code of Infractions (for example, littering and certain cases of rough sleeping and of begging) although some of it is regulated also by the Criminal Code (for example, graffiti). Additionally, according to a very recent decision by the Constitutional Court, local governments are entitled to regulate the 'rules of conduct' for the communities within their jurisdiction (Constitutional Court 29/2015).

Criminalisation of homelessness

The steps leading to the criminalisation of homelessness

The dispiriting story of the criminalisation of homelessness in Hungary began between 2008 and 2011 when several local governments (both in and outside of Budapest, for example in the Eighth District of Budapest or in the city of Kaposvár) decided to declare certain types of undesirable behaviour as 'administrative offences' within their own jurisdiction. Until the recent legislative changes in 2012, local governments were allowed to declare any act of their choice as an 'administrative offence' as long as it was limited only to their own jurisdiction. They were free to do so since neither the Code of Infractions nor the Criminal Code or the Constitution said anything about the required level of regulation regarding these kinds of behaviour. In the long list of acts that were criminalised this way between 2008 and 2011, we could thus find examples such as 'taking litter out of a trashcan', 'begging in public places', 'placing private property on public property' and 'using public places for living purposes'. It should be noted that the local governments seemed to select the acts for criminalisation and even the wording for the description of these offences quite randomly (to give an example, different local governments used different words to refer to the act of 'dumpster diving', which made it difficult for people to comply with the law). The penalty for the violation of such local offences was a fine.

At the end of 2011 (in November and December) the Parliament passed the amendment of the Code of Infractions, making the 'repeated violation of a local regulation regarding the prohibition of using public places for living purposes' part of the Code. Immediately after this, in December 2011, the Constitutional Court ruled in the case of one of the local governments that its prohibition regarding 'dumpster diving' was unconstitutional and therefore annulled this specific local regulation (Constitutional Court 176/2011). One year later, in November 2012, the Constitutional Court, following the principles of its decision from 2011, ruled that the above-mentioned amendment of the Code of Infractions was also unconstitutional and annulled that amendment (Constitutional Court 38/2012).

Following the decision of the Court, in March 2013, the Parliament passed a law that amended the Constitution, namely the infamous Fourth Amendment of the Constitution.[1] This amendment allowed the Parliament as well as local governments to declare the conduct described as 'using public places for living purposes' illegal in order to protect public order, public safety, public health and the cultural heritage in some public places. Even though it is not possible to criminalise the above-mentioned conduct – essentially, homelessness – in all public places, the fact that the legislator felt that this amendment needed to be made and this issue needed to be dealt with on a constitutional level clearly shows the attitude of the government and the Parliament towards homeless people. This can be seen also from somewhat cynical comments included in the proposal of the amendment: the commentary mentions the fact that criminalisation of homelessness is only possible in order to protect public order, public safety, public health and the cultural heritage and only in places which are specifically described by the law, which – according to the commentary – is essentially a guarantee of the protection of homeless people from being banned without a good reason. The criminalisation proposed is therefore to be understood as being for their own good.

In September 2013, the Parliament amended the Code of Infractions so that it now declares the conduct of 'using public places for living purposes' as illegal in places that are part of the World Cultural Heritage Site or any other place that is specified as a so-called protected zone by the local government within its own jurisdiction. Persons who commit this offence can be sentenced to community work, and if they are not willing to do the work, then a fine can be imposed. If they do not pay the fine, they will have to spend a certain amount of time in prison (with the amount of time depending on the amount of the fine that would have to be paid). Persons who commit this offence three times within six months can be immediately sentenced to spend time in prison.

In December 2013, the local government of Budapest passed the order listing the areas of the city where the behaviour described above is illegal (Assembly of Budapest 77/2013). Homeless people were effectively banished from most of the inner-city areas of Budapest. The whole area of the Fifth and Thirteenth Districts (out of the twenty-three districts of Budapest) became a 'protected zone', roughly meaning that homeless people could be fined upon merely entering those districts. Of course, luckily, the reality is not so harsh – most police officers appear reluctant to comply with the new regulations, and even if they do, most of the time they choose not to fine the homeless people but to simply ask them to leave.

In September and December 2014, the Supreme Court decided that most parts of the above-mentioned local government order were against the law and annulled them. Its arguments were based on the previous decisions of the Constitutional Court on the topic of criminalising homelessness, and in accordance with those, the Supreme Court stated that in general the law could not make homelessness a state in which a person had to choose between using social services and staying in public spaces and therefore risking punishment. At the same time, the Court acknowledged the right to prohibit 'rough sleeping' in places where it explicitly endangered public order, public safety, public health, or the cultural heritage. The Court also pointed out that the prohibition – both the list of areas where 'rough sleeping' was illegal and the reason for each of the areas to be included on the list – needed to be very detailed and clear. Homeless people cannot be banished either from the whole jurisdiction of a local government or from the whole town (Supreme Court Köf.5.020/2014/6 and Köf.5055/2014/2). Since then, the local government of Budapest has passed a new order, listing the areas where rough sleeping is illegal (Assembly of Budapest 27/2015).

Legal consequences of the current regulation regarding homelessness in Hungary

The definition of an infraction can be translated roughly as 'an act/conduct of a criminal nature that is dangerous to the society but the level of this danger is not as great as to make it necessary to declare it a crime'. This definition defines infractions in comparison with criminal offences by saying that they are minor or petty offences. Although it is stated that these acts are not dangerous enough to merit inclusion in the Criminal Code, the definition makes it clear that these petty offences are of the criminal kind. What makes its criminal nature even more obvious is the fact that in the case of most of these offences it is possible to apply imprisonment as punishment (although it can only be imposed by the court). Moreover, in the case of every infraction, non-payment of the fine can translate to incarceration (also only imposed by the court). So while we can see that the Code of Infractions has the characteristics of a code of minor offences, the acts prohibited by it are not all of the same criminal kind. Yet, in all cases – be it petty theft or homelessness in the designated areas – the same procedures apply. The procedure is more similar to the administrative one than to the criminal one. The court, when transforming the fine into imprisonment (when the fine is left unpaid), is only required to ask for the reasons behind the non-payment of the fine. As it does not inquire further into the matter, it is possible to be incarcerated on the basis of the Code without the court actually taking a close look at the case, since its procedure at that stage allows it to presume that the fine was lawful. So in general, the Code of Infractions creates a scenario where it is possible for a person to be given a prison sentence without a court looking into the details of the offence. While it is possible to make an appeal against the decision of the administrative authority, in which case the court would review the case, the matter depends on people deciding to make an appeal or not. As many do not, this de facto means that in the context of the local criminalisation of homelessness, it is possible for homeless people to go to prison simply because the local government decided to declare a certain area a 'protected zone'.

Relevance

How does this case illustrate the further blurring of the lines between criminal and civil/administrative law – and between criminal law and social policy law? As mentioned before, infractions are now essentially defined and treated as minor crimes. Some of them, indeed, are types of crimes. For example, in the case of theft, if the stolen goods are worth less than a certain amount of money, this is classified in Hungarian law as an infraction, while if they are worth more than a certain amount, the offence is treated as a criminal offence. The same can be said about many other crimes: less serious cases of the same conduct are typically treated as infractions. This shows that the distinction between an infraction and a criminal offence is not very clear indeed. Of course, this can be seen as a good thing, as committing an infraction does not give offenders a criminal record and the legal consequences of it are then in this respect less serious. The problem, however, is that the difference in consequences can be overrated. While it is true that the maximum amount of time that can be spent imprisoned for a single infraction is sixty days, this sentence does not sound that much better than a sentence for a minor criminal offence if we consider that those days have to be spent in a general prison.

The other critical issue in the case of infractions is the procedure. Essentially this is an administrative procedure. While the prison sentence can only be imposed by the court, the fine and community work can also be imposed by the 'local office of the government'. In reality this means that when, for example, someone is not able or willing to pay a fine imposed by the 'local office', the court will immediately transform it into incarceration without applying most of the guarantees of a criminal procedure.

So why is the case of homelessness relevant in this regard? The answer to this question is that no matter how one looks at it, the current regulations mean that a person, solely based on the fact that he or she is homeless (or more precisely that he or she is perceived by the authorities to be homeless) can eventually serve a sentence of up to two months in prison. The legislator has thus effectively decided to create a possibility for local governments to have the power to determine whether they want to allow certain people into their territory or not. And making these sections part of the Constitution itself (as described above) can also be seen as a symbolic act on the part of the legislator to show that if the Constitutional Court judges something to be 'unconstitutional' based on its human rights requirements and general principles, it is very easy then to make it 'constitutional' by changing the Constitution itself.

Understanding the reasons for and problems with the criminalisation of homelessness in Hungary[2]

Fear of crime

There have been many studies on the topic of fear of crime, trying to determine the roots of this phenomenon and find the main contributing factors to this very specific type of fear. Xu, Fiedler and Fleming (2005) refer to Trojanowicz and Bucqueroux (1992), who argue that when citizens think about the effectiveness of police work, they usually do not theorise about (serious) crime but are more concerned about the state of their neighbourhood and the quality of life there. They also suggest that empirical studies point in the direction of local disorder being a very important contributing factor to the fear of crime (Xu et al. 2005: 152). Borbíró (2014: 43) also points out that the orderliness of the area where people live – regarding both the physical landscape and the social structure – shapes the way they feel about crime, affects their fears and anxieties and, ultimately, their quality of life. In terms of leadership and political decision making, this has two main consequences, both of which are based on the fear of the community members and on the conclusions they may draw if they assume that crime rates are rising and that they are not safe walking on the streets or even in their own homes.

First, people might conclude that the perceived high crime rate is the fault of either the police, who are unable to protect the people and prevent crimes, or the political leaders (both at the national and the local level), who are not 'tough enough' on crime in their legislative decisions. Being perceived as ineffective is naturally political leaders' greatest fear, since it can result in the loss of office. This can by itself lead to the toughening of attitudes on crime and particularly on street crime and behaviour that can be seen as disorderly. The reason behind this is that measures implemented in order to take on street crime and disorder are among the most visible forms of policing (cf. the zero tolerance policing policy implemented in New York City during the mid-1990s).

The second consequence is that this also makes the political leaders realise that as long as people are scared, they will look for protection and security. This is part of the explanation of why in all election campaigns the topic of criminal policy has a central role. Furthermore, the crime situation is often described as deteriorating, regardless of the actual trends in crime rates based on the available statistics or new research data. This fits into the 'culture of fear' (Furedi 2002). As long as people feel scared enough, their leaders can get away with almost anything – even with measures that contribute to the reduction of rights (e.g. privacy) as long as they promise safety and security. Some may still say that the phenomenon in question, the criminalisation of homelessness, is valuable, as it and other similar measures have the potential to decrease fear of crime, just as Wilson and Kelling (1982) maintained in their 'broken windows' theory. However and at the same time, we can argue that such measures can be counterproductive, as they can also increase the fear of crime, especially when people encounter one of the criminalised behaviours. Criminalisation itself carries the message that an act poses a danger to society and that this danger is so great that the legislature felt the need to express their disapproval at the highest level (that of criminal law) or – in the Hungarian case – on the 'second highest level', the level of infraction law.

When describing the role of mass media in the forming of middle-class attitudes towards crime, Garland points out that knowledge about criminal justice and crime is not shaped by 'accurate information' but rather by a 'culturally given experience' (Garland 2002: 158). If this is the case, then the frequent use of the expression 'homeless criminality' – referring to crimes that are assumed likely to be committed by homeless people – by the media and politicians (for example, during the debate about criminalising homelessness [Parliament 2011])[3] might shape the opinions of people regarding crime as well, leading them to think that 'homeless criminality' is an actual existing phenomenon and that it is something to be concerned about. In this context, homeless people can even start to be seen as a 'criminal class', leading to the re-emergence of the long-abandoned concept.

The criminalisation of acts such as begging and rough sleeping clearly fuels this phenomenon.

All of this is relevant for us because in the 2011 parliamentary debate on criminalising rough sleeping, one of the arguments offered in favour of the proposal was that citizens might be 'scared' in the presence of homeless people (Parliament 2011).[4] If citizens think of homeless people as potential threats and risks and wish to distance themselves from potentially dangerous strangers (Hodgetts et al. 2011: 1944), the fear induced by this train of thought can indeed lead to their desire for this risk to be eliminated. However, the claims made in the Parliament about some citizens being scared of homeless people were not supported by any empirical evidence (neither during the debate nor since).

The politics of urban space – the promise of safety and security, urban aesthetics, commercial attractiveness of urban spaces and political success

According to Tosi, the poor have traditionally been seen in some policing models as 'a danger' or 'an object of fear and disgust' (Tosi 1996: 91). Once they are seen as a danger, criminal policy will react accordingly. In that way, a group of people who are already socially marginalised tend to also suffer punishment for their status and will be unable to change the status quo. This can reinforce the duality of 'us' versus 'them', the distinction between law-abiding citizens and the dangerous 'others', and consequently the societal exclusion of the latter.

Lefebvre (1996: 67) suggests that 'city and urban reality are related to use value' and that in urban politics, use value can be destroyed by 'subordinating the city and urban reality', referring to the fact that exchange value can be considered much more important in a market economy. When talking about city spaces, 'use value' can manifest itself in various kinds of different uses by all the different actors. The key question is, however, from the regulators' perspective: what are the things that potentially increase or decrease use value? In the 2011 parliamentary discussion regarding the behaviour termed 'repeated violation of a local regulation regarding the prohibition of using public places for living purposes', which basically refers to rough sleeping, many members of Parliament – including the one who proposed the bill – were arguing that the public was scared of homeless people, that people do not want to let their children play near them, that homeless people make public spaces unusable merely by their presence and that this is a particular problem in Budapest, where there are many homeless people in areas that are popular among tourists.[5] First, this rhetoric makes it clear that homeless people are not seen as part of the community but as outside elements who happened to wander into the territory, inhabited and used by the members of the community. Secondly, it becomes obvious that homeless people were in this debate perceived as elements of the environment that would disturb the peace of other people, including tourists, hence decreasing the use value, since the use of public space by homeless people is not considered as 'valuable use'. The success of a mayor – or a local government – is partly determined by how fast the city is developing, what new projects are going on, whether there are new and more work opportunities, and so on. In order to achieve these, the city needs to appear inviting and attractive in the eyes of potential investors, property buyers, various industries and tourists. As Stuart (2014: 1911) points out, when high-income earners move to the suburbs, the managers of the city try to boost industries like tourism or conventions and meetings. They try to attract the 'good consumers' and deflect the 'flawed consumers', as Crawford (2011: 483) puts it. Sampson and Raudenbush (1999: 604) also point to the symbolic meaning of disorder that can influence the activity of the aforementioned groups. If things appear to be in a certain order that is set by the regulators of urban space, it suggests they have control over the territory, and that can give potential newcomers the promise of safety. Factors of attractiveness of city spaces for these groups include security (Innes 2003: 99) – or the perception of a certain area as secure and safe – and the fit with the aesthetic preferences of the politically important groups and classes. The presence of homeless people does not fit this 'ideal' townscape, in which the city is imagined without incivilities. When speaking of urban aesthetics, Ferrell argues that homeless people 'engage a set of symbolic codes' both voluntary and involuntary (Ferrell 2001: 43). And the presence of some (or most) of these codes usually does not fit with the idea of city aesthetics of the owners (or controllers) of city spaces. The homeless – as seen from the Hungarian case – were regarded as making the townscape 'unusable' due to their presence, hence the politicians tried to eliminate the phenomenon by choosing the easiest solution: criminalisation. On top of that, homeless people represent visible poverty that can reflect badly on political leaders and leading forces in general.

Hodgetts et al. argue that instead of the concept of 'social distance as a cognitive construct', it could be more beneficial to discuss 'social distancing as an everyday practice' (Hodgetts et al. 2011: 1740) and in this interpretation a so-called 'social distancing event' is when, for example, a person acts in order to physically stay away from homeless people (Hodgetts et al. 2011: 1742). The authors also point out that social distancing can result in anti-homeless regulations (Hodgetts et al. 2011: 1751). Indeed, if we go with the concept of social distancing, we can understand the spatial exclusion of homeless people as 'social distancing events' as well, only that these events are now part of the legal system and so they not only give authorisation to the police to order homeless people to leave a certain area or to apply criminal sanctions against them, but also give people encouragement and moral justification to perform social distancing acts themselves. In this case social distancing happens on two levels. One is the above-mentioned spatial distancing resulting in spatial exclusion. According to Crawford, exclusion actually became a very important tool for managing public spaces (Crawford 2006: 464), and as a result the socially excluded will be 'locked out of key strategic public spaces' of the carceral city (Innes 2003: 100). The other is more of an emotional distancing, where – just as in Young's concept of the exclusive society (Young 1999) – homeless people become outsiders and excluded from society, resulting in a status quo where there is an 'us' and a 'them'. Spatial exclusion, according to Crawford, can be thought of as a form of crime prevention, as regulations that result in it ban the targeted people from certain spaces in order to prevent the appearance of the unwanted behaviour (Crawford 2008: 778).

Of course, the spatial exclusion of homeless people from certain parts of the urban space cannot be achieved only by regulating incivilities. It can be done by modifying already existing – or creating new – city spaces where the undesirable activities cannot be or are harder to perform. As Johnsen and Fitzpatrick (2010: 1707) point out, street activity can be 'designed out' this way. Risk that needs to be designed out no longer includes only serious crimes but also petty crimes and incivilities like homelessness. This can include a wide range of inventive measures: for example, in the case of Budapest (and undoubtedly many other cities), benches with two or three 'armrests' or tiny 'spikes' in the middle of the seat that make lying down on them impossible or at least highly uncomfortable.

Another aspect, worth a brief mention, is the effectiveness of the police, who are often used to achieve political success, as crime control and public safety have a significant role in politics (Gönczöl 2002: 198). The indicators of effectiveness vary, but the number of arrests is often used as one – and homeless people, indeed, are a group that are visible, easy to arrest and subject to a criminal procedure.

The focus on order and control

The 2011 parliamentary discussion used the expression 'homeless criminality' to refer to crimes that were – or were assumed to be – committed by homeless people. Homelessness has been said to lead to the committing of many different crimes. The aim of the new regulations was introduced as giving public spaces back to the law-abiding citizens (Parliament 2011).[6] This argument clearly portrays homeless people as risks to other members of the society and their presence as something that poses a threat to security, which should therefore be eliminated from city spaces. Walby and Lippert refer to Graham's characteristics of new military urbanism when they argue that in the 'urban threat discourse', every element present in the urban environment is evaluated from the point of risk analysis (Walby and Lippert 2013: 209–210; Graham 2010). This idea very much resembles Rudolph Giuliani's life-quality measures in the 1990s in New York, which aimed to 'reclaim public spaces' (New York City Police Department 1994). Similarly to this, Crawford (2011: 484) argues that there is a growing trend of urban strategies that aim to 'reclaim civility order and security', while Smith (1996) talks of the emergence of the 'revanchist city', which is about taking back the city spaces from the groups who 'stole it' from the 'middle and ruling class' inhabitants. During the Hungarian parliamentary debate, a very serious violent crime committed by homeless people was referred to in order to prove the existence of 'homeless criminality'. The rhetorical move that uses one incident to generalise across the board fuels moral panic (Cohen 2011) and can result in the attribution of the negative characteristics of a few members (those who committed the crime) to all members of the group.

Regulations that criminalise acts such as 'using public spaces for living purposes' or 'placing private property on public spaces' aim to achieve control over these spaces. They also, at least partially, eliminate freedom of movement of certain groups of people, because they basically forbid homeless people to access these areas. This ban is not explicit, since the law does not specifically say that homeless people cannot go to this or that street or square or sit on a bench and so forth. However, if we consider that homeless people tend to keep all their personal belongings with them and they have no other choice but to place them on public spaces every now and then, we can clearly see the discriminatory nature of such regulations. Novoszádek (2012: 17–18) argues that a very important element in the rhetoric of criminalisation is the belief that homeless people have a place to go even if they are banned from certain areas. And such a belief unmistakably implies that being a homeless person is a choice. In Hungary, the only other choice would be – aside from placing their belongings on someone else's property, which is also illegal – the use of homeless shelters. But the current system of homeless shelters, with separate day and night shelters, cannot really serve as a true alternative to living on the streets, since there are significantly fewer places in shelters than would be necessary, and most of the night shelters have to be left in the morning, and in order to use them again, a new registration is required on the next day. Just as Ferrell points out, as a result of these kind of regulations, homeless people will end up being 'perpetually in the wrong place', where they have no right to be anymore (Ferrell 2001: 43). Garland suggests that freedom and control coexist inseparably in today's society – different groups enjoy freedom to different extents, and for some excluded groups there is only control (Garland 2002: 198). In our case, homeless people are one of the latter groups. In the exclusionary context of regulating space and banishing those who do not behave in a certain way, in order for the group of the well-behaved to enjoy their freedom, people who do not comply with their norms have to leave the space and never return – at least until they change their behaviour.

Juhász argues that by declaring certain areas of the city 'homeless-free zones' – which is essentially what happens as a result of the Hungarian regulations in question – lawmakers distinguish between two categories of people, namely, those who deserve the protection of their spaces and those who do not (Juhász 2014: 50). This categorisation not only makes the perceived differences between homeless and non-homeless people stronger but also gives the impression that the rights of homeless people deserve a lesser or no protection if it seems that they collide with the interests of other users of city spaces.

Homeless people make a group that is easy to police, owing to their visibility and the vulnerable position they are in. This results in the emergence of 'reassurance policing' in Hungary – often done via visible policing and anti-social behaviour agendas (Barker and Crawford 2013: 12–14) – since the criminalisation of homelessness creates the legal background and authorisation for the police to perform visible policing on a visible group whose presence is considered to influence fear of crime and feelings of safety in a certain neighbourhood or city. Lápossy and Szajbély (2014: 53) stress that even the real potential of applying fines or other sanctions creates a threatening situation that violates the human dignity of this vulnerable group of people. The potential is indeed real, regardless of whether the patrolling police officers actually use these measures or not.

Crawford argues that when regulating anti-social behaviour in the UK, the language suggests that the regulation is based on – or is at least according to – the '*perceived* needs of the regulated' (Crawford 2009: 813). In the case of Hungary, this makes us wonder whether the 'perceived needs' are not perhaps merely perceived by the regulators (and hence are merely *their* perceived needs). This seems to be the case, since no empirical research has been conducted on the part of the legislator in order to find out whether people really support the criminalisation of homelessness, whether the residents really perceive the presence of homeless people as a threat or the sharing of the city space with them as an inconvenience.

Using criminal policy – and exclusion – as a tool for solving social problems

At first sight it can seem curious that punitive criminal policies and inclusive social policies can both be employed simultaneously to react to homelessness. Each of them represents a very distinct way of thinking about those who are in need or those who are different from the majority and who are living on the margins of society. Beckett and Western (2001: 44) suggest that penal institutions and welfare 'comprise a single policy regime' to deal with the socially marginal and depending on the inclusiveness or exclusiveness of the regime, one set of tools becomes dominant. Stuart (2014: 1909) suggests that the regulation of visible poverty – which homeless people represent – nowadays tends to lead to spatial exclusion instead of reintegration. Criminalising and punishing acts like rough sleeping, begging, dumpster diving or trash picking fits the punitive trend. If legislators decide to interpret a certain visible form of poverty as a behaviour that poses a danger to society, to public order or public safety – and public health, as it was concretely stated in the Hungarian proposal and later Act that criminalised rough sleeping – it is a decision that turns a social problem into a criminal one. Many Hungarian scholars have pointed out the recent changes in the criminal policy trends (see, for example, Kerezsi 2012, Lévay 2012, Borbíró 2014) and the criminalisation of homelessness is a striking example of that. The criminalisation of homelessness in Hungary can also be considered an example of the trend, which Garland (2002: 142) terms 'the strategy of punitive segregation'. The said criminalisation has the potential to achieve segregation on two different levels: firstly, on the level of the use of city space by banishing homeless people from certain parts of the city, and, secondly, on the level of society by being able to eventually imprison homeless people, thereby eliminating them from society. In *Visions of Social Control*, Cohen discusses two different ways of social control deployable in social space: inclusion and exclusion (Cohen 1985: 218–219). The banishment of homeless people from certain city spaces through regulations – and their strict enforcement – is definitely exclusion.

It is interesting to take a look at the potential consequences of committing the offences in question. As mentioned before, the violation can eventually (if fines are not paid or work sentences are not complied with) lead to a short-term prison sentence (in some cases of repeat offending, a prison sentence is possible right away). It remains unclear what the legislator is trying to achieve with the possibility of prison sentences in this regard. If we consider that according to the Prison Code (Act CCXL of 2013 on the Implementation of Punishments), one of the most important goals of imprisonment is to help the prisoner successfully reintegrate into society and become a law-abiding citizen, it is clear that in the case of homelessness these goals will not be met, as homeless people will still be homeless after getting out of prison (and subsequently be criminalised for it).

The other very important aspect of criminalisation is the stigmatisation effect. Both the Constitutional Court (Constitutional Court 166/B/2011) and the ombudsman (Ombudsman AJB-1232/2011) stressed that the inclusion of behaviours like 'taking things out of the trashcan' in the Code of Infractions stigmatises homeless people by declaring an element of their daily life illegal. As Cohen writes, those who get out of the criminal justice system will often have 'tags and labels which they may find quite difficult to shake off' (Cohen 1985: 42).

Another argument mentioned during the parliamentary discussion on the criminalisation was that criminalisation was actually in the interests of the homeless people, that is, it is meant to protect their human rights and human dignity, because living on the streets and eating out of a trashcan violates those rights.[7] Protecting human rights is certainly a noble purpose; however, why not choose the measures of social policy rather than criminal policy in order to achieve these goals? Moreover, is the protection of the rights of homeless people truly the aim of these kind of regulations? The answer to the second question probably lies in the first one: if the goal is to protect their human rights, then the chosen solution would lie in the area of social policy.

Writing in 1999, Ferge suggested that the thousand-year-old phenomenon of the 'undeserving poor' had made a very strong comeback. When talking about the undeserving poor in the context of punishment and welfare in late modernity, Garland argues that theories such as the 'rational choice theory' and 'responsibilization of individuals' and the concept of the threatening underclass not only influence criminal policies but also policies concerning the poor (Garland 2002: 196). He further points out that until recently (2001), the criminal policies of the twentieth century were for a long time influenced by a 'social style of reasoning'. Now, however, we can witness the rise of an 'economic style' of reasoning when dealing with such issues (Garland 2002: 188–190). Indeed, there could be a cold, economic reasoning, based on a short-term cost-benefit analysis, behind the choice to deal with homelessness through criminal law rather than through welfare and social policy reforms. Criminalisation – at least in the short term – costs less than spending resources on welfare.

As pointed out by many scholars (Christie 2000, Gönczöl 2002, Wacquant 2009, Borbíró 2014), there is a tendency in some Western countries to use criminal policy (including imprisonment) instead of social policy to 'solve' social problems – or more likely to make them invisible. According to Borbíró (2014: 42), the purest types of exclusive criminal policies handle the perceived sources of tension in society by using the tools of criminal law rather than welfare measures. These thoughts may sound exaggerated when talking about the criminalisation of homelessness but we have to consider the underlying reasons and motivations of the legislator, the preambles of the bills themselves, and the tendencies in the criminal policy that currently characterise Hungary. Homelessness is a social issue, and its criminalisation obviously cannot offer a long-term solution to this social problem; it can only delay the arrival of the real solution. The Constitutional Court clearly stated, for example, that the conduct described as 'taking litter out of the trashcan' is rather a result of a very serious, life-threatening situation than the personal choice of a person. The Court also stressed that while helping people in bad situations was the duty of the welfare system, its capacities were limited and so there would always be people who remained without the help they needed, who would not or could not get benefits. For such people the aforementioned behaviour is therefore a means to stay alive (Constitutional Court 166/B/2011).

Conclusion

By examining the underlying reasons of the criminalisation of homeless people in Hungary, it becomes clear how factors such as the fear of crime, the promise of safety, the concept of urban order and the importance placed on the commercial attractiveness of urban spaces, as well as the replacement of social policy with criminal policy to handle social problems, can lead to the criminalisation of an especially vulnerable group of socially marginalised people. Criminalisation seemingly promises a quick, simple, relatively cheap and effective solution to the problem that the presence of homeless people – as one of the most visible signs of poverty – may create for certain city leaders, regulators, politically influential members or groups of mainstream society. However, criminalising conduct such as rough sleeping, 'placing private property on public property', dumpster diving, trash-picking or begging not only violates constitutional and human rights principles but also creates a new category of offenders, a group of people who are in breach of law merely by dint of being at a certain public location where their presence is not wanted – due to commercial, aesthetic and quality-of-life reasons of the powerful majority. As a result, homeless people are being punished and excluded from society and urban spaces essentially because of their unfortunate life situation.

Notes

1 It should be noted that for amending the Constitution (or for creating a new one for that matter), the Parliament needs two thirds of its members to vote in favour of the proposition. Since the general elections of 2010, the governing parties have had this majority.

2 The concept of this typology has been partly introduced in Hungarian in the following paper: Podoletz, L. (2014) 'A hajléktalanság kriminalizálásának XXI. századi problémája a közveszélyes munkakerülőkről szóló 1913. évi XXI. törvénycikk tükrében' [The Problem of Criminalization of Homelessness in the 21st Century in the Light of Act 1913/XXI], in P. Bárd, P. Hack and K. Holé (eds.) *Pusztai László emlékére*, Budapest: Némedy Nyomda.

3 See, for example, Transcripts of Parliamentary Debates, Day 119, 17.10.2011, comments 58 and 340.
4 See, for example, Transcripts of Parliamentary Debates, Day 119, 17.10.2011, comments 276, 316, 322–324.
5 See, for example, Transcripts of Parliamentary Debates, Day 119, 17.10.2011.
6 See, for example, Transcripts of Parliamentary Debates, Day 119, 17.10.2011, comment 58.
7 See, for example, Transcripts of Parliamentary Debates, Day 119, 17.10.2011, comment 228.

References

Act II of 2012 on Infractions, Infractions Procedure and the Infractions Database (2012. evi II. törvény a szabálysértésekről, a szabálysértési eljárásról és a szabálysértési nyilvántartási rendszerről), *Magyar Közlöny* [Hungarian Gazette] 2012(2), 6 January 2012.

Act C of 2012 on the Criminal Code (2012. évi C. törvény a Büntető Törvénykönyvről) *Magyar Közlöny*, 2012(92), 13 July 2012.

Act CCXL of 2013 on the Implementation of Punishments (2013. évi CCXL. törvény a büntetések, az intézkedések, egyes kényszerintézkedések és a szabálysértési elzárás végrehajtásáról), *Magyar Közlöny*, 2013(218), 23 December 2013.

Amster, R. (2008) *Lost in Space: The Criminalization, Globalization and Urban Ecology of Homelessness*, New York: LFB Scholarly Publishing.

Barker, A. and Crawford, A. (2013) 'Policing urban insecurities in British cities', in R. K. Lippert and K. Walby (eds.) *Policing Cities*, New York: Routledge.

Beckett, K. and Murakawa, N. (2012) 'Mapping the shadow carceral state: Toward an institutionally capacious approach to punishment', *Theoretical Criminology*, 16(2): 221–244.

Beckett, K. and Western, B. (2001) 'Governing social marginality: Welfare, incarceration, and the transformation of state policy', *Punishment and Society*, 3(1): 43–59.

Borbíró, A. (2014) 'Amikor a kriminálpolitika a probléma – A hajléktalanság kriminalizációja és az exkluzivitás veszélyei', *Fundamentum*, 18(3): 41–45.

Christie, N. (2000) *Crime Control as an Industry – Towards GULAGs, Western Style*, Suffolk: Routledge.

Cohen, S. (1985) *Visions of Social Control*, Cambridge: Polity Press.

Cohen, S. (2011) *Folk Devils and Moral Panics*, New York: Routledge.

Constitutional Court Decision 166/B/2011. Online. Available at: http://public.mkab.hu/dev/dontesek.nsf/0/FEDB8B6BA8D0C1D5C1257ADA00526424 (accessed 15 February 2016).

Constitutional Court Decision 176/2011 (XII. 29.), *Az Alkotmánybíróság határozatai*, 20(12): 1362. Online. Available at: www.mkab.hu/letoltesek/abk_2011_12.pdf (accessed 15 February 2016).

Constitutional Court Decision 38/2012 (XI. 14.), *Az Alkotmánybíróság határozatai*, 21(10): 660. Online. Available at: www.mkab.hu/letoltesek/abk_2012_10.pdf (accessed 15 February 2016).

Constitutional Court Decision 29/2015 (X. 2.), *Az Alkotmánybíróság határozatai*, 24(19): 1340. Online. Available at: www.mkab.hu/letoltesek/ab_2015_19_alairt.pdf (accessed 15 February 2016).

Crawford, A. (2006) 'Networked governance and the post-regulatory space: Steering, rowing and anchoring the provision of policing and security', *Theoretical Criminology*, 10(4): 449–479.

Crawford, A. (2008) 'Dispersal powers and the symbolic role of anti-social behaviour legislation', *The Modern Law Review*, 71(5): 753–784.

Crawford, A. (2009) 'Governing through anti-social behaviour: Regulatory challenges to criminal justice', *British Journal of Criminology*, 2009(49): 810–831.

Crawford, A. (2011) 'From the shopping mall to the street corner: Dynamics of exclusion in the governance of public space', in A. Crawford (ed.) *International and Comparative Criminal Justice and Urban Governance*, New York: Cambridge University Press.

DeVerteuil, G., May, J. and von Mahs, J. (2009) 'Complexity not collapse: Recasting the geographies of homelessness in a "punitive" age', *Progress in Human Geography*, 33(5): 646–666.Ferge, Zs. (1999) 'Szegénység és bűnözés, azaz: van-e dezintegrációs és decivilizációs veszély?', *Belügyi Szemle*, 37(2): 3–27.

Ferrell, J. (2001) *Tearing Down the Streets: Adventures in Urban Anarchy*, New York: Palgrave.

Fundamental Law of Hungary (Magyarország Alaptörvénye), *Magyar* Közlöny, 2011(43), 25 April 2011.

Furedi, F. (2002) *Culture of Fear*, London: Continuum.

Garland, D. (2002) *The Culture of Control: Crime and Social Order in Contemporary Society*, Chicago: University of Chicago Press.

Gönczöl, K. (2002) 'A nagypolitika rangjára emelkedett büntetőpolitika', *Jogtudományi Közlöny*, 57(5): 197–204.

Graham, S. (2010) *Cities Under Siege: The New Military Urbanism*, New York: Verso.

Herbert, S. (2008) 'Contemporary geographies of exclusion I: Traversing Skid Road', *Progress in Human Geography*, 32(5): 659–666.

Hodgetts, D., Stolte, O., Radley, A., Leggatt-Cook, C., Groot, S. and Chamberlain, K. (2011) '"Near and far": Social distancing in domiciled characterisations of homeless people', *Urban Studies*, 48(8): 1739–1753.

Innes, M. (2003) *Understanding Social Control: Deviance, Crime and Social Order*, Berkshire: Open University Press.

Johnsen, S. and Fitzpatrick, S. (2010) 'Revanchist sanitisation or coercive care? The use of enforcement to combat begging, street drinking and rough sleeping in England', *Urban Studies*, 47(8): 1703–1723.

Juhász, G. (2014) 'A hajléktalanok mint alkotmányos tényezők', *Fundamentum*, 18(3): 46–51.

Kerezsi, K. (2012) 'Grandpa's fashion in the New Year – Innovative theoretical thoughts vs. simplistic crime prevention practices in Hungary', in P. Hebberecht and E. Baillergeau (eds.) *Social Crime Prevention in Late Modern Europe: A Comparative Perspective*, Brussels: VUB Press.

Lápossy, A. and Szajbély, K. (2014) 'Korlátozott terek – Szociális jogok az érdemesség és a kriminalizáció árnyékában', *Fundamentum*, 18(3): 52–57.

Lefebvre, H. (1996) *Writings on Cities*, Oxford: Blackwell.

Lévay, M. (2012) 'Human rights and penalization in Central and Eastern Europe: The case of Hungary', in S. Snacken and E. Dumortier (eds.) *Resisting Punitiveness in Europe? Welfare, Human Rights and Democracy*, New York: Routledge.

Livingstone, D. (1997) 'Police discretion and the quality of life in public places: Courts, communities, and the new policing', *Columbia Law Review*, 97(3): 551–672.

May, J. (2015) '"Gone, leave, go, move, vanish": Race, public space and (in)visibilities', *Social Identities: Journal for the Study of Race, Nation and Culture*, 21(5): 489–505.

Millie, A. (2008) 'Anti-social behaviour, behavioural expectations and an urban aesthetic', *British Journal of Criminology*, 48: 379–394.

Nagy, M. (2012) 'Quo Vadis Domine? Elmélkedések a szabálysértések helyéről a 2012. évi szabálysértési törvény kapcsán', *Jogtudományi Közlöny*, 67(5): 217–226.

New York City Police Department (1994) *Police Strategy No. 5: Reclaiming the Public Spaces of New York*, New York: New York City Police Department.

Novoszádek, N. (2012) 'Az Alkotmánybíróság határozata a guberálás szabálysértéssé minősítéséről', *JeMa – Jogesetek Magyarázata*, 3: 12–19.

Ombudsman Report on Constitutional Court Case AJB-1232/2011. Online. Available at: www.ajbh.hu/documents/10180/107993/201101232.rtf/d2e4f024–0ac0–45f3-b157–6de57a2b394c;jsessionid=3905EE6E70EB5FED574658225AAB522D?version=1.0 (accessed 15 February 2016).

Order of the Assembly of Budapest 77/2013. (XII. 3.). Online. Available at: http://budapest.hu/Lapok/Kozgyules/Rendelettar.aspx (accessed 15 February 2016).

Order of the Assembly of Budapest 27/2015. (V. 29.). Online. Available at: http://budapest.hu/Lapok/Kozgyules/Rendelettar.aspx (accessed 15 February 2016).

Podoletz, L. (2014) 'A hajléktalanság kriminalizálásának XXI. századi problémája a közveszélyes munkakerülőkről szóló 1913. évi XXI. törvénycikk tükrében' [The problem of criminalization of homelessness in the 21st century in the light of Act 1913/XXI], in P. Bárd, P. Hack, K. Holé (eds.) *Pusztai László emlékére*, Budapest: Némedy Nyomda.

Sampson, R. J. and Raudenbush, S. W. (1999) 'Systematic social observation of public spaces: A new look at disorder in urban neighborhoods', *American Journal of Sociology*, 105(3): 603–651.

Smith, N. (1996) *The New Urban Frontier: Gentrification and the Revanchist City*, New York: Routledge.

Stuart, F. (2014) 'From "Rabble Management" to "Recovery Management": Policing homelessness in marginal urban space', *Urban Studies*, 51(9): 1909–1925.

Supreme Court Decision Köf.5.020/2014/6. Online. Available at: http://lb.hu/hu/onkugy/kof502020146-szamu-hatarozat (accessed 15 February 2016).

Supreme Court Decision Köf.5055/2014/2. Online. Available at: www.lb.hu/hu/onkugy/kof505520142-szamu-hatarozat (accessed 15 February 2016).

Tosi, A. (1996) 'The excluded and the homeless: the social construction of the fight against poverty in Europe', in E. Migliore (ed.) *Urban Poverty and the Underclass*, Oxford: Blackwell Publishers.

Transcripts of Parliamentary Debates, Day 119, 17 October 2011 (Országgyűlési naplók, 119. ülésnap, 17 October 2011). Online. Available at: www.parlament.hu/orszaggyulesi-naplo-elozo-ciklusbeli-adatai (accessed 15 February 2016).

Trojanowicz, R. and Bucqueroux, B. (1992) *Toward Development of Meaningful and Effective Performance Evaluations*, East Lansing: Michigan State University, National Center for Community Policing.

von Mahs, J. (2005) 'The sociospatial exclusion of single homeless people in Berlin and Los Angeles', *American Behavioural Scientist*, 48(8): 928–960.

Wacquant, L. (2009) *Prisons of Poverty*, Minneapolis: University of Minnesota Press.

Walby, K. and Lippert, R. K. (2013) 'Municipal corporate security and risk migration companies in Canadian cities: A new military urbanism?', in R. K. Lippert and K. Walby (eds.) *Policing Cities*, New York: Routledge.

Wilson, J. Q. and Kelling, G. L. (1982) 'Broken windows: The police and neighborhood safety', *Atlantic Monthly*, 249(3): 29–38.

Xu, Y., Fiedler, M. L. and Fleming, K. H. (2005) 'Discovering the impact of community policing – the broken windows thesis, collective efficacy, and citizens' judgement', *Journal of Research in Crime and Delinquency*, 42(2): 147–186.

Young, J. (1999) *The Exclusive Society: Social Exclusion, Crime and Difference in Late Modernity*, London: Sage Publications.

Part II

Social control and representations of incivilities

6 Normalisation of behaviour in public space

The construction and control of 'public nuisance' in Belgium

Stefaan Pleysier

Local governance of safety

In most West European countries, the governance of safety and public nuisance tops political priorities both at the national level and at the community level. The growing attention for public safety issues in our cities and streets seems to have the scope of a societal quest. In line with these observations, a number of scholars proclaim a shift from traditional (penal) welfarism to a risk society and culture of control (Garland 2001, Boutellier 2002). Floating on neoliberal and neo-conservative agendas, this shift is paralleled by a new discourse where notions such as 'privatisation', 'commercialisation', 'responsibilisation', etc., enter the debates and quickly gain ground (van Swaaningen 2004, Schuilenburg and van Swaaningen 2013). Under these circumstances and over the last couple of decades, the governance of safety has moved away from a state monopoly and relatively exclusive task of the police to a mission and shared responsibility of the local community at large and a growing number of public-private partnerships (Hughes and Edwards 2002, van Swaaningen 2004, Crawford 2006).

Belgium is no exception to the above-mentioned more general trends. Although crime, public safety and anti-social behaviour in Belgium relate to the powers of the federal government, local communities and authorities have increasing possibilities to deal with these issues in a relatively autonomous way. In local communities and cities, we indeed witness the emergence of a neoliberal, managerialist discourse and a growing number of new services and strategies in the domain of public safety and order (Enhus 2006, Pleysier, De Pauw and Deklerck 2009). It is exactly this 'downsizing' and growing diversification and pluralisation of actors and mechanisms of control and surveillance at the local level that is generally described as the 'governance' of public safety (Crawford 2006, Schuilenburg 2012).

In what follows, I will first of all offer an overview of the system of administrative sanctions in Belgium. In essence, this system captures the above-described tendency towards more autonomy for local communities to deal with issues of public safety and nuisance on their territory. More specifically, and this will be elaborated on below, the emergence of administrative sanctions and new regulatory tools can, at least to some extent, be seen as indicative of a number of broader trends in society in general, and, more specifically, within the field of law enforcement and crime control. Based on these observations, this contribution concludes with the idea that criminological research should be more receptive to the specific dynamics of local policies and practices in the governance of safety.

The system of administrative sanctions in Belgium

A short history

In line with the above and more general observations, Belgium has since 1999 and later adopted federal legislation offering local communities and authorities the possibility to deal with public safety, nuisance and anti-social behaviour in an autonomous way (Cops, Put and Pleysier 2012, Devroe 2012, Pleysier 2015). Cities and communities are able to draft their own community or police codex and enforce and penalise infractions to that code with a system of administrative sanctions. In the last couple of years and after several legislative amendments, this system of administrative sanctions has been adopted and implemented in a large number of Belgian cities and communities.

The system of administrative sanctions and related legislative initiatives can be described as the outcome of a quest of former federal governments to deal with the issue of public safety and nuisance in a fast and efficient manner. This quest was facilitated by at least two elements that stirred both the political debate and public opinion. First, the impact of public nuisance on individuals was 'empirically discovered' in a first edition of the Belgian Safety Monitor, a large-scale victim survey administered by the federal police, in 1997. This study revealed that for at least part of the population, the experience of public nuisance and disorder is strongly related to the citizen's fear of crime (Devroe 2012). A second element that facilitated legislation on a system of administrative sanctions was a generally assumed feeling of impunity. The argument was that due to the workload within the traditional judicial system, perpetrators of public nuisance and disorder 'got away' without sanction or further prosecution of their behaviour, which seemingly put a large burden on 'harmonious life' in the community at large.

A first federal law was adopted in 1999, but it needed several legislative amendments in 2004 and 2005 before the system of administrative sanctions gained interest and was applied in Belgian cities and communities.[1] This law is a typical example of so-called 'framework legislation': it delineates general principles, responsibilities, powers and procedures but does not contain detailed rules. Hence, this federal legislation offers a framework to communities to adopt local regulations in order to deal with issues of disorder, public nuisance and petty crime on their territory. Roughly speaking, two categories of infractions can be distinguished. A first group contains incidents of social disorder and public nuisance, and disturbances of the public order and peace in the community. Municipalities can sanction these infractions in a completely autonomous way, as long as this type of behaviour is identified and penalised in the local community or police codex. A second set of infractions can equally be adopted in local legislation and administratively sanctioned, but these deal with infractions that are also penalised by criminal law. These 'mixed' infractions can be sanctioned by the local community if the priority for prosecution through criminal law is not initiated within the associated time limit. This second category contains acts of vandalism, night-time noise, insults, petty theft, etc.

Infractions to the community or police codex are generally registered by police officers, appointed community servants or public transport servants. Their report is then transferred to the sanctioning servant of the community, who judges the receptiveness of the report and feasibility of a sanction and administers the sanction itself. Possible administrative sanctions, stipulated within the 1999 legislation (up until the new 2014 legislation, see below) were a fine (maximum €250), mainly for individual citizens, and, oriented towards local trade and commerce, the suspension or withdrawal of a licence or permit and the closure of an establishment. Furthermore, minors under the age of 16 could not be administratively sanctioned, the maximum fine was half of the maximum for adults, and there was an obligatory offer of mediation in order to avoid a fine and be in line with the Belgian youth law (and the educational objective of sanctions or measures in the case of minors). Finally, one was and still is able to appeal an administrative sanction to the police court in the case of adults, or to the youth court in the case of minors (16 or 17 years old).

In principle, the system of administrative sanctions offers local governments a legitimate tool in order to tackle specific incidents of disorder and public nuisance on their territory. Compared with, for example, the Anti-Social Behaviour Orders, or ASBOs, in England and Wales, the system of administrative sanctions is a relatively 'light' instrument, largely based on fines, in order to deal with undesirable behaviour that arguably has a negative impact on the individual's fear of crime and on the harmonious public life in a community. 'Recidivist' individuals, who repeatedly breach local regulations, can at most be sanctioned with a new administrative sanction. In England and Wales, breaching ASBOs, which are civil orders, can result in a criminal sanction. According to Crawford, over three-fifths (63 per cent) of adults and over two-fifths (42 per cent) of juveniles who breached their ASBO between 2001 and 2006 were given a custodial sentence (Crawford 2009: 825).

Current legislation

Since January 2014 a new federal law on the system of administrative sanctions has come into effect. These legislative changes, announced at the end of 2011 in the agreement of a new federal government under Prime Minister Elio Di Rupo, have been subject to a vivid debate over the last two years in the media and public opinion. The debate polarised around a number of adjustments and new features in the 2014 law. A first change in the new legislation that stirred the public debate is the lowering of the minimum age from 16 to 14. I will come back to this lower minimum age and the position of minors in the system of administrative sanctions later in this contribution. Secondly, a number of important changes in the range of possible administrative sanctions have been adopted. The maximum amount of an administrative fine is now €350 for adults and €175 for minors. Also, the range of alternative sanctions that can be imposed (mainly in order to avoid a fine in the case of minors) is extended: the offer of mediation (obligatory for minors) was already possible, but the new legislative framework also suggests the possibility of community service (a maximum 30 hours for adults and 15 hours for minors). Furthermore and specifically for minors within the system of administrative sanctions, the new law adopted a procedure for parental involvement; the sanctioning servant is able to drop further procedures if he or she is satisfied with the 'pedagogical interventions' of parents towards their minor child. A third new element in the margin of the 2014 law is a specific article that offers mayors the possibility to impose a designated public place ban on individuals who disturb public order in specific places. This ban, which is as such not an administrative sanction but a power ascribed to the mayor, can be imposed on individuals for a period of one month with the possibility of prolonging this period twice. And finally, the list of possible 'mixed' infractions is extended, mainly with a number of infractions related to anti-social behaviour in traffic. As for the first category of 'simple' infractions of disorder and public nuisance, there is no limited list within the federal law. The federal legislator has left this first category of infractions to the discretionary power of the individual cities and municipalities, which, as already mentioned above, are able to sanction behaviour in this category as long as it is defined and penalised in the local community or police codex.

As mentioned, this new legislation and the system of administrative sanctions as such has been criticised and discussed in the media and public opinion over the last two years. Although this polarised debate between advocates and opponents of the system often missed depth and profoundness, the main critiques touched ground. Roughly speaking they focused on judicial caveats in the legislation, and social and ethical concerns surrounding the system of administrative sanctions (Cops et al. 2012, Cops and Pleysier 2014, Pleysier 2015). One of the major judicial critiques on the system of administrative sanctions is the observation that local communities tend to jeopardise the traditional separation of powers, or 'trias politicas', by being the legislator, officer, prosecutor, judge, mediator and executor of the sanctions or the beneficiary of the fines, all at the same time (Cops et al. 2012). Furthermore, questions were raised concerning legal equality and certainty. Belgium counts 589 local communities, of which each community could, based on and within the boundaries of the federal legislative frame, draw up its own set of regulations, making it obviously difficult and virtually impossible to assume that citizens are, first of all, aware of these regulations and, secondly, sanctioned in a similar way for similar behaviour across different communities.

This also touches upon the social and ethical critiques that were raised about the system of administrative sanctions. As mentioned before, the legislative federal framework does not provide a list of the types of behaviour that can be sanctioned, leaving this to the discretionary power of local governments. What is defined as 'public nuisance' is indeed a subjective and individual assessment of behaviour as an intolerable or unacceptable burden on 'harmonious life' in the public domain. Although the federal framework confines administrative sanctions to the domain of the 'material public order', there is a self-evident threat that the system would slip towards the unauthorised domain of the 'moral public order'.[2] More in general, and I will come back to that later, new regulatory tools such as the administrative sanctions tend to organise and 'normalise' social life in the public domain based on an essentially normative notion of what is 'undesirable' or 'unacceptable' in a certain situation or context (Dixon, Levine and McAuley 2006, Boutellier 2011, Schuilenburg 2012). Moreover, this subjective normativity could lead to a disproportionate focus on the most vulnerable groups in our society; the danger indeed is 'that the behavioural expectations of the majority are seen as "social", while those of minority or marginalised "outsider" groups are regarded as anti-social' (Millie 2009: 16).

New regulatory tools in a pre-crime society

As mentioned before, neither this system of administrative sanctions in Belgium nor other new regulatory tools in the field of local safety and public nuisance in general appears in a sociological vacuum. The emergence of these instruments and strategies can indeed be understood against the backdrop of a diagnosis of our late modern society (van Swaaningen 1997, Schuilenburg and van Swaaningen 2013). According to Zygmunt Bauman, we live in a 'liquid society' in which individuals struggle to balance new freedoms and possibilities on the one hand and our modern quest for certainty, security and safety on the other (Bauman 2000). The erosion of solid ground and traditional routines and the growing liquidity of all aspects of life and society have promoted the control of risks and the precaution principle as the *leitmotiv* of a fearful society.

Within the field of law enforcement and crime control, we see that the focus of attention has shifted from 'crime and punishment' through 'risk and control' to 'uncertainty and precaution' (Boutellier 2011: 66; Pleysier 2014). Zedner (2007, 2009) captured the above-mentioned broader trends under the notion of a transformation of a 'post-crime' to a 'pre-crime society'. In a pre-crime society, law enforcement is no longer based on the transgression of (criminal) law, but on the reduction of insecurity and unsafety, and therefore the early detection and intervention of potential risky behaviour. A pre-crime society operates under the precaution principle and aims at the 'governance of the unknowable' (Zedner 2009: 128). The dominant logic is pre-emptive, hence the emergence of new mechanisms of control and surveillance. In a pre-crime society the focus of attention will be on registration, detection and control of future risks and (potential) risky behaviour of individuals and groups. Furthermore, a pre-emptive logic will transform the traditional idea of prevention to the early detection, intervention and regulation of risky behaviour. Willem Schinkel (2011) argues that the emergence of new forms of regulation and prevention bend towards the idea of repression. He refers to this as 'prepression', as the 'pro-active repression that attempts the timely suppression of certain forms of life' (Schinkel 2011: 372; Pleysier 2012, 2013). This prepression is not prevention 'as we know it', but the repression of 'risky causal chains' supported by new technologies of registration, archiving and control, and the suppression of alternative 'possible worlds'. Zedner (2009: 74) also mentioned the arrival of new preventive measures that 'seek to anticipate and forestall harms long before they occur', in order to maximise security in a proactive manner.

Prepression and the proactive (or pre-emptive) logic of early detection and intervention has led to a 'politics of behaviour' aimed at controlling and regulating undesirable and risky behaviour of individuals and groups in the public domain. In the Netherlands, Bas van Stokkom (2013) recognises these politics of behaviour in the expansion of legislation and powers to the local police and policy in deploying reactive and proactive strategies of regulating unwanted and undesirable conduct in public. In a similar way, Crawford (2009) describes how anti-social behaviour in England and Wales is tackled by ASBOs, which perfectly fit the pre-crime logic. According to Crawford (2009), anti-social behaviour serves as a precursor to crime, prompting pre-emption and prevention. Inspired by the 'broken windows' theory, anti-social behaviour is seen as a first step in a developmental trajectory for both individuals and communities, and therefore is countered by ASBO legislation in order to prevent, at the individual level, 'more serious offending' and to 'nip individual criminal careers in the bud', and at the community level, to halt spirals of decline into disorder, fear and crime (Crawford 2009: 816).

A similar line of argument can be recognised in the Belgian system of administrative sanctions and in the, as described above, new legislation since January 2014. More specifically, and preceding the new law, several mayors from larger cities in Belgium pled in favour of lowering the age of administrative sanctions to young people causing public nuisance to the age of 14 or even 12, whereas the age limit had previously been set at 16 (Cops et al. 2012, Pleysier 2015). The argument was that if we do not stop these youngsters and intervene at an early age, 'things will go wrong'. In the final draft of the 2014 law, the former minister of interior, Joëlle Milquet, indeed lowered the age to 14 and stated that the system of administrative sanctions is a necessary means to 'prevent a spiral of delinquency' (Pleysier 2013). These arguments illustrate a prepressive approach towards disorder and anti-social behaviour, grounded in the idea that no alternative worlds exist. It promotes a vision where night-time revels and noisy enjoyment, urinating in public spaces and so forth inevitably will lead to criminal careers unless communities intervene at an early stage using administrative sanctions to stop the assumed spiral of decay and delinquency. This reasoning not only highlights the argument that anti-social behaviour needs 'nipping in the bud' in order to prevent worse from happening, but also supports a deterministic approach towards human agency that can be ascribed to a pre-crime society (Crawford 2009, Zedner 2009).

In a similar manner, Ashworth and Zedner (2012) ask themselves to what extent it is justified to intervene at an early stage and stigmatise and criminalise behaviour in order to prevent uncertain future risks and harms that 'might' be done. In line with this, and inspired by J. S. Mill's principle of liberty, Peršak proclaims the harm principle indeed 'as the main justification for state intervention into the autonomous sphere of the individual' (Peršak 2007: 13). In our discussion on the system of administrative sanctions, this argument is reflected in the aforementioned confinement of administrative sanctions to the domain of the material public order. Indeed, mere disturbances of the moral public order lack the aspect of harm, or are at most limited to a future and uncertain harm, which renders state (or in this case, municipal) interventions highly problematic. This brings Ashworth and Zedner (2012: 554) to the conclusion that adequate limiting principles should be in place in order to confine the risk of an 'overexpansion of the criminal law on preventive grounds'. Moreover and in relation to the ASBOs in England and Wales, they warn against the ambiguity of the prohibition of conduct that 'may not be a criminal offense in its own right (e.g. entering a shopping mall, jumping noisily on a trampoline)', as 'particularly in these days of over-criminalization', the 'arguments for criminalizing it are not sufficiently strong' (Ashworth and Zedner 2012: 564).

The normalisation of behaviour in public

The strategy to detect and intervene early against the 'undesirable' behaviour is often accompanied with what Boutellier (2011) has called a 'moral inversion'. The combination of new regulatory tools and the aforementioned subjective normativity has sharpened selective practices of preventative exclusion in the public domain 'that seeks to govern future behaviour rather than regulate past conduct' (Crawford 2011: 502–503). Building on Goffman's *Behaviour in Public Places* (1963) and *Relations in Public* (1971), Dixon et al. (2006) argue that certain behaviour is classified and labelled as a nuisance or 'incivility' because it is seen as an infraction of the moral order in public life. Conduct, according to Dixon et al. (2006: 188; Pleysier 2015) becomes 'situationally inappropriate' or 'unacceptable'. Adam Crawford has illustrated this in England and Wales by referring to the emergence of a number of wide-ranging restrictions such as designated public place orders, dispersal powers, drinking bans, etc. (Crawford 2009, 2011). Schuilenburg (2012) mentioned similar mechanisms of 'selective exclusion' in the Netherlands (Schuilenburg and van Steden 2014, 2014b; Wesselink, Schuilenburg and Van Calster 2009). In the margin of the new legislation on administrative sanctions in Belgium, I referred in the above to a new power given to the mayor allowing him or her to impose a designated public place ban on individuals who disturb public order in specific places. Several cities and communities also have drinking bans that prohibit drinking alcohol in a designated public area, which can be enforced as an administrative sanction.

Although these new regulatory tools are not overtly or explicitly aimed at specific individuals or groups in our society, in their consequence they do refer to and jeopardise the position of certain societal groups in the public domain (Crawford 2009). In line with Adam Crawford (2009), van Stokkom (2013) argued that these regulatory tools embody a 'politics of behaviour' and growing intolerance towards undesirable behaviour in public space. Mainly in larger cities in the Netherlands, he observes a growing tendency towards offensive practices that are deployed in order to ban and exclude a variety of 'defiant' citizens (beggars, homeless people, prostitutes, addicts, loitering youth, etc.) from the public or semi-public domain (van Stokkom 2013, 2011). These 'exclusionary' practices (e.g. a collective shop ban, pub ban and public transport ban) were also explored by Schuilenburg, who described these as illustrations of emerging new civil and administrative instruments aimed at regulating access to and behaviour in semi-public space (Schuilenburg 2009, Wesselink et al. 2009, Schuilenburg and van Steden 2014a, 2014b). It becomes clear that crime and safety are seemingly convenient pretenses to control and exclude certain 'undesirable' individuals and groups – for example, the homeless, illegals, beggars, prostitutes from (certain parts of) the public domain. The exclusion of these groups is not in the first place based on their threat to the public order and safety, but grounded in the fact that they seem to violate unspoken norms that regulate public life in the city centre (Dixon et al. 2006, Crawford 2011).

In Belgium, several cities resorted to the system of administrative sanctions as a helpful solution to recover an abolished criminal statute that penalised begging and vagabondage in the public domain (Pleysier 2015). In doing so, the police or community code of those cities penalised begging in a specific perimeter or designated area of the city or community. Local authorities defend this ban by referring to the supposed fact that begging is often a pretext for pickpocketing and shoplifting, which feeds the above-mentioned idea that in order to prevent theft, one has to intervene on the 'antecedent' behaviour, i.e. begging. The Belgian Council of State previously recalled the municipality of Brussels, which tried to ban panhandling in the city centre using similar codes and like arguments.[3] Furthermore, it might be considered somewhat strange that the undesirable behaviour, i.e. begging, is seemingly only undesirable and unwanted in specifically designated areas in the city. This reflects the above-mentioned idea of Dixon et al. (2006) that conduct and behaviour in public space is defined as situationally inappropriate based on normative definitions of place. Behaviour is defined as problematic and deemed punishable not because of the behaviour *in se*, but because it is 'out of place' (Dixon et al. 2006, van Stokkom 2013, Margier, Bellot and Morin 2014, Pleysier 2015). This refers to the fact that the perimeter of the ban on begging is most likely to be situated around the commercial city centre and shopping streets. In their Canadian study, Chesnay, Bellot and Sylvestre (2013) point to the fact that the visibility of homelessness urged cities to reaffirm the city centre as focused on consumption, leisure and luxury. The behaviour of homeless people, illegals, prostitutes and so forth, and their presence within the perimeter, defines them as 'out of place': they violate 'consumerist norms' in city centres (Dixon et al. 2006: 190). The idea of 'situationally inappropriate' behaviour (Dixon et al. 2006) refers again to Zygmunt Bauman (1997: 6), who stated that it 'is not the intrinsic quality of things which makes them into "dirt", but solely their location; more precisely, their location in the order of things envisaged by the purity-seekers'. The commercial centres of our cities are increasingly designed to be sterile, zero-friction zones, meant for leisure and consumption (Crawford 2011, van Stokkom 2013, Schuilenburg and van Steden 2014a). In these sanitised public spaces, homeless people, illegals, beggars and prostitutes are 'out of place', they are 'unappetizing polluting agents' (Bauman 1997: 6; van Stokkom 2013, Margier et al. 2014, Pleysier 2015).

This politics of behaviour not only point to mechanisms of selective exclusion or banning of impure and undesirable individuals from certain parts of the city, they also stigmatise and criminalise individuals and groups because of their 'otherness'. These mechanisms of 'othering' and 'exclusion' are closely interrelated: 'there are imaginary geographies which place imperfect minorities in marginalised locations: in a social elsewhere' (Ruggiero 2000: 1; see also Goodey 2002: 135). Their 'otherness' disrupts the orderliness of the sterile city centre focused on leisure and consumption; in those places, or more in general, in a consumerist society, 'flawed consumers are its most irksome and costly liabilities' (Bauman 2004: 39).

Conclusion: towards a new research agenda?

Based on the above observations and analysis of (the features of) the system of administrative sanctions in Belgium, I come to a conclusion. In this chapter I argued that we have seen in the recent years a growing tendency across and within cities and communities to tackle local safety and public nuisance issues and design new regulatory tools to do so in a rather autonomous way. To a large extent, it is this localisation, downsizing and diversification of power that is referred to as the 'governance' of public safety (Crawford 2006). These processes, however, confront us as criminologists with a growing awareness of the limitations of a traditional approach to the topic and the urge for a new research agenda.

As Crawford (2011: 16) states, criminological research is all too much focused on a state-centric approach 'by focusing policy analysis on national government instruments and statements; notably legislation, protocols and guidance'. Instead, we could benefit from an approach in which we focus on how these governmental instruments and legislation are, on the one hand, influenced by 'international pressures and global influences' and, on the other hand, implemented, and to some extent hollowed out, by 'local political cultures' (Crawford 2006). The aim in this contribution was indeed to illustrate how broader sociological trends and transformations in the field of law enforcement and crime control seem to permeate and influence the local governance of urban safety and the emergence of new regulatory tools such as the system of administrative sanctions in Belgium. However, in order to fully understand how these systems work and are at the same time 'resisted, refashioned and played out in different ways in particular locales', we need to be cognizant and sensitive 'to the manner in which central government edicts are refracted and reinterpreted through local traditions and political cultures' (Crawford 2011: 16; Crawford 2002).

At least to some extent, the importance of these local constellations and new regulatory tools aimed at delivering urban safety reflects the image of what Schuilenburg (2015) calls 'security assemblage'. An assemblage is described as 'a short-lived or durable constellation of territories, rules and authorities' and provides us with a model that 'allows a better comprehension of the complexity of ongoing changes in reality' (Schuilenburg 2015: 129). In the introduction to Schuilenburg's book (2015), David Garland argues that the conception of an assemblage is indeed appealing, as it allows a dynamic approach to security and recognises the premise 'that our societies have undergone a shift from a criminal justice system of crime control, monopolised by the state and its uniformed police, to a hybrid system in which multiple actors and agencies have become jointly responsible for delivering security' (Garland 2015: 1).

This process of localisation and hybridisation of crime and safety policies, and the necessity to grasp this within criminological research, is also reflected in a recent ruling of the Constitutional Court in Belgium.[4] In the aftermath of the new federal law on the system of administrative sanctions, a conglomerate of human and children's rights organisations, labour unions and individuals brought a case before the Constitutional Court in which they asked the Court to assess, among others, the legitimacy and necessity of lowering the minimum age for administrative sanctions from 16 to 14, the protection of minors within the system, the compliance of the system with Article 6 of the European Convention on Human Rights (the right to a fair trial before an independent and impartial judge) and with the principles of the separation of powers, of legal equality and certainty. On many of these objections, the Constitutional Court ruled that the federal law on the system of administrative sanctions was not at odds with most of the complaints (Weis 2015). However, as it was a framework law, the Constitutional Court simultaneously pointed to the importance of (a review of) the implementation of the system of administrative sanctions and the local practice within those cities and communities that adopted the system.

In that respect, not only will the courts have to focus on local practices and 'security assemblages' in order to 'judge' those, but also criminologists will equally have to show interest 'in how the implementation of programs and the operationalisation of policy involve unprogrammed choices and departures from the organisational script' if they wish to improve their understanding of these new regulatory tools set in motion in order to tackle local safety and public nuisance issues (Garland 2015: 3; Schuilenburg 2015).

Notes

1 After these legislative changes in 2004 and 2005 the popularity of the system of administrative sanctions rose quickly. Whereas before 2005 only 28 per cent of the communities in the Flemish part of the country had implemented the system of administrative sanctions and a community codex, this increased to 62 per cent in 2007 and 79 per cent in 2011. By the end of 2013, 84 per cent of all communities in the Flemish part of the country had adopted the possibility to penalise public nuisance by administrative sanctions.

2 The confinement of the system of administrative sanctions to the material public order implies that infractions have to deal with a clear and visual disturbance of or harm to the public order, such as nighttime revelry, vandalism or nuisance (Lierman and Van de Weyer 2014). A disturbance of ideas, feelings or emotions alone cannot lead to an administrative sanction. For instance, the presence of minors or drugs in a pub as such

is an issue of moral public order and therefore, by law, not the subject of the system of administrative sanctions. In a similar way, local codes that constrain the consumption of alcohol amongst young people as such, without the external element of disturbance or harm to the public order, lack the necessary condition of material public (dis)order.

3 Arrest Council of State (Raad van State), Nr. 68.735, 8 October 1997.

4 Arrest Constitutional Court (Grondwettelijk Hof), Nr. 44/2015, 23 April 2015.

References

Ashworth, A. and Zedner, L. (2012) 'Prevention and criminalization: Justifications and limits', *New Criminal Law Review*, 15(4): 542–571.

Bauman, Z. (1997) *Postmodernity and Its Discontents*, Cambridge: Polity Press.

Bauman, Z. (2000) *Liquid Modernity*, Cambridge: Polity Press.

Bauman, Z. (2004) *Wasted Lives*, Cambridge: Polity Press.

Boutellier, H. (2002) *De Veiligheidsutopie*, Den Haag: Boom Juridische Uitgevers.

Boutellier, H. (2011) *De improvisatiemaatschappij. Over de sociale ordening van een onbegrensde wereld*, Den Haag: Boom Lemma.

Chesnay, C. T., Bellot, C. and Sylvestre, M.-E. (2013) 'Taming disorderly people one ticket at a time: The penalization of homelessness in Ontario and British Columbia', *Canadian Journal of Criminology and Criminal Justice*, 55(2): 161–185.

Cops, D. and Pleysier, S. (2014) 'De wet op de gemeentelijke administratieve sancties (GAS-wet). Een korte introductie', *Agora*, 30(1): 30–33.

Cops, D., Put, J. and Pleysier, S. (2012) 'De GAS-wetgeving als instrument voor de aanpak van overlast. Bedenkingen bij en suggesties voor een integraal en onderbouwd overlast-beleid', *Panopticon*, 33(6): 552–563.Crawford, A. (ed.) (2002) *Crime and Insecurity. The Governance of Safety in Europe*, Cullompton, Devon: Willan Publishing.

Crawford, A. (2006) 'Networked governance and the post-regulatory state? Steering, rowing and anchoring the provision of policing and security', *Theoretical Criminology*, 10(4): 449–479.

Crawford, A. (2009) 'Governing through anti-social behaviour: Regulatory challenges to criminal justice', *British Journal of Criminology*, 49(6): 810–831.

Crawford, A. (2011) 'From the shopping mall to the street corner: Dynamics of exclusion in the governance of public space', in A. Crawford (ed.) *International and Comparative Criminal Justice and Urban Governance*, Cambridge: Cambridge University Press.

Devroe, E. (2012) *A Swelling Culture of Control? De genese en toepassing van de wet op de gemeentelijke administratieve sancties in België*, Antwerpen: Maklu.

Dixon, J., Levine, M. and McAuley, R. (2006) 'Locating impropriety: Street drinking, moral order, and the ideological dilemma of public space', *Political Psychology*, 27(2): 187–206.

Enhus, E. (2006) 'Politie en nieuwe functies in veiligheid: communicerende vaten?', *Orde van de Dag*, 33: 33–38.

Garland, D. (2001) *The Culture of Control. Crime and Social Order in Contemporary Society*, Oxford: Oxford University Press.

Garland, D. (2015) 'Introduction', in M. Schuilenburg (ed.) *The Securitization of Society. Crime, Risk and Social Order*, New York: New York University Press.

Goffman, E. (1963) *Behaviour in Public Places. Notes on the Social Organization of Gatherings*, New York: Free Press.

Goffman, E. (1971) *Relations in Public. Microstudies of the Public Order*, New York: Basic Books.

Goodey, J. (2002) 'Whose insecurity? Organised crime, its victims and the EU', in A. Crawford (ed.) *Crime and Insecurity. The Governance of Safety in Europe*, Cullompton: Willan Publishing.
Hughes, G. and Edwards, A. (eds.) (2002) *Crime Control and Community. The New Politics of Public Safety*, Cullompton: Willan Publishing.
Lierman, S. and Van de Weyer, P.-J. (2014) 'Recente ontwikkelingen in de rechtspraak en de wetgeving over algemene bestuurlijke politiebevoegdheden van de gemeente', in VRG-Alumni (ed.) *Recht in beweging – 21ste VRG Alumnidag 2014*. Antwerp: Maklu.
Margier, A., Bellot, C. and Morin, R. (2014) 'L'itinérance en milieu urbain. Deux voies de normalisation', *Le sociographe*, 48: 21–32.
Millie, A. (2009) *Anti-Social Behaviour*, Maidenhead: Open University Press.
Peršak, N. (2007) *Criminalising Harmful Conduct: The Harm Principle, Its Limits and Continental Counterparts*, New York: Springer.
Pleysier, S. (2012) 'Kind als gevaar. De nieuwe preventie en criminalisering van gedrag', *Tijdschrift voor Jeugd en Kinderrechten*, 4: 278–288.
Pleysier, S. (2013) 'Kinderen als 'crash test dummies'. Keerzijde van de lokroep naar vroegtijdige interventie', *Tijdschrift voor Jeugd en Kinderrechten*, 3: 252–265.
Pleysier, S. (2014) 'Veiligheid en voorzorg in tijden van onzekerheid', in J. Maesschalck, S. Parmentier, D. Van Daele, J. Debacker and L. Mergaerts (eds.) *Waarheidsvinding en adviesverlening bij rampen. Naar een onderzoeksorgaan voor veiligheid in België?*, Leuven: Universitaire Pers Leuven.
Pleysier, S. (2015) 'Local governance of safety and the normalization of behavior', *Crime, Law & Social Change*, 64(4): 305–317. doi:10.1007/s10611–015–9592–4.
Pleysier, S., De Pauw, E. and Deklerck, J. (2009) 'Goed bestuur of doorgedreven veiligheidsfetisjisme? Patrick Dewael introduceert een opleiding "pré-politie en veiligheid"', *Panopticon*, 28(1): 54–64.
Ruggiero, V. (2000) *Crime and Markets: Essays in Anti-Criminology*, Oxford: Oxford University Press.
Schinkel, W. (2011) 'Prepression: The actuarial archive and new technologies of security', *Theoretical Criminology*, 15(4): 365–380.
Schuilenburg, M. (2009) 'De securisering van de samenleving. Over de relatie tussen veiligheidszorg, bestuur en quasistrafrecht', *Krisis. Tijdschrift voor actuele filosofie*, 3: 6–22.
Schuilenburg, M. (2012) *Orde in veiligheid: Een dynamisch perspectief*, Den Haag: Boom Lemma.
Schuilenburg, M. (2015) *The Securitization of Society: Crime, Risk and Social Order*, New York: New York University Press.
Schuilenburg, M. and van Swaaningen, R. (2013) 'Veiligheid in een laatmoderne cultuur', *Tijdschrift over Cultuur & Criminaliteit*, 3(2): 109–122.
Schuilenburg, M. and van Steden, R. (2014a) 'Praktijken van selectieve uitsluiting. Over de bescherming door en tegen veiligheidsassemblages', *Cahiers Politiestudies*, 30(1): 51–62.
Schuilenburg, M. and van Steden, R. (2014b) 'De collectieve Horeca Ontzegging: uitsluiting uit de publieke ruimte?', *Beleid en Maatschappij*, 41(1): 4–18.
van Stokkom, B. (2011) 'Dealing with defiant citizens: Building emotional intelligence into police work', in S. Karstedt, I. Loader and H. Strang (eds.) *Emotions, Crime and Justice*, London: Hart Publishing.
van Stokkom, B. (2013) 'Onveiligheid als stedelijkheidsfobie. Angst en onmacht in de hygiënische stad', *Tijdschrift over Cultuur & Criminaliteit*, 3(2): 137–154.

van Swaaningen, R. (1997) *Critical Criminology. Visions from Europe*, London: Sage Publications.

van Swaaningen, R. (2004) 'Veiligheid in Nederland en Europa; een sociologische beschouwing aan de hand van David Garland', *Justitiële Verkenningen*, 7: 9–23.

Weis, K. (2015) 'Grondwettelijk Hof verfijnt GAS-wet', *De Juristenkrant*, 309: 2.

Wesselink, L., Schuilenburg, M. and Van Calster, P. (2009) 'De Collectieve Winkelontzegging', *Tijdschrift voor Veiligheid*, 8(1): 6–19.

Zedner, L. (2007) 'Pre-crime and post-criminology?', *Theoretical Criminology*, 11(2): 261–281.

Zedner, L. (2009) *Security*, London: Routledge.

7 Understanding uncivil behaviour through urban space and culture

Anna Di Ronco

Introduction

The newly designed urban spaces and the modern architectures that can be found in city centres and in regenerated, high-end areas of the city reflect the wants and interests of the mainstream society in which they are embedded. Depending on what societal groups with decision-making powers need or want to do in such city areas, urban spaces (such as squares, city parks and parking lots) and buildings are assigned a particular function by urban planners and city administrators. Urban public spaces can be designed as residential, shopping, leisure, entertainment and business areas or incorporate a multitude of such functions. The way powerful groups see and wish to experience the redesigned or modern urban spaces influences the formation of expectations of how individuals should behave and appear within them. In other words, on the basis of the image or idea of specific urban zones that people with political capital have, the expectations are formed as to how such spaces should 'properly' be used by others and how individuals should conduct themselves and look in them. Such spatial representations (and the resulting societal expectations for that space) are also influenced by, and mediated through, cultural factors.

In such urban areas, the expectations of powerful majorities often oppose and potentially conflict with the 'cultural space' (Ferrell 1997) of marginalised individuals, or with the different meanings that the latter assign to space. Conflicting interpretations on the uses of space, including the aesthetic appearances of people within it or on the personal or group style, may also intersect with practices of social control, which are aimed to exclude and criminalise the 'deviant', 'antisocial' or 'uncivil'[1] minorities, who are deemed responsible for nuisance.

This chapter aims, firstly, to inspect how various criminological perspectives have investigated and explained deviant and criminal behaviour through space and culture. Secondly, by drawing on the results of two recently conducted comparative studies on the regulation, representation and law enforcement of two types of incivilities (street prostitution and public drunkenness), this chapter highlights the spatial and cultural elements that play a role in how 'incivilities' are socially constructed, seen and tackled by the authorities. It will argue that the expectations of powerful groups about particular urban spaces, which ultimately shape the social and law enforcement reactions to nuisance, are the result of the interplay between the way they see or experience those places and the country- and context-specific cultural factors. Implications for criminological research concerned with explaining incivilities and their regulations are discussed in the concluding section.

Criminology at the crossroads between space and culture

Space

Different criminological theories and perspectives have integrated the study of crime and deviance with the analysis of the urban space and of its physical features. The study of the spatial distribution of crime dates back to the 1930s and is traditionally associated with the work of the sociologists of the Chicago School, who carried out ethnographic and statistical research in the city of Chicago. In line with the findings of the most prominent writers within this school (e.g. Shaw and McKay), the space where criminality and deviance are high is characterised by elevated levels of social and economic deprivation (Newburn 2007). This is explained well by Burgess (1925) in his zonal hypothesis, which describes the city as developing in five concentric circles around the business district. The second zone, which is the space of transition between the business district and three residential areas inhabited by people of high social position, is characterised not only by the presence of highly transient populations of low social status but also of inadequate and deteriorated housing and buildings. It is in such socially disorganised and physically deprived areas that deviance and crime are understood to find the optimal conditions to flourish.

Unlike the early researchers of the Chicago School, the succeeding generations of Chicagoans did not empirically inspect and further theorise about the relationships between the physical traits of the urban environment and the occurrence of crime and deviance. Rather, they focused on the mapping of offenders' residences – a research method that exerted great influence on environmental criminology's later studies on the spatial location of offences in the city 'hot spots' (Brantingham and Brantingham 1981).

From the 1970s onwards, attention was again drawn to the physical features of space, by environmental criminologists and, among them, by opportunity-based theorists. They did so by casting the focus on the situational circumstances within which the crime event or vice (Felson 1994) takes place, which are understood as providing opportunities for offending. Opportunities to potential offenders are not only offered by the presence of vulnerable targets and victims in certain (routine) times and space settings. They are also provided by the existence of spaces that are easily accessible, left unsupervised, and that present a number of physical features that favour the committing of the criminal and deviant activity (Clarke 1995). To reduce crime opportunities and increase the perceived risks of being caught and sentenced, Situational Crime Prevention (SCP) techniques have been developed (Cornish and Clarke 2003). Among the SCP strategies that target the criminogenic space, there are also measures that rely on the improvement of the design of urban areas.

The idea that architectures may operate as a means of crime prevention was first suggested by the architect and city planner Oscar Newman (1972). By introducing the notion of 'defensible space', Newman suggested that particular architectural and physical characteristics of the residential area not only hamper the occurrence of crime (for example, by providing easily observable places facilitating the natural surveillance of residents) but also help people living there to build informal social networks and to develop a sense of ownership of, and attachment to, the place, which leads them to proactively monitor and protect the area. Newman's idea to work on architectural design to prevent and reduce crime was further developed in programmes known as Crime Prevention Through Environmental Design (CPTED) and by the work of Alice Coleman (1985) in the UK, which focused on the identification of the problems related to urban architecture and design that were prone to criminal and uncivil behaviour (Newburn 2007).

If well-designed urban environments may have a positive effect on residents and entice them to activate informal mechanisms of social control, dilapidated areas may lead to further abandonment and, worse, to the creation of favourable conditions for the occurrence of crime and deviance. Such a theory has been developed by two realist criminologists, Wilson and Kelling (1982), who in their 'broken windows' theory argued that people who see broken windows, abandoned buildings, graffiti, tags and other signs of decay in their neighbourhood will likely retreat from the public spaces, which will lead to the loosening of the informal systems of crime control, which are necessary for the containment of crime.[2] Despite emphasising the importance of looking at the level of physical disorder in an area to understand the incidence of crime and deviance, they provided a solution that did not centre on the improvement of the physical characteristics of space (Katyal 2002). Rather, they encouraged local authorities to adopt tough policies and hardcore law enforcement responses against uncivil behaviour in order to reduce crime in problematic neighbourhoods.

The spatial dimension of crime and deviance has also been addressed by critical criminologists. Under conditions of late modernity, they saw space as a locus of extensive, although often subtle, social and crime control, where the activities of monitoring and of crime prevention are carried out by agencies and actors that often differ from the competent governmental bodies (Cohen 1985, Garland 2001, O'Malley 2001). In other words, not only the police but also individuals and communities are considered responsible for crime prevention. Such agents accomplish the aim of securing the public and the private places through a variety of techniques, which include (but are not limited to) intensified guarding and patrolling by the police and by private security firms. Public, private and the increasingly present semi-private (or, following Shearing and Stenning (1985), 'hybrid') spaces are also protected through the manipulation of their physical and design features, that is, through the installation of locks, grills, alarms, systems of closed-circuit television (CCTV) and of other, even more sophisticated, monitoring technologies (Lyon 2004). The implementation of all these new modes of crime control is not equal in the urban territory: if they are prevalent in wealthy areas, they are less so in poor, dilapidated neighbourhoods, which are often left unmonitored. When actuarial strategies of crime control (Young 1999) are supplemented by punitive regulations targeting uncivil behaviour (Bannister, Fyfe and Kearns 2006) in the regenerated areas of the city, they produce the effect of socially and geographically excluding marginalised groups of people, who are pushed into other, less wealthy and less supervised urban areas (Davis 1990, Sibley 1995).[3]

Scholars working within cultural criminology have also addressed the spatial dimension of deviance. They focused on the spaces where hedonistic, pleasure activities are pursued by subcultural groups and where the same groups are subject to the criminalisation practices devised by the dominant majorities. They have, for example, analysed and explained deviance and social control practices in the Night-Time Economy (NTE). In night-time entertainment districts, they have, for example, studied the pleasure-seeking practices of street drinkers (Measham and Brain 2005) and the attitudes to deviance of different social groups (Demand and Landolt 2014), as well as the punitive policies and measures applied to deviant subcultures (for example, Hayward and Hobbs 2007, Crawford and Flint 2009).

Culture

A number of criminological theories and perspectives have emphasised the importance of culture and of cultural factors in understanding the meanings given to crime and deviance in different sociocultural contexts. Theories developing from the interactionist tradition in sociology, like the labelling theory, have viewed criminal and deviant[4] behaviour as socially constructed notions that are the 'product of culturally-bounded social interaction' (Newburn 2007: 8). Through action and interaction, individuals come to learn a specific set of cultural norms, codes and systems of meanings that shape their definition of acceptable or expected (and, by contrast, deviant and criminal) conduct in certain time and space settings. When such value systems are shared by the dominant social classes, deviant 'outsiders' (Becker 1963) are created, labelled and intensively penalised by them.

The idea that different social groups may have different cultures or adhere to different value systems has been developed by criminological perspectives drawing on the work of the Chicago School. What the sociologists working within this school found (mostly through their ethnographic work) was that the heterogeneous social groups living in the 'zone of transition' (Burgess 1925) embraced systems of meaning that were different, although stable and coherent, from those of the mainstream society. Within such groups, delinquency was seen as a stable attribute and as being culturally transmitted (Shaw and McKay 1942) onto the new generations together with the other codes and systems of meaning established in the group. This theorisation aligns with Sutherland's (1947) argument that values and meanings, as well as criminal techniques, motives and rationalisations, are learnt and internalised by the group's members through social interaction within the group. Criminal subcultures are not only associated with social groups who adopt different value systems than the ones embraced by the mainstream society (Cohen 1955). They are also formed as a consequence of the strain or of the blocked opportunities experienced by individuals in the process of achievement of socially recognised goals (Cloward and Ohlin 1960).

Cultural criminologists have in more recent years adopted a broad(er) working definition of culture, as they focused on the symbols and systems of meanings shared both by the urban subcultures and by the dominant groups (Webber 2007). Notwithstanding the broad interest in the cultures of different social groups, much of the research has concentrated around urban subcultures and, more accurately, around the specific aesthetic and behavioural style adopted by them. Style is viewed by cultural criminologists as an inherent feature of the urban subculture, which helps its members to acquire their identity within the group (Ferrell and Sanders 1995). It is also considered as the catalyst of (informal and formal) crime control responses, which are activated when the subcultural style collides with the 'aesthetic of authority' (Ferrell 1997) or with the mainstream aesthetic sensibilities and tastes. Apart from the aesthetic style of their members, urban subcultures and groups have also been studied as repositories of rituals, habits and practices that reflect their search for pleasure or risk-based experiences (Ferrell 1997, Lyng 1998).[5]

The interplay between space and culture

Criminological analysis of criminal and deviant activity has seldom linked the cultural representations of deviance and crime and the social control mechanisms devised against it with the space where uncivil behaviour happens to occur. Despite the fact that the connection between the spaces of criminality and the (sub)cultures of the people living there was made by the Chicago School, such a link has not prominently featured in the later work of criminological theorists and scholars, which has relied on either spatial or cultural variables. An interest in both spatial and cultural elements is partially present in the studies of cultural criminologists, which have often analysed deviant activities and the social reactions to them in areas of the city devoted to pleasure (for example, as already mentioned, in urban night-time districts). They have, however, tended to underexamine the complex net of cultural (as well as historical, political and socioeconomic) variables operating at the national, regional or city level, which shape groups' behavioural and aesthetic expectations for a particular urban space and, as a consequence, their attitudes to deviant and uncivil behaviour. This lacuna has recently been pointed out by Hayward (2012), who emphasised that it is important for cultural criminology and, more generally, for criminological research to inspect people's (affective/emotional) representations of space through the relevant cultural elements in order to develop an alternative, multifaceted understanding of the criminological space.[6]

This section is dedicated to presenting the results of two comparative studies on the regulation, societal representation and law enforcement of two types of incivilities (street prostitution and public drunkenness) that attempt to examine such culture–space linkages. Its purpose is to highlight the importance and role of local context-specific, as well as national, cultural factors in shaping the societal meanings given to different urban spaces, which, in turn, have an influence on the spatial location, societal representations of and reactions to uncivil behaviour in the same areas.

Street prostitution

The first study aimed to inspect the spatial location of, and the local responses to, street prostitution in different areas of the city and to detect the factors that played a role in shaping them (Di Ronco 2014). It did so by using Hayward's (2004) 'culture of consumption' model as a theoretical backdrop, which identifies three urban spaces where the deviant, uncivil activities of individuals (arising from their consumption and pleasure-seeking pressures) are subject to different levels of societal tolerance. These spaces are 'spaces of consumption and pleasure', 'centripetal spaces' and 'spaces of deprivation' (Hayward 2004). In these three urban areas the deviant activities that permit the individual consumer to reach an emotional state of pleasure and to fulfil his consuming desires are differently evaluated: in some places they are tolerated and even celebrated when they occur at particular times, whereas in other areas they are subject to penalisation. Such an evaluation depends (at least partly) on the physical and architectural characteristics that feature the urban environment. Deviant, uncivil, pleasure-seeking activities are socially accepted at night in places where pleasure has been physically incorporated, such as in 'spaces of consumption and pleasure', which are high-end areas of the city devoted to shopping during day hours and to entertainment at night. They are also tolerated in 'spaces of deprivation', or in run-down areas thriving on crime and deviance and lacking systems of social control. A lower level of tolerance of uncivil, deviant activities is usually present in 'centripetal spaces', which are inner-city spaces of shopping and residence, usually protected through SCP techniques and public forms of surveillance.

To inspect whether the culture-of-consumption model helps to explain the spatial presence of, and societal reaction to, street prostitution in different urban contexts, we selected three cities situated in three different European countries. They are the cities of Birmingham (UK), the Brussels Capital Region (Belgium) and Milan (Italy). These cities were chosen on the basis of demographic indicators (e.g. the number of residents, their religious and ethnic diversity, their mobility) and of indicators of governance (i.e. political leanings of the parties governing the cities), which reported similar data for all the three selected cities. The study subsequently identified and examined the three spaces containing the characteristics of Hayward's (2004) model in the selected cities.[7] To check whether the theoretical model contributed to explaining the presence of street prostitutes in certain urban areas, along with the societal attitudes to it, the study took into consideration the socio-economic, urban and architectural developments that occurred in the selected cities' areas in the past two or three decades, as reflected in the relevant literature, reports of national and international organisations and the data obtained from national and city experts, members of NGOs and residents' organisations.

A close analysis of the spatial location of street prostitution and of the social reaction to it in the three areas of the selected cities has shown some differences that explain the role that country- and city-specific cultural factors play in our understanding of regulated incivilities in the urban space. While street prostitution is present at nights in 'spaces of consumption and pleasure' of Birmingham (the Ladywood ward) and of the Brussels Capital Region (Avenue Louise), it is not present in similar areas of Milan (the Porta Nuova district) in any time span. Pleasure has been incorporated in the urban design of Porta Nuova, which registers the presence of, for example, night-time venues and disco clubs. Street prostitutes, however, are not to be found there. Sex workers are only present inside the clubs of the area as elegant escorts.

Furthermore, although present in 'centripetal spaces' of Milan (Navigli), street prostitutes (and their clients) are here deterred in a number of ways. Their presence on the streets is not only discouraged through specific design features of the urban environment, which facilitate the monitoring of the areas by formal and informal agencies of social control (for example, through CCTV cameras and improved street lighting) and limit their accessibility (for example, through electronic barriers and pedestrian precincts limiting vehicular circulation). Prostitutes soliciting for sex are also repressed through an intensified police presence and patrolling, which (at least until 2011, when the so-called 'anti-prostitution order' was in force) also translated into the application of punitive sanctions to them (City of Milan 2010).

In short, while in Milan the contested presence of street prostitutes in 'centripetal spaces' (Navigli) is a typical characteristic of inner-city areas of shopping and residence, which aligns with the 'culture of consumption' model (Hayward 2004), the absence of sex workers in 'spaces of consumption and pleasure' (Porta Nuova) at nights makes the area diverge from the said model.

A context-specific cultural element that helps to understand the absence of street prostitutes in 'spaces of consumption and pleasure' (Porta Nuova) and the societal negative attitude to the phenomenon of street prostitution in 'centripetal spaces' (Navigli) of Milan is the prostitutes' aesthetics and its importance. In Milan, street prostitution is a phenomenon that is highly contested by residents' organisations, which consider it as a phenomenon undermining 'people's quality of life and the liveability of public spaces' (Fondazione Padri Somaschi – Servizio Bassasoglia, in Di Ronco 2014: 163). More specifically, what seems to compromise people's life quality and the liveability of space is the visible presence of prostitutes indecently dressed on the public streets. This aesthetic component emerges, for example, from the anti-prostitution order in force in the city until 2011 (City of Milan 2008), which targeted and penalised prostitutes on the basis of 'their attitude, dress code and manners of approaching', rather than on the basis of the activity of soliciting clients.[8] In other words, such a regulation assumed that any woman standing on the street and showing a specific dressing style and attitude is actually a prostitute (Parmigiani 2008). As such, she 'deserves' a sanction.[9]

The way people look at, and respond to, the sight of prostitutes in urban areas at the reach of upper and middle classes is also explained through the national attitudes to sex, sexuality and gender. For example, when Italian people were asked, they expressed the belief that Italians have a negative attitude to overt declarations of sexual preferences by individuals and that women are perceived to be more discriminated against in Italy than in other European countries (Eurobarometer 2012; FRA 2012). Italy, moreover, has certain social expectations of the role that the 'respectable woman' should play within society (Quassoli 2004; Crowhurst 2012), which are frustrated when prostitutes are seen in spaces of the upper and middle classes.[10]

In light of the reduced number of responses provided by the inquired local authorities and organisations, the study only limitedly reconstructed the societal attitudes to street prostitution against the backdrop of city-specific cultural elements. More specifically, the limited amount of information provided did not allow us to further elaborate on the importance of people's aesthetic appearances in certain urban areas of Milan, which was considered in the study as a city-specific cultural element. Due to these limitations, the study has mainly relied on the analysis of the attitudes embraced at the national level (such as attitudes about gender, sex and sexuality), which (at least to a certain extent) are usually mirrored also at the local level. What the city- and country-specific cultural factors that have been presented in this study suggest, however, is that there are specific expectations that powerful majorities hold towards the way women should look and behave in 'nice-looking' areas attended by the middle and upper classes. These expectations are met, in high-end areas of Milan (Porta Nuova), through the missing presence of street prostitutes and, in well-kept areas of the city centre (Navigli), through the adoption of (design-based) displacing strategies and the application of sanctions.

Public drunkenness

The second comparative study attempted to explain the reality of the nuisance of public drunkenness as well as police officers' representations of and enforcement responses to it in nightlife locations of two cities: Ghent (Belgium) and Trento (Italy). It did so by empirically testing two hypotheses.

First, drawing on the literature suggesting the existence of different 'cultures of drinking' in the 'dry' (northern, central, eastern and) western parts of Europe and in 'wet' countries of the south of the region (Anderson and Baumberg 2006, Calafat et al. 2010), it was hypothesised that a distinct reality of the nuisance of public drunkenness was present in the nightlife locations of the two cities. More specifically, it was expected that in cities belonging to the 'dry' drinking culture of western European countries, the consumption of alcohol, although being less frequent, would involve higher intoxication levels and a greater number of uncivil behaviour than in the 'wet' southern drinking cultures.

Second, to explain police representations of the nuisance of public drunkenness and their responses to it, we drew on the literature, which suggests that the aesthetic characteristics of certain groups of people have an impact on police officers (Ferrell 1995, 1996; Ferrell and Sanders 1995) and that such an impact varies across different social contexts (Jordan 2000, Masuda et al. 2008, Millie 2008). Such an impact was thought to be more prominent in Italy, where scholars have long described the policing strategies targeting the minority groups (Melossi 2000, Quassoli 2004, Parmigiani 2008) who are seen to have different aesthetic and behavioural characteristics than the mainstream population. In Belgium, by contrast, policing strategies are said to be less biased toward outer appearances, but rather to be driven by an aggregation of factors (Snacken 2007, Easton and Ponsaers 2010). It was therefore hypothesised that the aesthetic style of street drinkers would play a more powerful role in shaping police officers' representations of the nuisance of public drunkenness, as well as the policing responses against it, in Italian, rather than in Belgian, cities.

On the basis of the two formulated hypotheses, the cities of Ghent, in Belgium, and Trento, in Italy, were selected for conducting the empirical part of the research. These two cities were selected because they presented a number of similar characteristics, such as the presence of a high number of students and the existence in the municipal regulation of a set of provisions sanctioning the (alcohol-related) uncivil behaviour of individuals and regulating the night-time activities of licensed premises (e.g. the selling of alcoholic beverages and the playing of music at night). These two cities were also selected on the basis of the living experiences of the researcher who carried out the study, who (at the time the research was started) had lived in Trento for five years and has lived in Ghent for three years. This on-site knowledge of the cultural and context-specific factors was thought to aid the researcher in the analysis of the empirical data (which was collected through observations and interviews with police officers) in reducing the chances of misinterpretation of data.

Through systematic observations carried out in each of the two nightlife areas (situated in the Vlasmarkt, in Ghent, and in Santa Maria Maggiore Square, in Trento) located in the centre of the two cities for seven subsequent evenings,[11] it was found that the nuisance of public drunkenness did not substantially differ in the two cities, as similar levels of intoxication and of disorderly behaviour were registered there.[12] By contrast, semi-structured interviews[13] with eight police officers in Ghent and with nine agents in Trento, who were tasked with tackling incivilities, highlighted the differences in their representations of, and responses to, public drunkenness as a nuisance. Officers in Ghent associated the nuisance of public drunkenness happening at night in the selected nightlife area with the excessive behaviour of people (conduct that bothered others, or that jeopardised the personal integrity of the self or of others), whereas in Trento they connected it to the presence of certain groups, namely students, punks and members of anarchic movements, immigrants and homeless.

In Trento, punks, immigrants and homeless were also described by three agents through a direct reference to their aesthetic appearances, as well as to their 'typical' behaviour and attitudes. For example, they identified nuisance groups like punks by 'the way they are dressed' and described homeless people causing alcohol-related disorder as 'shabbily dressed'. As emerges from the following fragment, disorderly immigrants were also portrayed by one of the officers through reference to their manners and physical appearances: 'you can spot them from the attitudes they have, from their large, broad and strong build. . . . [T]hey are mostly from Eastern Europe and former Yugoslavia [. . .] but they can also have other nationalities'.

One of the police officers in Trento also referred to the aesthetic characteristics of punks in an indirect fashion, by opposing the 'beauty' of the urban environment of the city centre (where the nightlife location is found) to the un-styled presence of punks, which was seen to 'degrade [. . .] the beauty of the historical monuments located in the area'.

Of the nine police officers interviewed, however, only a limited number of them made a reference to the aesthetic and behavioural characteristics of such groups of people: while three officers referred to them directly, one did so indirectly. Such a reference may, therefore, also be explained by a number of other factors, such as the personal biases and stereotypes of the interviewed police officers, their limited language or articulation skills and their tendency to give answers that are thought to be socially expected from them. An uneven representation of the nuisance of public drunkenness (which is based on the conduct adopted by people, in Ghent, and on the belonging to a certain group, in Trento) may also be explained through other cultural factors that were not included in the study, such as the specific culture of policing, which may differently shape the police practices and strategies to deviant and criminal behaviour in the two cities.

The study also found that police agents both in Ghent and in Trento rarely enforced national and local regulations addressing the phenomenon of public drunkenness as a nuisance. They, however, attributed different motivations to such a low level of intervention. While the Ghent police officers associated their intervention only with the excessive behaviour of individuals (or with behaviour that was thought to exceed the expected standard of drinking in public spaces) and so their sparse intervention was explained by the need to prevent drunk people from harming others or themselves, in Trento their formal responses were said to be inhibited by practical factors, such as the limited number of agents working during the night shift. Notwithstanding these practical constraints, police officers in Trento considered public drunkenness, as well as the nuisance connected with it, as one of their top priorities due to the high number of complaints and requests for intervention filed by the residents on a daily basis. Responses to such concerns and complaints were given by police agents through the adoption of alternative strategies, which included the fining of the bars around which incivilities occurred and an intensified patrolling of the area.

According to the interviewed Trento police agents, the tolerance levels of residents in the area to public drinking, drunkenness and connected nuisance behaviour were very low. They linked the negative attitude of people living there to a number of context-specific factors, such as the recent introduction of happy hours and parties for students, which have changed the traditionally accepted patterns of drinking in the city and led to the occurrence of episodes of physical and social disorder (which were previously absent, or less frequent, in the same area). Such factors help to explain why residents did not tolerate (or socially approve of) newly introduced drinking habits in that particular space at night: they had different expectations of how people should consume alcohol and behave in that place and at specific times, which drew on the social habits and practices that were well established in the past years.

In conclusion, the results of this study show that cultural factors, such as the importance of the aesthetic style of certain groups of people for some police officers in Trento, shape police representations of nuisance in night-time areas of the city centre. Furthermore, they suggest that policing strategies are in the same areas influenced by the perceived attitudes of dominant social groups (as reflected in the views of the residents residing in the well-off properties that surround the areas examined), whose expectations for the use of public spaces are moulded by context-specific cultural components.

Conclusion

Defining and controlling criminal or deviant behaviour are performed differently depending on the social and cultural contexts where they occur.

Definitions of deviance may be formed nationally at the level of the central government or at the level of the regions, territories or municipalities which have constitutionally been given regulatory autonomy by the central state. In Western democracies, the national parliament is usually the body in charge of shaping the definition of criminal activity, which is assumed to reflect the cultural values and sensitivities of the social groups with policymaking influence. Not all the definitions of what is punishable are, however, elaborated at the national level. Especially in the area of incivilities, the competence to define anti-social or uncivil behaviour is often given to local authorities (as, for example, in Belgium and Italy), who in turn refer to cultural values and systems of meanings, beliefs and customs that are well established in the locality.

As the results of the two studies described in this chapter suggest, the definitions of and the societal responses to incivilities very much vary between cities and, within them, between the different 'spaces of consumption and pleasure', 'centripetal spaces' and 'spaces of deprivation'. Such differences depend on the way in which national and context-specific cultural factors play out in the urban space. More accurately, definitions of and reactions to uncivil behaviour vary in the different areas of the city on the basis of the dominant cultural representations of space, which shape the way groups with decision-making powers expect such spaces to be used and people to behave and look within them.

The importance of how people appear in certain wealthy areas of the city has been highlighted in the examples of Milan and Trento (Italy). In Milan, for instance, a special significance is attributed by powerful social groups to the way people look in certain 'nice looking' urban areas. People who are indecently dressed (as street prostitutes are considered to be) are absent in high-end zones of the city and are intensively penalised in spaces of the historic city centre. The aesthetic component has also been found to play a role in shaping some of the police officers' views on the nuisance of public drunkenness in the central nightlife location of Trento; they described the groups of people causing alcohol-related disorder through their attitudes and aesthetic styles.

The importance of such an aesthetic component is, however, not undisputable. In Milan, for example, the relevance of such an element was inferred from the municipal anti-prostitution order (City of Milan 2008), which was in force until 2011. Due to the limited information provided by the interviewed civil servants, police officers, NGOs and residents' associations, it was, however, not possible to further elaborate on the importance of this component. Also in Trento the significance of group style in shaping police officers' representations is not conclusive, since only a limited number of police officers referred to the aesthetic and behavioural characteristics of certain groups deemed to be causing nuisance. The role of such an element, therefore, may well be the product of the personal stereotyped vision of the individual police officer, or of the specific policing culture, and cannot be easily generalised.

The spatial distribution, societal representation and law enforcement of street prostitution and public drunkenness in certain areas of Milan and Trento have also been explained through other national and context-specific cultural elements. For example, local responses to street prostitutes in high-end areas and in the historic city centre of Milan have been connected to the national attitudes to sex and sexuality and to the image and social role that is recognised for women in Italy. The importance of context-specific factors was highlighted in the example of Trento, where the changes in the drinking habits of young people in the central night-time area conflicted with the customs of the dominant social classes and led to the adoption of alternative policing responses against alcohol-related disorder. Local attitudes to the nuisance of public drunkenness are also informed by the drinking customs and habits of powerful groups, which shape the significance given to the consumption of alcohol and to the uses of public spaces. All such shared symbols and systems of meaning influence the societal expectations of how people should behave, at least in places attended by the powerful middle and upper classes.

To conclude, local representations of incivilities and responses to them vary in the different 'cultural spaces' of the city: they are the result of the cultural representations of space and, as such, reflect the meanings given to that particular city segment and the expectations arising from it. Contemporary cultural accounts of incivilities and their regulations should therefore investigate how people represent the urban spaces at the micro level of the community, the area, the district, the neighbourhood and (if relevant and appropriate) even at the level of the single road or street. The way people see and experience such spaces, in fact, not only synthesises their emotional or affective perceptions and visions. It also reflects the cultural shared background of beliefs, values, and traditions that are embedded in, and are important for, their social group(s) of reference. For this reason, it might be useful to draw also on other disciplines and perspectives that engage with exploring the affective representations of urban spaces and architectures, such as urban studies (and, within them, urban anthropology), and with inspecting space through culture, such as cultural geography.[14] The results and literature available from these and other disciplines may help to offer a further understanding of the complex relations between space and culture, which influence our vision of, and reaction to, incivilities in the urban space.

Notes

1 In this chapter, deviant, anti-social, uncivil (as well as nuisance and disorderly) are used interchangeably as synonyms.

2 The 'broken windows' theory of crime was later superseded by Sampson and Raudenbush (1999), who explained criminality in problematic neighbourhoods of Chicago through the structural deprivation and low levels of social cohesion that exist in such areas, which lead to reduced expectations for the presence of informal controls in the public space.

3 An example on the policies and punitive measures implemented in (traditionally tolerated) urban red-light districts with the aim to displace sex work is offered by the work of Hubbard (2004).

4 Also the definition of anti-social behaviour has been connected by British scholars with the (local) context where it occurs. See, among others, Whitehead, Stockdale and Razzu (2003), and Millie (2008).

5 For example, they have inspected and explained the emotional altered states sought by young people at nights. See, among others, Maesham and Brain (2005).

6 A similar invitation to critical theorists of social control to read local, and even neighbourhood-based, responses to crime and deviance through the (national political) culture and the '"structures of feelings" of different societies', was made by Loader and Sparks (2002: 104).

7 Spaces of consumption and pleasure were found in the Ladywood ward in Birmingham, in Avenue Louise in the Brussels Capital Region and in Porta Nuova in Milan. Areas resembling the characteristics of centripetal spaces were Balsall Heath (in Birmingham), the Alhambra Quarter (in the Brussels Capital Region) and in the Ticinese–San Lorenzo neighbourhood (in Milan). The adjacent wards of Soho and Lozells (in Birmingham), the area surrounding the Boulevard du Roi Albert II (in Brussels) and the bordering neighbourhoods of Loreto and Buenos Aires (in Milan) matched the characteristics of 'spaces of deprivation'.

8 Point 2 of the order (City of Milan 2008: 3) reads as follows: '[I]t is prohibited in the whole municipal territory to negotiate and agree on sexual services with individuals who solicit for sex on the streets or who with their attitude, dress code and manners of approaching express the intent to offer sexual services'.

9 From 2012, the Belgian city of Ghent has included in the municipal regulation a provision imposing on the prostitutes working in the red-light district a specific dress code (Boels 2014). As Weitzer and Boels (2015) reported, window prostitutes who wear scant clothes and attract the attention of potential clients with gestures and signs are viewed by police officers as both a nuisance and the cause of the further nuisance of clients. To fully or more properly understand the relevance of such an aesthetic element in this urban (cultural) setting would require the carrying out of ethnographic fieldwork in this city zone and the analysis of such obtained data through the cultural and context-specific factors that are of relevance there.

10 A reference to the breach of middle-class norms and values was also made clear by the anti-prostitution order of the city of Milan (City of Milan 2008: 1), which described the phenomenon of street prostitution as 'being morally harmful, as it offers an altered image of personal relations and annulment of human dignity and freedom, which give rise in the community to a sense of discomfort and of decline of social values'.

11 Observations were carried out in two areas of the cities that had been identified by police officers as being famous for their nightlife and associated with alcohol-related disorder. Before midnight, they were the area of the Vlasmarkt in Ghent, and the spaces surrounding Santa Maria Maggiore Church in Trento. After midnight, they were the adjacent spaces of the Oude Besteenmarkt (in Ghent) and of the Via delle Orfane and Vicolo Colico (in Trento), where most of the late nightlife entertainment occurred. Observations were performed in 2014 from 22 to 28 August in Ghent, and from 2 to 8 September 2014 in Trento. They were carried out from 10 pm to 1 am for seven subsequent evenings. (For more on methodology, see Di Ronco [forthcoming]). Through the aid of a coding sheet (as well as of field notes, videotaping and photographing), I observed and measured the number of people present in the areas at different times, their average age and gender, the level of intoxication reached by them and the occurrence of uncivil behaviour. Disorderly behaviour was associated mainly with people littering, urinating, causing loud noise, yelling, loudly disputing and engaging in physical assaults, violence and vandalism.

12 The study has a number of limitations. In order to be able to observe the typical drinking modes and patterns adopted by people in the two nightlife locations, we selected week(s) when no special events, festivals or celebrations were held. The data, in both cities, were collected, however, during a period of time when a limited number of students were present in the two cities due to the ending of the holiday period. In other periods of the year, when students are more present in the two localities, as well as during other seasons and according to the weather conditions, the drinking modes and patterns may substantially change in the two cities' areas and lead to different results.

13 Interviewed police officers belonged to the Lokale Politie, in Ghent, and to the Polizia Locale, in Trento, which are bodies that are competent to sanction cases both of public drunkenness and of nuisance behaviour connected to the consumption of alcohol. Police agents were purposively selected according to their competencies in enforcing regulations on public drunkenness. They were eight in Ghent, and nine in Trento. The questions of the semi-structured interviews focused on inspecting police agents' representations of the nuisance of public drunkenness and their enforcing attitudes to alcohol-related disorder.

14 An invitation to cultural criminology to consider the body of knowledge of cultural geography and, within it, of the non-representational theory, has also been made by Hayward (2012).

References

Anderson, P. and Baumberg, B. (2006) 'Alcohol in Europe: A public health perspective. A report for the European Commission'. Online. Available at: http://ec.europa.eu/health-eu/doc/alcoholineu_content_en.pdf (accessed 1 June 2015).

Bannister, J., Fyfe, N. and Kearns, A. (2006) 'Respectable or respectful? (In)civility and the city', *Urban Studies*, 43(5–6): 919–937.

Becker, H. S. (1963) *Outsiders: Studies in the Sociology of Deviance*, New York: Free Press.

Boels, D. (2014) 'Prostitution and its relations with informal economies', in N. Peršak and G. Vermeulen (eds.) *Rethinking Prostitution: From Discourse to Description, from Moralisation to Normalisation?*, Antwerp: Maklu.

Brantingham, P. J. and Brantingham, P. L. (1981) 'Notes on the geometry of crime', in P. J. Brantingham and P. L. Brantingham (eds.) *Environmental Criminology*, Prospect Heights: Waveland Press.

Burgess, E. W. (1925) 'The growth of the city: An introduction to a research project', in R. E. Park and E. W. Burgess (eds.) *The City*, Chicago: University of Chicago Press.

Calafat, A., Blay, N. T., Hughes, K., Bellis, M., Juan, M., Duch, M. and Kokkevi, A. (2010) 'Nightlife young risk behaviours in Mediterranean versus other European cities: Are stereotypes true?', *European Journal of Public Health*, 30: 1–5.

City of Milan (2008) 'Disposizioni per contrastare la prostituzione su strada e per la sicurezza urbana'. Online. Available at: www.cocomi.it (accessed 12 June 2015).

City of Milan (2010) 'Dispositivo Servizi Mirati. Antiprostituzione'. Online. Available at: http://st.ilfattoquotidiano.it (accessed 12 June 2015).

Clarke, R.V.G. (1995) 'Situational crime prevention', in M. Tonry and D. Farrington (eds.) *Building a Safer Society*, Chicago: University of Chicago Press.

Cloward, R. and Ohlin, L. (1960) *Delinquency and Opportunity: A Theory of Delinquent Gangs*, New York: The Free Press.

Cohen, A. K. (1955) *Delinquent Boys: The Subculture of the Gang*, London: Colher-Macmillan.

Cohen, S. (1985) *Visions of Social Control: Crime, Punishment and Classification*, Cambridge: Polity Press.

Coleman, A. (1985) *Utopia on Trial: Vision and Reality in Planned Housing*, London: Shipman.

Cornish, D. B. and Clarke, R.V.G. (2003) 'Opportunities, precipitators and criminal decisions: A reply to Wortley's critique of situational crime prevention', *Crime Prevention Studies*, 16: 41–96.

Crawford, A. and Flint, J. (2009) 'Urban safety, anti-social behaviour and the night-time economy', *Criminology and Criminal Justice*, 9(4): 403–413.

Crowhurst, I. (2012) 'Approaches to the regulation and governance of prostitution in contemporary Italy', *Sexuality Research and Social Policy*, 9(3): 223–232.

Davis, M. (1990) *City of Quartz: Excavating the Future in Los Angeles*, New York: Verso.

Demant, J. and Landolt, S. (2014) 'Youth drinking in public places: The production of drinking spaces in and outside nightlife areas', *Urban Studies*, 51(1): 170–184.

Di Ronco, A. (2014) 'Regulating street prostitution as a public nuisance in the "culture of consumption": A comparative analysis between Birmingham, Brussels and Milan', in N. Peršak and G. Vermeulen (eds.) *Rethinking Prostitution: From Discourse to Description, from Moralisation to Normalisation?*, Antwerp: Maklu.

Di Ronco, A. (forthcoming) 'Public drunkenness as a nuisance in Ghent (Belgium) and in Trento (Italy)'.

Easton, M. and Ponsaers, P. (2010) 'The view of the police on community policing in Belgian multicultural neighbourhoods', in M. Cools, B. De Ruyver, M. Easton, L. Pauwels, P. Ponsaers, G. Vande Walle, T. Vander Beken, F. Vander Laenen, G. Vermeulen and G. Vynckier (eds.) *New Empirical Data, Theories and Analyses on Safety, Societal Problems and Citizens' Perceptions*, Governance of Security Research Papers series 3, Antwerp: Maklu.

Eurobarometer (2012) 'Discrimination in the EU in 2012. Report'. Online. Available at: http://ec.europa.eu (accessed 1 June 2015).

Felson, M. (1994) *Crime and Everyday Life. Insights and Implications for Society*, Thousand Oaks: Sage.

Ferrell, J. (1995) 'Culture, crime and cultural criminology', *Journal of Criminal Justice and Popular Culture*, 3(2): 25–42.

Ferrell, J. (1996) 'Crimes of style: Urban graffiti and the politics of criminality', in J. Ferrell and C. R. Sanders (eds.) *Cultural Criminology*, Boston: Northeastern University Press.

Ferrell, J. (1997) 'Youth, crime, and cultural space', *Social Justice*, 24(4): 21–38.

Ferrell, J. and Sanders, C. (1995) *Cultural Criminology*, Boston: Northeastern University Press.

FRA [European Union Agency for Fundamental Rights] (2012) 'EU LGBT survey. Technical report. Methodology, online survey, questionnaire and sample'. Online. Available at: http://fra.europa.eu (accessed 12 June 2015).

Garland, D. (2001) *The Culture of Control*, Chicago: University of Chicago Press.

Hayward, K. J. (2004) *City Limits: Crime, Consumer Culture and the Urban Experience*, London: GlassHouse Press.

Hayward, K. J. (2012) 'Five spaces of cultural criminology', *British Journal of Criminology*, 52: 441–462.

Hayward, K. J. and Hobbs, D. (2007) 'Beyond the binge in 'booze Britain': Market-led liminalization and the spectacle of binge drinking', *British Journal of Sociology*, 58(3): 437–456.

Hubbard, P. (2004) 'Cleansing the metropolis: Sex work and the politics of zero tolerance', *Urban Studies*, 41(9): 1687–1702.

Jordan, P. W. (2000) 'Aesthetics and cultural differences', *Proceedings of the Human Factors and Ergonomics Society Annual Meeting*, 44(32): 6–77.

Katyal, N. K. (2002) 'Architecture as crime control', *Yale Law Journal*, 111: 1039–1139.

Loader, I. and Sparks, R. (2002) 'Contemporary landscapes of crime, order, and control: Governance, risk, and globalization', in M. Maguire, R. Morgan and R. Reiner (eds.) *The Oxford Handbook of Criminology*, Oxford: Oxford University Press.

Lyng, S. (1998) 'Dangerous methods: Risk taking and the research process', in M. S. Hamm and J. Ferrell (eds.) *Ethnography at the Edge: Crime, Deviance and Field Research*, Boston: Northeastern University Press.

Lyon, D. (2004) 'Globalizing surveillance: Comparative and sociological perspectives', *International Sociology*, 19(2): 135–149.

Masuda, T., Gonzalez, R., Kwan, L. and Nisbett, R. E. (2008) 'Culture and aesthetic preference: Comparing the attention to context of East Asians and Americans', *Personality and Social Psychology Bulletin*, 34(9): 1260–1275.

Measham, F. and Brain, K. (2005) '"Binge" drinking, British alcohol policy and the new culture of intoxication', *Crime, Media, Culture*, 1(3): 262–283.

Melossi, D. (2000) 'The other in the New Europe: Migrations, deviance, social control', in P. Green and A. Rutherford (eds.) *Criminal Policy in Transition*, Oxford: Hart Publishing.

Millie, A. (2008) 'Anti-social behaviour, behavioural expectations and an urban aesthetics', *British Journal of Criminology*, 48: 379–394.

Newburn, T. (2007) *Criminology*, Abingdon: Willan Publishing.

Newman, O. (1972) *Defensible Space: Crime Prevention Through Urban Design*, New York: Collier.

O'Malley, P. (2001) 'Policing crime risks in the neo-liberal era', in K. Stenson and R. Sullivan (eds.) *Crime, Risk and Justice*, Cullompton: Willan Publishing.

Parmigiani, F. (2008) 'Le implicazioni costituzionali del potere sindacale di ordinanza', Ph.D. thesis, Verona: University of Verona.

Quassoli, F. (2004) 'Making the neighbourhood safer: Social alarm, police practices and immigrant exclusion in Italy', *Journal of Ethnic and Migration Studies*, 30(6): 1163–1181.

Sampson, R. J. and Raudenbush, S. W. (1999) 'Systematic social observation of public spaces: A new look at disorder in urban neighborhoods', *American Journal of Sociology*, 105(3): 603–651.

Shaw, C. R. and McKay, H. D. (1942) *Juvenile Delinquency and Urban Areas*, Chicago: University of Chicago Press.

Shearing, C. D. and Stenning, P. C. (1985) 'From the panopticon to Disney World: The development of discipline', in A. Doob and E. Greenspan (eds.) *Perspectives in Criminal Law*, Ontario: Canada Law Book Inc.

Sibley, D. (1995) *Geographies of Exclusion: Society and Difference in the West*, London: Routledge.

Snacken, S. (2007) 'Penal policy and practice in Belgium', *Crime and Justice*, 36(1): 127–215.

Sutherland, E. H. (1947) *Principles of Criminology* (4th ed.), Philadelphia: Lippincott.

Webber, C. (2007) 'Background, foreground, foresight: The third dimension of cultural criminology?', *Crime, Media, Culture*, 3(2): 139–157.

Weitzer, R. and Boels, D. (2015) 'Ghent's red-light district in comparative perspective', *Sexuality Research and Social Policy*, 12: 1–13.

Whitehead, C.M.E., Stockdale, J. E. and Razzu, G. (2003) *The Economic and Social Costs of Anti-Social Behaviour*, London: London School of Economics.

Wilson, J. Q. and Kelling, G. (1982) 'Broken Windows: The police and neighborhood safety', *Atlantic Monthly*, 249(3): 29–38.

Young, J. (1999) *The Exclusive Society: Social Exclusion, Crime and Difference in Late Modernity*, London: Sage.

8 Media representations of incivilities in the British and Flemish press

Nina Peršak

Introduction

The security discourse, and its lower-order category – the incivilities discourse, which pervades the contemporary 'risk society', is an efficient tool of political power and a stimulant of feelings of belonging to a particular community, which often paves the way for various laws and policy against 'otherness'. Security is a value, a legal good (*Rechtsgut*), protected by numerous laws, and a basic human need. It is, however, also an industry, a business that feeds on the individual's fears, and one of the most abused terms of today. As 'security' is an extremely emotive word, capable of stopping short the logical mental or cognitive reasoning process, it represents a jewel in the thesaurus of securitising rhetoric, which holds also other entries, such as 'risk', '(dis)order', 'efficiency' and 'threat'. In the name of security, governments with law-and-order orientations tend to expand the field of the prohibited by including minor, socially undesirable or uncivil conduct that is normally a part of everyday experience in a modern, pluralistic, urban society.

This experience may be a source of fear and anxiety, particularly to those not accustomed to (or happy about) living in an urban environment.[1] In late modernity or 'liquid modernity' (Bauman 2004), in which the only constant is that there is no constant, existential anxiety – which is part of the human condition – is heightened, owing to increasingly fragmented lives, which are no longer necessarily structured around notions of a divinely constructed world that would give them a sense of meaning and make them feel safe in this uncertain world (Bauman 2004, Kanduč 2005). In this light, the criminalisation of various indecent or annoying but harmless acts – incivilities, disorder or anti-social behaviour (ASB)[2] – can be explained as an attempt to establish order in this insecure world through the extension of the notion of 'victim'. The observed culture of victimhood (Furedi 1997, Spalek 2006, Brooks 2015) pervading Western society further fuels the expansion of the victim status and, through this extension, the notion of crime. But how does the anti-social behaviour come to be seen as criminal?

One way of examining how people may attain a notion of the world in which the (merely) anti-social becomes akin to criminal is through the longitudinal content analysis of the most influential national press. In order to understand how social representations of a 'problem' come about, it is useful to observe the 'constructors'. The media or the press, for example, is one such constructor, whose operating tactics have attracted much scientific attention (for example, Ericson, Baranek in Chan 1991, Eldridge 1999, Reiner, Livingstone and Allen 2000, Reiner 2002, Roberts and Hough 2005). The dominant political ideologies such as 'law and order' when conveyed through mass media are powerful discourses capable of creating or re-interpreting social representations. Social representations are, in turn, capable of influencing the individual's behaviour (Moscovici 1976, 1984). Newspapers not only influence or 'cook opinions' (O'Connell 1997) but also affect the moral development of their readership. Cultural and sub-cultural values are also conveyed through the media. A newspaper, for example, thus becomes a vehicle through which the normative precepts – i.e. what is permitted, what is not and, moreover, how one should respond to certain violations of normative rules – are conveyed, rendering the representations with which the newspaper operates essentially normative. Moreover, the media itself teaches its readers how others think and feel about a certain social issue and, at least implicitly, suggest how they should therefore feel about it themselves. On the other hand, the media also presents the views of the public (and of specific groups of people, such as politicians and important media figures through interviews and opinion columns). It is therefore also a vehicle through which some voices are heard or heard more, while others are not, or are heard less.

After a short methodological section, this chapter presents the results of three studies that longitudinally examined the British and Flemish press, respectively. The research on the representations of the 'anti-social' in the British press was conducted within the context of social psychology (specifically theory on social representations)[3] in 2007, inspecting a decade-long development and usage of the word 'anti-social'. Settling in Belgium in 2011, I observed a similar phenomenon of punitive regulation of incivilities with almost identical inception dates, which made me wonder about the representations of incivilities in Belgium. In 2012, a grant[4] from Ghent University (located in Flanders, the Dutch-speaking region in Belgium) enabled my researchers and me to pursue this query further, focusing specifically on the Flemish press coverage of incivilities or 'nuisance' (*overlast*), as they call it. The two Belgian studies presented focused on the sanctioned or regulated incivilities, especially on the role of the courts in this area and on the voices of criminal justice scholars, respectively. In the concluding part of the chapter, the results are further discussed, together with the limitations of research and some comparative observations. The chapter ends by emphasising the importance of studying media representations of incivilities (or of any 'social problem') and proposes some ideas for further research.

Methods: content analysis of the press

British press

In order to find out whether the representations of the anti-social (or their elements) have changed through time and, if so, how, longitudinal content analysis of

British national newspapers (broadsheets and tabloids) for the period 1996–2006 was conducted (Peršak 2007). This period was chosen to include the dates of anti-social behaviour legislation (1999 and 2003) and a few years before and after that for comparison. For each year, a week starting from 15 March to 21 March (inclusive) has been chosen to gather the articles.[5] This week was selected in view of it being unremarkable, mid-season with no important holidays or events, which might have increased ASB or made its epiphenomena more irregular or uncharacteristic.

Articles were accessed through the Lexis-Nexis Butterworths electronic database, comprising thirteen British national papers with their Sunday editions: The Guardian, The Times and The Sunday Times, The Observer, The Business, The Independent and The Sunday Independent, The Daily Telegraph and The Sunday Telegraph, The Daily Mail and The Mail on Sunday, The People, The Daily Star and The Sunday Star, The Express and The Sunday Express, The Sun, The Mirror and The Sunday Mirror, and News of the World. The sample was collected on the basis of a keyword search; the keywords being 'anti-social' and 'antisocial'.[6] Although no limit was placed on the news format, certain articles were later excluded (letters to the editor), as the link between them and the papers which published them was too weak to warrant inclusion in the sample. Other units eliminated from the collected sample included duplications of texts (only one article of the two or more was kept; if one of the two was longer [usually in the later edition], the longer one remained in the sample) and irrelevant articles (for example, where the word 'anti-social' appeared only in passing and no code could be applied to it). This resulted in 146 articles, out of the original 205. As we got less than 10 articles for the years 1996, 1997, 1999, 2000 and 2003, the search was extended past 21 March in order to obtain further articles, amounting to 10 articles for each of those years. The final sample thus encompassed 168 articles (units of analysis): 1996 (10), 1997 (10), 1998 (10), 1999 (10), 2000 (10), 2001 (14), 2002 (16), 2003 (10), 2004 (21), 2005 (34) and 2006 (23). There were 89 quality paper articles and 77 tabloid articles.

The codes were selected to fit the purpose of our research, namely, to discern the existing and changing elements of representations of the 'anti-social'. Following the advice of Bauer (2000: 145) that complex coding is more likely 'to suit only a small historical window' and hence that a simple coding frame is preferred for a longitudinal study in order to 'avoid anachronisms', five basic codes were developed: (a) *who*: the anti-social subject or perpetrator of the anti-social behaviour or act; (b) *what*: the anti-social act or activity the 'who' is or has been involved in; (c) *jeopardised*: those who are seen as being under threat from ASB; (d) *reasons*: a general word for causes, triggers, motives, etc. of ASB; and (e) *solutions*: the proposed or used responses to ASB.

The qualitative research computer software ATLAS/ti was employed to code the text with these pre-existing codes (closed coding), which had been ultimately developed after piloting. The codes have been used to obtain the material deemed to represent the five basic elements of the representation of 'anti-social'. The outputs (retrieved coded text) have then been analysed, further coded or subcategorised if necessary in order to distil the underlying themes or group the similar results together. On some occasions, where the frequency of a certain word (or words) seemed particularly important, the ATLAS/ti programme's Search function was used to seek out all instances of the relevant word throughout the sample. The inter-rater reliability was established by another rater coding 20 per cent of the overall sample, based on the full description of the codes and calculating the Cohen's *kappa* coefficient for each individual code.[7] The overall reliability was .75 (excellent reliability).

Even though our research was primarily of an exploratory nature, there were some starting hypotheses present that guided the analysis, namely: (1) that the legislation had something to do with the rise of the 'anti-social' in the British press, (2) that the representation has changed through time, moulded also by government legislation and policies, and (3) that there were differences between broadsheets and tabloids (re)presenting the same 'problem'.

Flemish press

The study by Vander Beken and Vandeviver (2014) was conducted within the research on legitimacy (Peršak 2014) and examined the discussions about the legitimacy of the Belgian system of local administrative sanctions, or GAS (*Gementelijke Administratieve Sancties*, municipal administrative sanctions). This system has been used to tackle incivilities since its introduction in 1999.[8] The authors scanned 2,694 articles on local administrative sanctions, published in a selection of Flemish newspapers between 1 January 1999 and 31 December 2013. The newspapers inspected included the paper editions of De Morgen, De Standaard, De Tijd, Gazet van Antwerpen, Het Belang van Limburg, Het Laatste Nieuws and Het Nieuwsblad (these seven Flemish newspapers were indexed without interruptions since the inception of the Belgian incivilities or GAS legislation). This mixture of broadsheets and tabloids was accessed through the Mediargus online database. In the quantitative part of their study, they inspected the number of articles on the selected topic and the evolution of the publishing frequency throughout time. Search strings used were related to 'local administrative sanctions' and local administrative sanctions in combination with the word 'judge', to flesh out articles relating to specific criticisms voiced against this new system. Many authors, for example, considered it problematic that municipal authorities had seemed to usurp the role of a judge in these procedures, thus jeopardising the principle of separation of powers. The qualitative part of their study focused mostly on editorials and opinion articles that discussed local administrative sanctions in order to outline the media debate on this issue and how the media debate changes over time. The relevant articles were grouped together according to three criteria: (a) the period in which they were published, (b) the tone of the article, and (c) the group whose opinion is represented (Vander Beken and Vandeviver 2014).

A study by Di Ronco (forthcoming), carried out under the research grant on incivilities mentioned above, looked more in-depth into those incivilities that were regulated and fined though the GAS system as well as into the role of criminal justice experts in the media discussion surrounding these regulated incivilities. The content analysis of news published in a selection of newspapers during the most inflated month (the month of the year which yielded the most hits) of the years between 1998 (a year before the adoption of the GAS legislation, i.e. Law of 13 May 1999) and (inclusive) 2014 included coding for: (a) the *newspapers* that mostly covered stories on regulated incivilities over time; (b) *year* of publication; (c) the *main actors* (*'who'*) involved in the media discourse on regulated incivilities; (d) the *problems* described; and (e) the *solutions* that were offered to resolve such problems. In the first part, quantitative data acquired from the results of the coding were presented; in the second, more qualitative part, themes that seemed recurrent over the years were examined in more detail. In order to inspect the role played by criminologists and criminal justice experts within such themes, the original sample was supplemented with the inclusion of other articles (throughout the year) where such agents were given voice.

Newspapers were accessed through the GoPress (former Mediargus) database and included De Standaard, Het Nieuwsblad, De Morgen, Het Laatste Nieuws, Gazet van Antwerpen, and Het Belang van Limburg. De Standaard and De Morgen are considered quality papers or broadsheets, while the rest are considered popular press (Raeymaeckers 2005) – although not quite 'tabloid' (in the British sense). The keywords used for the selection of units were a combination of 'GAS OR administrative' AND 'fine OR fines OR sanction OR sanctions' in the first search, expanded by 'criminologist' OR 'professor' OR 'researcher' for the second search. After cleaning the initial sample (removing the doubles and irrelevant articles), the final sample (for the first coding) consisted of 444 newspaper articles. The second keyword search (with the inclusion of experts) resulted in 43 relevant items. As 8 among these were already included under the first search, and therefore already in the sample of the years' most inflated months, only 35 were therefore new (belonged to the other months), making the overall sample count 479 items. The distribution per year was as follows: 1998: 2; 1999: 7(8); 2000: 4; 2001: 4; 2002: 15(16); 2003: 5(7); 2004: 14(16); 2005: 24(25); 2006: 37(40); 2007: 18(19); 2008: 19(21); 2009: 22(24); 2010: 21(22); 2011: 28(34); 2012: 74(77); 2013: 78(86); 2014: 72(74).[9] Nvivo software was used for computer-assisted content analysis and 10 per cent of the initial sample (of 444 items) was coded by a second coder to establish inter-coder reliability. The overall Cohen's *kappa* calculated for three codes (Who, Problem and Solution) was 0.647, denoting substantial or good agreement.[10]

Results

The British press

Quantitatively, one of the first things to notice has been an exponential rise in the use of the word 'anti-social' (or 'antisocial') throughout the examined years.

Rising slowly from 1995, the usage of the word 'anti-social' increases sharply after 2001. As not all newspapers were included in the database at the same time

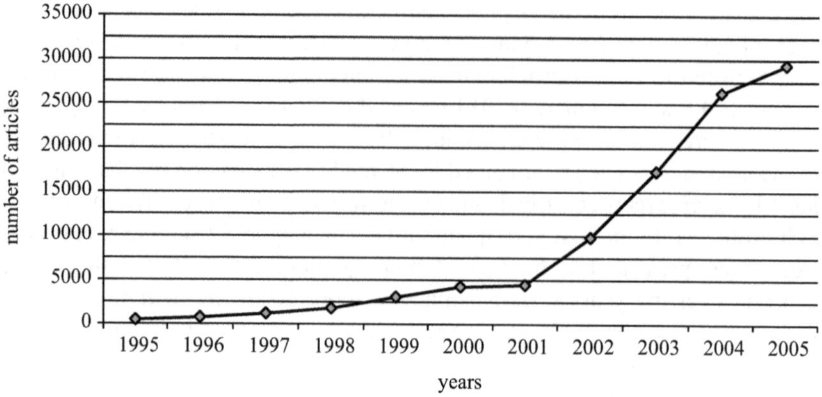

Figure 8.1 'Anti-social' (or 'antisocial') in British newspapers between 1995 and 2005.
Source of data: Factiva database

(e.g. The Telegraph was added to the Factiva database on 1 November 2000), this rise could partly (but to a minor degree) be attributed to the later date of inclusion of certain papers into the database. However, a very similar rise of the 'anti-social' utterances was observed when we looked only at those newspapers which had been included in the database from the outset, e.g. The Guardian.

Furthermore, the qualitative content analysis of our sample of newspaper articles in the British national press during this time also showed significant changes in the substance of media representations of the 'anti-social'. The anti-social behaviour legislation (specifically, the Crime and Disorder Act of 1998 and the Anti-Social Behaviour Act of 2003), aiming to make people or communities feel safer and nicer, certainly seemed to have made its impact, influencing the number and content of those representations in an interesting way.

The offender (who)

As to the Subject or offender, that is, as to *who* is considered 'anti-social' or is reported as doing or having done something 'anti-social', the analysis revealed that the mentioned ASB legislation not only re-moulded the representation of the anti-social but also that this reshaping steered the original representation towards the one encompassed in the legislation, consequently narrowing it down to the one connected with (only) behaviour or conduct of human beings. As this was one of the hypotheses, the sample was purposely gathered by using only the keyword 'anti-social' (or 'antisocial'), not 'anti-social behaviour' in order to be able to observe the possible changes in the linkages and meaning of the word.

The overall picture reveals that those who were labelled as anti-social need not be humans, or alive for that matter. The 'anti-social', when used for the above-mentioned objects and non-humans, turns out to be equivalent to 'anti-human'.

Thus, a 4 x 4 is, for example, an 'anti-social vehicle' because it does not care (or cares less than other vehicles) about other people, the planet or zebra crossings; certain hours are anti-social because they mean people have to work during hours which are traditionally reserved for family, home, playing with children or relaxing; adult male orangutans are anti-social because, unlike their baby orangs, they become aggressive and hostile towards people. When it comes to anti-social humans, three major groups can be distinguished: (a) children (mostly distinguished by age group), (b) adults (mostly distinguished according to what they do for a living, their profession or job (e.g. a rock star, a former cleric, a self-styled artist, a Labour councillor, broadcasters, entrepreneurs) or according to their membership in a particular anti-social group (habitual drunkard, doggers, muggers and winos, road and air-ragers, prisoners, 'middle-class, pushy mothers', certain tube travellers, neighbours) or (c) abstract notions, such as the 'underclass' (a class of people who are poor and deemed a corrupting, anti-social group outside society) or 'anti-social elements' (a dehumanising or depersonalising term for people involved in anti-social behaviour).[11]

A longitudinal overview reveals the rise of a 'thug', 'tearaway' and 'yob'.[12] In our sample, the usage of these labels, in the first few years, is almost non-existent (perhaps also due to the lack of tabloids in our 1996 and 1998 sample), then sporadic, with a particular rise in 2002.[13] Tabloids, as can be expected, dominate in the use of these emotive and populist terms. Incidentally, the populist language involving 'yobs' and 'thugs' was thriving even in the Home Office (2004a, 2004b, 2004c) documents. While The Guardian avoids these labels the most (using it only once), The Mirror employs them the most, using all three labels and a few more. In one of its articles ('Voice of the Mirror: Get tough with yobs like these', published on 20 March 2002), for example, it likens two anti-social brothers, aged 15 and 17, to Attila the Hun. They are described as thugs, yobs, thieves, bullies, a two-boy crimewave, monsters and 'a perfect example of why law and order is breaking down in Britain'. The custom of using such strong language usually goes hand in hand with appealing for harsher punishment, as in this case, where the court is praised for stripping them of their right to anonymity but criticised for not sending them to prison, which is, in The Mirror's view, 'what should have happened to them'.

However, it has to be noted that tabloids are not the only media using this emotionally charged language. What is most evident in the case of a 'yob' is that four different broadsheets (The Times, The Observer, The Independent and The Telegraph) or their Sunday editions used the term in 2003 or later, and the proportion of tabloids to broadsheets using the term is evening out (10:6 in total and 5:6 after 2002). From this, it can perhaps be concluded that the image of the offender (usually a juvenile) has undergone a shift even in daily quality newspapers. This happened more in the case of The Independent than The Guardian, which remained fairly stable. Perhaps the difference between The Independent and The Guardian can be explained by the readership profile they address. Even though both are considered more left-wing or 'left of the centre' (Fox 2004: 223), The Guardian is considered more left than The Independent. In crime and disorder issues, in particular, the gap between them seems bigger in the time interval studied.

The anti-social activity (what)

In the mentioned period, the law in England and Wales defined 'anti-social' quite vaguely as anything that caused or was likely to cause 'harassment, alarm or distress' to persons not of the same household. However, even if the law had been less vague, most people might still have got the first (and only) idea of ASB from experience and from reading and hearing about the real-life examples portrayed every day in the media. What was the image of the anti-social in the press? Considering that the anti-social Subject (the 'who') need not be a human being doing something anti-social, as we have seen above, but a tree or an animal, a supermarket or prison, the activities listed as anti-social (or 'what') encompassed two groups: other, more passive types of acts or activities in which people engage or do not engage (e.g. 'not joining in conversations') and anti-social conduct in which other subjects (not people) engage or which are imputed (personified) onto them (group A), and the human's anti-social behaviour as covered by the ASB legislation (group B).

Out of 22 purely group A articles, the large majority (18) were found in quality newspapers, while the large majority of group B offences (41 out of 63 articles) belonged to tabloids. It would seem, therefore, that tabloids tended more often to use the term 'anti-social' in the official, governmental sense, denoting particular types of human behaviour, as typologised, for example, in the Home Office document (2004d). However, even if we look at broadsheets only, one could discern a marked increase in group B acts in 1999, somewhat levelling off in the following years, then again an increase in 2003 and a widening of the gap between the groups in favour of group B from then onwards.

One plausible explanation for this shift in 1999, i.e. group B gaining influence over group A, could lie in the then pending legislation, namely, the already mentioned Anti-Social Behaviour Orders (ASBOs) that were introduced by the Crime and Disorder Act of 1998 and were about to come into force on 1 April 1999. Similarly, the additional thrust in 2004 can perhaps be attributed to the effects of the Anti-Social Behaviour Act of 2003 and its surrounding political agenda (encapsulated in the white paper *Respect and Responsibility – Taking a Stand Against Anti-Social Behaviour*). The law – whether one sees it as an articulation of politics or as an independent actor – seems to have given the press a new, more precise language of ASB, limited the list of options (group A) to which the language of ASB can be applied, thus steering it into a particular direction, into a narrower and more defined narrative of the anti-social.

The victim (to whom)

Those jeopardised by anti-social acts include, first and foremost, the community, which is always, without exception, presented as a good thing. Community as a victim consists of good, law-abiding, honest residents who are being attacked by the anti-social enemy, who is in this case an outsider, somebody not being part of this community, or consists of a good, law-abiding majority that is, alas, ridden with the internal anti-social enemy who aims to destroy it from within. This duality can be exemplified by the following passages:

> Meanwhile, it is quiet today over on Antonio Street. Mulling over the outcome, Sergeant Ward says that he believes the asbos have had the desired effect. There is a sense of relief in many homes on the street, he says. 'Some of these residents have lived here 20 or 30 years, and they remember the days when if there was a problem they could talk to each other and it would be dealt with. It's true, it's a rough area. But they see this as a way of retrieving their community' (The Guardian, 16 March 2004).

In this case, there is a problem in the midst of the community. While the said community used to deal with this internal matter by its members talking it through and dealing with it, now they reach for an ASBO in order to 'retrieve' – i.e. recover, repossess, take back – the community, which has apparently been snatched away from them. The 'unretrieved' community, in other words, is nonetheless 'community', despite its anti-social inhabitants who destroy it from within.

> Cars used by boy racers to terrorise communities can now be seized by cops. [. . .] 'That is why we have given the police powers to seize the vehicles which are causing misery. I know this move will be welcomed by communities' (The Sun, 18 March 2005).

In this second example, on the other hand, it is the outsiders – boy racers – who terrorise communities. If boy racers were considered part of the community, it would have been difficult to conclude that taking the vehicles from them was a move that would be 'welcomed by communities'. 'Communities' in this case clearly do not include boy racers – the latter are something external, the outsiders jeopardising the former.

Other victims ('jeopardised') mentioned often include children or a certain group of people, such as families, neighbours, tenants. The latter are often qualified as 'law-abiding', which acts as the antithesis of 'anti-social'.

The reasons (why)

In trying to make out some shape in the kaleidoscope of reasons (causes, triggers or factors for the anti-social behaviour), four main types of explanations have emerged: (a) social (related to housing, education, parenting, society, culture, etc.); (b) individual or personal (reasons which are considered to lie within the anti-social individual); (c) psychological and biological (such as emotional abuse, stress, depression, impulse control disorder – which trace the causes of ASB to its psychological or biological roots); and (d) systemic (institutional, legal or structural reasons).

The results reveal a slightly greater tendency for broadsheets to provide reasons: only 54.5 per cent of broadsheet articles dealing with ASB do *not* provide reasons, compared with 75.6 per cent of tabloid articles. Another way is to look at it through language: in more than half of the cases (16 of 27) that mention either 'thug', 'tearaway' or 'yob', or a combination of those, no reasons are provided. Out of these 16, the large majority (13) belong to tabloids.

Looking at the reasons on the whole, the 'social reasons' are by far the largest group (35 articles mention them, although not exclusively), 'psychological and biological' reasons follow them with 16 articles, 17 were 'systemic' and 4 'individual or personal'. Broadsheets are twice as worried about social factors than are tabloids (30 vs. 14). Tabloids (and more right-of-centre quality papers) are critical of actors who do not use ASBOs or use them too leniently. When it comes to blaming ASB on the inefficiency of the judicial branch or law enforcement or law itself (i.e. on the 'system'), the tabloids and right-wing broadsheets dominate. The changes in 'drinking laws', i.e. laws regulating pubs and bars' opening hours, laws regulating the issuing of licences to new pubs and bars, etc., are, however, a concern of a bigger number of broadsheets.

It is also interesting to note what is happening within the most numerous group of reasons – social reasons.

Table 8.1 features a detailed list of various social reasons mentioned – broken down by year and the type of newspaper. As can be seen, the popular press is mostly worried about bad parenting and family problems as well as about alcohol consumption and its effects on anti-social behaviour. The latter became a major topic of discussion (for the quality press as well) in 2004, when new laws aiming to curb binge drinking (in order to reduce anti-social behaviour) were introduced. The quality papers, on the other hand, are interested also in broader structural reasons, such as the economic, market mentality, which damages society, makes it more violent and its underclass greater and more desperate and pressures parents into working long hours and thus having no time for their children, who consequently suffer from emotional neglect and extreme pressure. They also mention negative social phenomena such as alienation on the part of local ethnic communities and exclusion of the poor or the poorer, critically speak of the schools' practice of expulsion and find other agents (airlines, big manufacturers, mobile technology, the drink trade and its power) and other social agencies responsible – the latter for failing to help an anti-social individual while there was still time, the former for enabling ASB in their own way. None of these topics, however, attract any of the tabloids.[14] Furthermore, television, media portrayals of ASB and the effects of video and Internet games on children seem to be a bigger source of worry for the broadsheets, even though these worries are somewhat more concentrated in the first couple of years.

As regards other categories of reasons, in the 'psychological and biological' category, negative childhood experiences (such as abuse, neglect and school victimisation) feature in the first six years, while the later years pay more attention to spelling out the immediate emotions and their stimuli, which precipitated anti-social behaviour. Still, as the overall sample of articles displaying this type of reason is relatively small (16), the above observation may not hold with a bigger sample. The vast majority of newspaper accounts containing this type of

Table 8.1 Types of social reasons mentioned and their prevalence in UK broadsheets and tabloids

Type of 'Social Reason'	*Year*											*Total No. of Reasons Mentioned*
	96	*97*	*98*	*99*	*00*	*01*	*02*	*03*	*04*	*05*	*06*	
1 Unemployment, poverty, deprivation, disadvantage	●				○		●	●				4
2 Housing							●					1
3 Deficiencies in parenting and family				○	○ ○ ○		○		●	●		7
4 Alcohol, drinking and drinking culture					●				○ ○ ● ● ● ● ●	○	○	10
5 Other agents					●				●	● ●		4
6 Lack of alternatives	●						●		○			3
7 TV, video and Internet games	● ● ●	●					○				○ ●	7
8 School (expulsion, education)	●				○				●			3
9 Economic, market mentality	● ●											2
10 Other agencies	●											1
11 Other negative social phenomena							●	●				2
Total	9	1	0	1	7	0	6	2	11	4	3	44*

Legend:
○ Reason mentioned in a popular press article (total no.: 14)
● Reason mentioned in a quality press article (total no.: 30)
* The total number of social reasons mentioned (the number is higher than the total number of articles addressing social reasons (35), as 5 articles mention two reasons and 2 articles mention three)

reason belong to the quality papers. The 'individual or personal' reasons form the smallest group (4); however, this may be due to the fact that this category was employed only where a certain reason could not be generalised or comfortably put in any of the other categories of reasons. Of course, many other reasons, such as 'social' or 'psychological', can also become in a sense 'individual' when they meet together in one particular individual and play a role in her anti-social behaviour. 'Systemic' reasons (17) include institutional, legal or other systemic reasons, where institutions such as courts or police or other elements of the legal system, such as the law or lawyers, are held responsible for ASB. ASBOs were either not working or not strong enough, institutions were chastised for being slow to take up ASBOs or for being ineffective (i.e. not jailing those who break an ASBO), other laws such as those dealing with pubs' and bars' opening hours and relaxed licensing laws were also to blame (particularly from 2004 onwards). These reasons appeared the most in tabloids and more conservative broadsheets.

The solutions (what to do)

Solutions to the problem of incivilities often overlap with the above-described reasons. They may be presented as the antithesis of reasons, yet solutions do not appear to be derivatives of reasons, but are usually the article's main point. In some cases one gets the impression that reasons are in fact constructs of their solutions. Here we spot two main types, namely the (more) repressive and (more) progressive or liberal solutions, the criterion for distinguishing between them being the punishment or some other suggested punitive limitation of freedom. The oft-mentioned more repressive solutions include issuing ASBOs, evictions for anti-social tenants, targeting parents, threatening to shoot vandals (and shooting them), jailing the offenders when they breach their ASBOs, naming and shaming the young offenders (stripping them of their anonymity), carrying out swift justice for offenders and confiscating vehicles. The articles putting forward such solutions tend to engage in 'othering' (Lister 2004). The more progressive solutions suggest education, more research, talking, counselling, turning aggression into creativity, anger management, returning the wealth to the poor, prison reform in the direction of reminding the prisoner that he remains a citizen, rehabilitation, increasing awareness and debate on ASB, providing bus service for late-night revellers to get home safe and more community-oriented actions and programmes.

It is interesting to note that the proportion of progressive solutions compared with repressive ones is about two to three (in the overall sample) but that the large majority of the progressive ones belong to broadsheets (32 vs. 9), while the more repressive ones are more likely to be found in tabloids (35 vs. 24). Longitudinally, the years 1996 and 1998 stand out for their number of progressive solutions mentioned, while it all changes in 1999, with all solutions for that year being more on the repressive side.

The Flemish press

Flanders is one of the three regions of Belgium, the other two being Wallonia (French-speaking) and Brussels (bilingual, i.e. French- and Dutch-speaking). Its 'municipal' approach to the regulation of incivilities dates back to 1998 and as such overlaps with the British anti-social behaviour legislation of 1998. As noted by Vander Beken and Vandeviver (2014), the Flemish press has been covering the developments in the area of municipal administrative sanctions (GAS) well, with a total of 2,694 articles published in the first fourteen years (1999–2012). The authors have distinguished three periods, corresponding to initial introduction of the system (1999–2004), amendments to it in terms of extending its applicability (2005–2011) and suggested further amendments, increasing the fines and lowering the age limit (2012). The first period did not produce many articles (only 21 over the whole six years), which, according to the authors, could be explained by the limited implementation of the GAS system. With the increase in implementation, the second period saw a steady increase in the number of articles, from 120 in 2005 to 425 in 2011 (on average, 296 per year). The GAS sanctions have become topical. In 2012 (the third period, the last year studied), the number rose even more – to 598 articles. Despite this fact, articles that discuss the role of the judge in the application of GAS amount to only 108 (or 4.01 per cent of the total number). Although this judicial role attracted much debate in the legal circles as a procedural concern with this system – municipal authorities acting as judges, not only defining undesirable behaviour but also imposing the sanction for it, without the 'constitutionally required independence' (Vander Beken and Vandeviver 2014: 39) – the media did not place much importance on the lack of a proper judge in the GAS system. The issue of 'judicial involvement' is mentioned the most in the first couple of years (1 out of 3 articles in 1999 and 2000 focus on this topic), but the interest quickly dies away, with only 5 per cent of articles in 2012 touching upon the subject (ibid.: 42).

In their qualitative part of the study, inspecting predominantly editorials and opinion articles on the topic of GAS, the authors observe that the press in the first period widely support the GAS idea, reporting only a few criticisms, which question the system as being parallel to the criminal justice system and voice concern with the legal safeguards included in the GAS system. In the second period, following the 2004 and 2005 amendments, the media proclaims GAS a success in the face of the fact that more municipalities implemented the system. Critical stances are observed to be more or less missing, while newspapers welcome the tool that 'deals with impunity' and 'promptly' sanctions incivilities, which are also reported as 'widespread' and 'drastically rising' (ibid.: 44). In 2012, however, the tune changes. This period is, according to the authors, characterised by 'misuse, protest and distrust throughout society' (ibid.: 44). Critical voices are predominant. They question the frequency of the use of fines in cases where they are not necessary as well as the target, arguing that the sanctions target people that in their view do not really need to be subjected to such sanctions, such as the young and the socially vulnerable. They question its costs, the absurdity of some prohibited incivilities and, in general, the repressiveness of the system and people. The authors also note that critiques can be heard from a variety of actors, such as a youth movement organisations, various social and cultural organisations, politicians and mayors.

The second study, by Di Ronco (forthcoming), went more in-depth into the notion of 'regulated incivilities (or regulated nuisance), examining what sorts of problems are noted in this respect and what sorts of solutions are proposed for them, as well as whose voice is heard in the press, and in particular whether criminal justice experts are present and listened to. The most reported 'regulated incivilities are noise nuisance, followed by illegal dumping and littering, violent and aggressive behaviour, theft and burglaries, parking offences, urinating, public drinking, drunkenness and abuse of drugs. However, not only conduct but certain people as well have been designated as a 'problem', most notably the young (108 items). Other 'problems' mentioned include legal issues, mostly dealing with the application of GAS sanctions or implementation of administrative measures (163 items), such as concerns about the intensified control (e.g., surveillance by CCTV) and extending the scope of GAS regulations. Legal amendments proposed and the legal definition of nuisance are also mentioned, as well as the problem of impunity when cases of incivilities are dismissed rather than processed.

Among 'solutions', the issuing of administrative fines to problematic individuals (266) and the adoption of other types of administrative measures against them (122) take precedence over all others, such as extending the application of GAS fines to new types of behaviours or to different categories of individuals (107), the adoption of regulations enforced through administrative sanctions for those municipalities that have not adopted the system yet (96) and preventive measures (94) such as teamwork among different public authorities, local projects not envisaging a sanctioning response, the recruiting of additional or new personnel and so forth.

One recurrent theme, which Di Ronco spots occurring throughout the years, is 'getting tough on polluting behaviour'. For dirty cities, more repressive interventions are offered as the prevalent solution. The other more frequent narrative is 'setting limits to the excessive GAS system and finding alternatives'; this one, however, emerges only in the last four years examined (2011–2014). Drawing on newsmaking criminology, which examines the use of mass communication media by criminologists 'for the purposes of interpreting, informing and altering the images of crime and justice, crime and punishment, and criminals and victims' (Barak 2001: 190), Di Ronco further examined whether and to what extent the views of criminology and criminal justice experts were present in the newspapers, and concluded that overall they have not been very successful in conveying their message. Who is listened to the most? In Di Ronco's sample, mayors are given voice the most (in 174 articles), followed by the aldermen, police officials, various politicians, MPs, public prosecutors and other public officials. Representatives of important organisations (of cities, labour unions, trade and sport) are also present. Further down the line are individuals, such as managers, employers, and residents. Experts in criminology and criminal justice are present nearly as much as students – in only 8 newspaper items. When the experts' voices are heard, however, they mostly act as a counterbalance to the claims made by others. Specifically, the experts have challenged the prevailing representation of the problems linked to regulated incivilities and of their solutions by drawing on research results and legal principles. They have also advocated other normative solutions and a thorough analysis and revision of the GAS system. However, owing to the very limited number and form of the experts' interventions (short quotes rather than longer commentaries), they seem not to have been effective in shaping cultural constructions of regulated incivilities (ibid.).

Discussion and conclusion

Rather than having to do with the actual rise in the anti-social conduct, the observed rise of the 'anti-social' in the British press between 1996 and 2006 was hypothesised to be related to the governmental production of certain legislation, which in turn fixed the label 'anti-social behaviour' in the minds of the public. That there could not be such a rise in the actual behaviour that could be deemed anti-social (e.g. littering, fly-tipping, etc.) follows from comparison with another type of deviance – crime. Considering the steady drop in the level of crime since the mid-1990s (Bottoms 2006: 256), one could thus argue that it is very unlikely that anti-social behaviour would rise, particularly in such an exponential way. The results of the content analysis of the British press suggest that it was in fact legislation, and subsequent government actions, that have instigated an increase, and moreover, moulded the content of the representations of the 'anti-social'.

Looking at the context within which these changes occurred, the sharp rise after 2001 can probably be most directly linked to New Labour's active encouragement of the wider use of ASBOs through guidances, instructions, legislative changes and publicity campaigns (Burney 2005: 33, 91). Furthermore, wider structural factors such as the political climate regarding criminal justice issues, i.e. the law and order mentality, which spilt over from the USA, with its rather punitive stance and 'broken windows' thesis (Wilson and Kelling 1982)[15] as its justification, could have been further fuelling the rhetoric of the anti-social. Certain unpleasant, fear-instigating events (notably 9/11) could also have had a knock-on effect in the sense of people becoming more afraid of (and perhaps less willing to tolerate) other socially unpleasant human behaviour. They may have also become more sensitised to socially undesirable phenomena through the preceding media portrayal.

The reshaping that has taken place in the eleven-year period has steered the original representation towards that articulated in the ASB legislation, which means that it has narrowed it down to the one concerned with human behaviour and moreover behaviour in a particular (officially defined) way. This marked shift occurred in 1999 and re-occurred (or got refuelled) in 2003, overlapping with ASB legislation (Crime and Disorder Act in 1998 and Anti-Social Behaviour Act in 2003). While broadsheets were slower to pick up on the new representation and continued to use it in the 'old', broader way, tabloids quickly and more consistently embraced the new meaning, endowing it with legitimacy. By picking up the government-induced representation and moulding the existing representations to fit the governmental, 'official' one without much criticism or scepticism, the press thus actively contributed to the legitimising process of the ASB legislation.

Negative emotive words, such as 'thug', have also progressively begun to be used (more by tabloids than broadsheets, though) to describe the anti-social offender, mirroring the language of the government documents. In the early years, this helped to solidify the negative image of the Other and clear the path for harsher, additional punitive 'solutions' and the extension of censure to come. These 'commonly used populist adjectives in anti-social behaviour discourses', as Squires and Stephen (2005: 126) observe, 'serve to reinforce notions of *dangerous Other* and cement ready acceptance of another, exponentially intrusive, measure to contain "out of control" youngsters'. Through time they become self-evident truths, taken for granted, which enables the authoritative systems of classification and demarcation between 'us' and 'them' to be seen as natural rather than constructed (Valentine 1998). Through contrastive identification (ibid.) or identification of 'us' against 'them', they moreover reinforce the identity of the Self (or 'us'). The Self is contrasted with the anti-social Other and therefore needs no specification and consequently invites no scrutiny.

The British quality papers displayed a greater tendency to give reasons or explanations for ASB. They were more interested in social (and particularly in the structural) and psychological reasons compared with tabloids, which (together with right-wing broadsheets) were more likely to place the blame on courts and local councils for not imposing enough ASBOs or not sending the offenders who break them to jail. How governmental agendas define the social-problem-of-the-day was clearly seen from 2004 news accounts, when new drinking laws (and their connection to ASB) were being discussed – almost entirely monopolising the 'reasons' debate, giving drinking and its laws high visibility, and invisibility or marginal visibility to other reasons, thus determining the sayable-representable and narrowing the representation (in its 'reasons' element) even further. Although the solutions to the 'anti-social' problem drastically tipped the balance in favour of the more repressive responses in 1999, the quality press, unsurprisingly, dominates in the more progressive ideas, while tabloids proved to be in general more punishment oriented and overall supportive of the government.

The results of the analysis of the Flemish press highlight some other interesting points. The authors suggest that the public or media opinion changes when it hits home, that legal concerns (e.g. about the procedure or non-involvement of a judge in issuing a sanction) do not feature very prominently in the media discussions on the legitimacy of the GAS system but that the focus is rather on the consequences of such a system, i.e. what it means for 'us' (Vander Beken and Vandeviver 2014: 46). This seems to suggest, on my reading, that the media (or the general, non-expert audience for whom the press writes) may worry more about the outcome than the procedure or the means to achieve something. It could also suggest that some legal intricacies are too complex for the media (or for its audience, as it envisions it) to be really interested in. The authors end their chapter by noticing – with some concern – that while some municipalities linked the development of this system to its security policy, others have not; the latter instilled the GAS system not for preventive purposes but 'as an autonomous instrument of a strict control policy' (ibid.: 47). This complements our observation in the beginning of this chapter: while worries about security can be a driving force behind the criminalisation of incivilities, security can also be just a rhetorical tool and criminalisation a tool of power – not having actually anything to do with security or prevention of undesirable conduct, but rather with political control.

In contrast to our British study, Di Ronco noticed no significant difference between the Flemish broadsheets and popular press in terms of its content – for example, in reasons or solutions proposed. This can perhaps be partly explained by the fact that the Flemish popular press cannot be easily equated with tabloids. They are more mid-market dailies, which report on political and socio-economic matters by appealing to a broad spectrum of the different social categories within the newspaper audience (Velders et al. 2013). She did notice, however, the difference in the amount of news on, or interest in, the topic of incivilities, with the popular press clearly in the lead: both Het Laatste Nieuws and Het Nieuwsblad had roughly twice as many articles discussing regulated incivilities than any other newspaper.

All three studies, however, suffer from some limitations,[16] which make confident generalisations impossible and conclusions tentative. If we attempted a more detailed comparison between these studies, we would, moreover, be constrained by additional limitations arising out of different objectives, different media characteristics (British tabloids vs. the Flemish popular press) and differences in the sample, its size and keywords used to draw a sample. Even though a comparison between all three studies can therefore be only very limited, a lot can be learned from all three as regards the changes in the press moulded by the onset (and subsequent amendments) of the law on incivilities. All three studies covered (or included in their coverage) the years 1999–2006, which were the first eight years of the life of legislation tackling incivilities in the two countries, and can therefore – in their own right – shed light on the representation, construction and development of the topic of incivilities in the print media in their respective countries.

What is interesting – comparatively – is that while the British press clearly focuses on behaviour – the term 'anti-social' is mostly linked to behaviour of people (except in the first, pre-ASBO years) or social disorder – the top three incivilities in the Flemish press, as they came out in the study by Di Ronco, are related to physical disorder, namely noise, illegal dumping and littering. Polluting behaviour is mentioned as a typical case of nuisance that is administratively sanctioned in Belgium. Uncivil or 'nuisance people', which would suggest more directly 'social' (or rather, anti-social) nuisance, are mentioned much less frequently. It would seem therefore that while England and Wales have been concerned with rude people, it is mostly dirt that bothers the Flemish. However, as Di Ronco's search was limited to regulated, fined incivilities (i.e. those that have been prohibited and can incur a sanction), not *any* type of incivilities (as in the British case of 'anti-social'), this can play a part. It could be that in Flanders physical incivilities are mentioned more because they are the ones that are fined the most or are more easily fined (perhaps as they are more stationary). To confirm or reject this hypothesis of a possible cultural difference in the (media) perceptions of incivilities, further research should compare the British sample with the Flemish sample sourced on '*overlast*' (nuisance, incivilities). Further research of media representations of incivilities could also include the inspection of the possible influence of newspaper ownership on the content of the press as well as include other media such as television and digital and social media (Facebook, Twitter, etc.), which are an increasingly popular platform for sharing and receiving information.

In the light of the existing research concerning media influences and the widespread phenomenon of populist politics, media representations have a significant political dimension to them. We live in social structures; we think and feel within the network of ideologically mediated symbols. Certain interested people, such as 'moral entrepreneurs' (Cohen 1972), can use the media to evoke certain emotions in the public in order to establish the right momentum or garner support for their future actions, e.g. for harsher criminalisation or more repressive measures against such behaviour. This is why the quantitative and qualitative research of media representations has an additional critical impetus in the field of criminology. Although the absence of the views of criminology and criminal justice experts, as observed in Flanders, who can be the voice of reason and constraint in this area of growing social control is to be regretted, finding (and researching) the silence can sometimes speak volumes. It also, however, reminds us of the changing nature of scientific communication and its societal impact: one of the challenges for further engagement of researchers in this field could also therefore include dissemination of their findings to the mass media or wider, non-expert audiences.

Notes

1 Félonneau (2004) has observed that those who dislike or reject the city (urbanophobes) clearly correlate with a weak urban identity and tend to overestimate uncivil behaviour in the city.
2 Of course, not all disorder or anti-social behaviour is harmless; the harmful anti-social behaviour, however, tends to be already criminalised.
3 This research is based on my second master thesis (master studies in social and developmental psychology, University of Cambridge). The results were later presented at the European Society of Criminology 2009 conference, but not published to date.
4 BOF Starting Grant, no. 01N01713 (project grant holder: Prof. Dr. Nina Peršak), Special Research Fund UGent.
5 Owing to the time limitations of the master studies, specifically the time frame dedicated to the writing of a master thesis, it was not possible to extend the sample by choosing a bigger time frame. Due to the lack of access to Factiva and LexisNexis databases, the study could also not be extended later. The rather small sample, which may not be representative for an entire year, is a limitation that is, however, duly noted.
6 Antisocial, written without a hyphen, is the American English spelling of the word. As both spellings are present in the British national papers, the search included both versions (using the OR operator).
7 For the individual codes: 'who' (.74), 'what' (.75), 'jeopardised' (.73), 'reasons' (.78), 'solutions' (.75).
8 See Chapter 6 (by Pleysier) on the Belgian system of regulation of incivilities.
9 The first number indicates the number of relevant items published in the year's most inflated month, the number in the parentheses includes the items where experts have appeared in the news in the other months of the year.
10 The inclusion of the codes 'Year' and 'Newspaper' into the calculation of kappa would have artificially increased the degree of overall agreement among coders, as they did not involve any margin of interpretation among coders, which is why they have been excluded from the calculation of the inter-rater agreement.
11 The Mirror, 25 March 1999: 'Park patrols are to be introduced to take back green spaces from anti-social elements. It is thought that Dubliners are being driven from the city's parks by muggers and winos, it was claimed yesterday.'
12 The said terms were located in the texts electronically by using ATLAS' Search function in the Edit menu.

13 Thug: twice in 1997, 1 in 2000, 1 in 2001, 5 in 2003, 3 in 2004, 2 in 2006 (only 2 out of 14 in broadsheets (Independent and Sunday Telegraph (lies in the margin between a tabloid and a broadsheet)). Tearaway: 1 in 1999, 3 in 2000, 3 in 2002, 1 in 2005, 1 in 2006 (2/9 in broadsheets). Yob: 1 in 2001, 4 in 2002 and every year since (6/16 in broadsheets).

14 The Mirror (18 March 2000) is worried about school or schooling but in a somewhat different sense: in a sense of providing a weak education and being a place where the bullying of a later offender took place.

15 In short, the 'broken windows' thesis claims that visible social disorder (e.g. a broken window), if not dealt with promptly, will subsequently cause more serious crime (all windows to be broken, the increase of violent, predatory crime, etc.).

16 The limitations of the British study on the anti-social include the limitation related to the size of the sample. In order to state some conclusions with more confidence, the study could profit from an increase in the sample size. Even though 'a simple increase in sample size alone does not necessarily imply that the research findings will be more valid', it may add 'greater breadth to the scope of the analysis' (Kelle 2000: 293). Vander Beken and Vandeviver only cursorily examined the newspaper items; a more detailed coding and establishing of its reliability may yield more precise or in-depth results. Both Belgian studies retrieved articles from a selection of seven or six (six overlapping) newspapers. Other newspapers not included in the study may have offered a somewhat different representation of nuisance-related problems and solutions; however, the newspapers included were those with bigger regional circulation, meaning they were more likely to impact on the audience. Di Ronco's study has relied on a sub-sample of articles published in a selection of Flemish newspapers in the years' most inflated months. While this made it possible to spot the 'hot topics' in the press, it runs the risk of inflating the importance of specific topics and events, which may not be representative for the remainder of the year. Furthermore, the intercoder agreement has only been calculated for the three main codes (on 10 per cent) and not for the subcodes.

References

Barak, G. (2001) 'Review essay', *Critical Criminology*, 10(2): 137–145.

Bauer, M. W. (2000) 'Classical content analysis: A review', in M. W. Bauer and G. Gaskell (eds.) *Qualitative Researching with Text, Image and Sound*, London: Sage.

Bauman, Z. (2004) *Identity: Conversations with Benedetto Vecchi*, Cambridge: Polity Press.

Bottoms, A. (2006) 'Incivilities', offence and social order in residential communities', in A. von Hirsch and A. Simester (eds.) *Incivilities: Regulating Offensive Behaviour*, Oxford: Hart Publishing.

Brooks, A. C. (2015) 'The real victims of victimhood', *New York Times*, 26 December 2015. Online. Available at: www.nytimes.com/2015/12/27/opinion/sunday/the-real-victims-of-victimhood.html?_r=0 (accessed 26 December 2015).

Burney, E. (2005) *Making People Behave: Anti-Social Behaviour, Politics and Policy*, Devon: Willan Publishing.

Cohen, S. (1972) *Folk Devils and Moral Panics*, London: MacGibbon and Kee.

Di Ronco, A. (forthcoming) 'Media representation of regulated incivilities in the Flemish press: Relevant actors, problems, solutions and the role played by experts'.

Eldridge, J. (1999) 'Risk, society and the media: Now you see it, now you don't', in G. Philo (ed.) *Message Received*, New York: Addison Wesley Longman Ltd.

Ericson, R. V., Baranek, P. and Chan, J. (1991) *Representing Order: Crime, Law and Justice in the News Media*, Milton Keynes: Open University Press.

Félonneau, M.-L. (2004) 'Love and loathing of the city: Urbanophilia and urbanophobia, topological identity and perceived incivilities, *Journal of Environmental Psychology*, 24: 43–52.

Fox, K. (2004) *Watching the English: The Hidden Rules of English Behaviour*, London: Hodder.

Furedi, F. (1997) *Culture of Fear: Risk-Taking and the Morality of Low Expectation*, London: Cassell.

Home Office (2004a) *Call for Local Heroes* (Press Release 216/2004, 29 June), London: Home Office.

Home Office (2004b) *Confident Communities in a Secure Britain: The Home Office Strategic Plan 2004–2008*, London: Home Office.

Home Office (2004c) *Confident Communities in a Secure Britain: Home Office Publishes Strategic Plan* (Press Release 237/2004, 19 July), London: Home Office.

Home Office (2004d) *Defining and Measuring Anti-Social Behaviour* (Home Office Development and Practice Report, no. 26), London: Research, Development and Statistics Directorate. Online. Available at: www.homeoffice.gov.uk/rds/pdfs04/dpr26.pdf (accessed 20 November 2015).

Kanduč, Z. (2005) 'Postmoderne nevarnosti, bojazni in "dobri sovražniki"', *Revija za kriminalistiko in kriminologijo*, 56(4): 337–347.

Kelle, U. (2000) 'Computer-assisted analysis: Coding and indexing', in M. W. Bauer and G. Gaskel (eds.) *Qualitative Researching with Text, Image and Sound: A Practical Handbook*, London: Sage.

Lister, R. (2004) *Poverty*, Cambridge: Polity Press.

Moscovici, S. (1976, orig. 1961) *La psychanalyse: Son image et son public*, Paris: Presses Universitaires de France.

Moscovici, S. (1984) 'The phenomenon of social representations', in R. M. Farr and S. Moscovici (eds.) *Social Representations*, Cambridge: Cambridge University Press.

O'Connell, M. (1997) 'The raw and the cooked – two types of public opinion', *Papers on Social Representations – Textes sur les Representations Sociales*, 6(1): 37–49.

Peršak, N. (2007) 'Representations of the anti-social', unpublished M.Phil. thesis, Cambridge: University of Cambridge.

Peršak, N. (ed.) (2014) *Legitimacy and Trust in Criminal Law, Policy and Justice: Norms, Procedures, Outcomes*, Farnham, Burlington: Ashgate.

Raeymaeckers, K. (2005) 'Letters to the editor: A feedback opportunity turned into a marketing tool. An account of selection and editing practices in the Flemish daily press', *European Journal of Communication*, 20(2): 199–221.

Reiner, R. (2002) 'Media made criminality: The representation of crime in the mass media', in M. Maguire, R. Morgan and R. Reiner (eds.) *The Oxford Handbook of Criminology*, Oxford: Oxford University Press.

Reiner, R., Livingstone, S. and Allen, J. (2000) 'No more happy endings? The media and popular concern about crime since the Second World War', in T. Hope and R. Sparks (eds.) *Crime, Risk and Insecurity*, London: Routledge.

Roberts, J. V. and Hough, M. (2005) *Understanding Public Attitudes to Criminal Justice*, Maidenhead: Open University Press.

Spalek, B. (2006) *Crime Victims: Theory, Policy and Practice*, Basingstoke: Palgrave Macmillan.

Squires, P. and Stephen, D. E. (2005) *Rougher Justice: Anti-Social Behaviour and Young People*, Devon: Willan Publishing.

Valentine, J. (1998) 'Naming the other: Power, politeness and the inflation of euphemisms', *Sociological Research Online*, 3(4). Online. Available at: www.socresonline.org.uk/socresonline/3/4/7.html (accessed 18 December 2006).

Vander Beken, T. and Vandeviver, Ch. (2014) 'When things get serious. Reflection on the legitimacy of local administrative sanctions in Belgium', in N. Peršak (ed.) *Legitimacy and Trust in Criminal Law, Policy and Justice: Norms, Procedures, Outcomes*, Farnham, Burlington: Ashgate.

Velders, K., Joye, S., Biltereyst, D., Bonte, T. and Delcart, E. (2013) '(Un)covering Poland between PR and presidency: A quantitative content analysis of print news coverage of the Polish EU presidency in Flanders', *Central European Political Studies*, 3: 109–120.

Wilson, J. Q. and Kelling, G. L. (1982) 'Broken windows: The police and neighbourhood safety', *Atlantic Monthly*, 249(3): 29–38.

9 Over-policed?

Tackling incivilities and the intersections with migration control

Joanne van der Leun

Introduction: tackling incivilities in the urban context

Social incivilities, understood as lower-level breaches of community standards, have received ample scholarly attention over the years, although mostly in the Anglo-American context, because they appear to signal crime and trouble (Hunter 1978, LaGrange, Ferraro and Supancic 1992), just like broken windows or other physical cues do. Activities such as loitering, hanging around and displaying improper behaviour have increasingly become the target of policies aimed at reducing fear of crime and insecurities (Garland 2001). This also holds for the Netherlands, where the government does not provide an explicit definition but describes social incivilities as 'behaviour systematically severely impacting on the wellbeing, and which is specifically targeted at specific persons'.[1] A more useful definition might be that of the European Commission (2000: 4), which defined anti-social conduct as 'conduct that without being a criminal offence can by its cumulative effect generate a climate of tension and insecurity'. Preventing and punishing these categories of behaviour have become crucial in times in which the police and other law enforcement agencies are under pressure to prevent crime from happening.

As the type of behaviour that comprises incivilities or anti-social behaviour are open to broad interpretation and are framed and criminalised differently across time and space (Peršak 2014: 22), this approach to security combines the broad interest in incivilities and sub-crime with the increased monitoring of 'suspect populations' and 'disorderly spaces' (De Leeuw and Van Swaaningen 2011, Van der Leun and Koemans 2013). The preventive aims of the new crime complex are therefore typically accompanied by new technologies and risk assessments (Feeley and Simon 1992, Dekkers and Van der Woude 2014). On the other hand, the discretionary judgements of police officers get a lot of weight, as the police are expected to intervene early and 'nip crime in the bud' (Svensson and Saharso 2015).

For decades, Dutch politicians supported the strong social character of crime policies and felt that (perceived) problems of incivilities, disorder, sub-crime or anti-social behaviour should not be dealt with under criminal law (Downes and Van Swaaningen 2007). This restraint tied in with the emphasis on regulated tolerance that characterised Dutch society for a long time (Buruma 2007, Engbersen, Van der Leun and De Boom 2007). In 1985, a governmental committee explicitly advised the Dutch cabinet not to address phenomena such as nuisance and disorder in the public domain with criminal law, in order to avoid over-criminalisation and escalation. Now, thirty years later, criminalisation is seen as an important tool to combat incivilities. In particular, in reaction to the events of 9/11, preventive powers of law enforcement have been seriously expanded (see the next section). In 2007, Den Boer (2007: 17) noted with respect to Dutch policy changes after 2011: 'With the relatively one-sided choice for repression and selective and proactive investigation, the Netherlands seems to have abandoned its traditional culture of trust, familiarity and tolerance'. Garland's influential observations regarding contemporary societies such as the US and the UK that came to be cultures of control also appears to be applicable to the Netherlands, with its rapidly changing crime policies in which tackling sub-crime and incivilities has moved to the fore (Van Swaaningen 2005, Daems 2009, Koemans 2010). The Dutch government has chosen to expand the traditional criminal law approach to misdemeanours (a category of behaviour that is deemed less serious than criminal offences) and criminalise social incivilities at the national level. Inspired by British examples, criminal law has also been supplemented with new possibilities of punishing behaviour under administrative law. Administrative legislation provides local authorities, which have strong powers with respect to security and public order, with more legal instruments (often dubbed administrative sanctions) to react to and prevent incivilities. In 2010, a law pertaining to severe anti-social behaviour, with many similarities to the British Anti-Social Behaviour Order (ASBO), was enacted.[2] This law consists of a civil order backed up by a criminal penalty (Koemans 2010). These forms of criminalisation do not imply that social policies have been abandoned, though. The Dutch approach to incivilities can best be described as a mix of repression and criminalisation on the one hand and social and urban restructuring on the other. A long-standing policy tradition under the label of Big Cities Policy (GSB) aims to improve disadvantaged urban neighbourhoods by focusing on the economic pillar, the physical infrastructure and the social infrastructure, and the national government has heavily invested in doing so for decades now (Van Kempen 2000).

Several authors have concluded that repressive policies aiming at incivilities are primarily concerned with governing troublesome youth, in particular when hanging around in public spaces (Crawford 2008, Bannister and Kearns 2013). Whereas this selective focus is indeed visible in the Netherlands, problems of incivilities and anti-social behaviour in the streets in the Netherlands are first and foremost associated with young male citizens with an immigrant background in distressed and multi-ethnic neighbourhoods. Notwithstanding the Big Cities Policy, this process is comparable to what has been noticed in the United States with respect to inhabitants of disadvantaged neighbourhoods, many of whom have a different ethnic or racial background than the dominant groups in society. In many large cities and in particular in diverse areas, hanging around in public spaces is reason enough for the police to intervene (Collins 2007).

The keen interest in people with a migrant background is directly linked to the social climate in the Netherlands more in general. Over the last two decades, tensions resulting from the persistently weak socioeconomic position of certain (ethnic) groups combined with public concern with the feasibility of the prevailing tolerant approach to immigration rose (Pakes 2004, Engbersen et al. 2007, Van der Leun and Van der Woude 2011). Tensions manifested themselves more intensely in specific urban areas than elsewhere in the Netherlands. Many diverse urban neighbourhoods contain a relatively high share of low-income families, including those with an ethnic minority background. The same neighbourhoods are also plagued by relatively high levels of disorder and crime and feelings of insecurity, and are highly policed. For many Dutch politicians, it has become self-evident that the authorities should not only fight employment, restructure housing stock and actively involve citizens in urban policies, but also act firmly against incivilities and social problems (Pakes 2005, Van Stokkom 2007, Van Swaaningen 2008). Already in 1995, the Social and Cultural Planning Bureau concluded that the mere presence of ethnic minority groups in areas increased feelings of insecurity among the traditional neighbourhood residents and gave them the impression that the neighbourhood was deteriorating (SCP 1995, Uitermark 2003). Tapping into these insecurities, which have been exacerbated over the years by fears of terrorism and cross-border crimes and the mediatised attention to high crime figures for some groups of immigrants, politicians have effectively called for broader powers for law enforcement and for a more repressive stance. We could argue that the expressive characteristics of the anti-incivilities agenda are accompanied by fear of outsiders in that its tools enable the targeting of those marginalised groups who (seemingly) exhibit behaviours that are seen as 'different' (Tonry and Bildsten 2009, Boone and Van Swaaningen 2013).

The present chapter will critically look at these developments from a 'crimmigration' control point of view: to what extent do these broad policing powers and the combat against incivilities lead to the selective de facto criminalisation of marginalised young people with a migrant background when using public space? And how does that impact upon the (perceived) selectivity with regard to people with a migrant background? The underlying aim is to turn the attention to a broader lens than the traditional rather narrow one which is advocated by human rights organisations, which emphasises police discrimination or institutionalised racism and tends to overlook wider societal processes including law making and policy drafting. By way of illustration of the dynamics that these policies can bring about, it will zoom in (a) on ID checks in the streets based on explorative qualitative fieldwork in six neighbourhoods in two large Dutch cities, namely Amsterdam and The Hague, and observation of police–citizens encounters in these same neighbourhoods in The Hague, and (b) on surveillance of irregular migrants. But first, we will depict the legal framework of expanding law enforcement powers.

Powers, legitimisations and selectivity

In addition to far-reaching urban renewal programs with a combination of urban restructuring, social policies, repression and the introduction of restraining orders after the British example (Van der Leun and Koemans 2013), a number of fairly recent legislative changes have evidently broadened the scope for action for law enforcement officials (Van der Woude and Van der Leun 2013). These changes include the introduction of preventive stop and search powers as of 2002. Before, law enforcement officials could carry out searches if there was a reasonable suspicion of a criminal offence (Art. 27 in relation to 55b of the Code of Criminal Procedure). Since 2002, the legal basis for stop and search powers can be found in both the Municipalities Act[3] (Art. 151b) and the Weapons and Ammunitions Act[4] (Art. 50–52). The powers to stop and search are vested in mayors by means of a by-law,[5] which they can decide on after having consulted the municipal council and the public prosecutor. The mayor can designate certain areas as 'security risk zones' in which anyone can be subjected to a 'preventive search' by police officers during a fixed period of twelve hours. Under authority of the public prosecutor, the police can search any individual as well as goods and vehicles without having concrete grounds for suspicion (Van der Woude and Van der Leun 2013).

Within the context of counterterrorism, police officers can also perform preventive searches without a preceding order by the public prosecutor. These searches can take place in permanent security areas that are considered at risk. Over the years, these powers have been expanded. A crucial body of law enabling these preventive searches is the Dutch counterterrorism legislation: in response to the 2004 terrorist attacks in Madrid, the Investigation and Prosecution of Terrorist Offences (Extension of Powers) Act was implemented[6] (see also Van der Woude 2010).

In addition to these wide stop and search powers in designated areas, police officers and other law enforcement officials exercise several broader powers, which relate to concerns about irregular migration and residence. Cases in point, which are relevant for the present chapter, are immigration controls and identification checks, which have both been expanded against the background of concerns about migration. The most recent significant adaptation of the aliens legislation, the Netherlands Aliens Act of 2000,[7] which came into force in 2001, includes several renewed provisions (Sections 50 and 53) for police and immigration authorities to carry out house searches for illegally residing immigrants and also broadened the scope for stopping people in the street to ask for their identity and nationality. Police officers are the ones who are vested with the surveillance of illegal residence in the Netherlands and they can stop people in the streets when there is a reasonable suspicion that such persons are unlawfully residing or in order to prevent illegal residence of persons after they have crossed the border (section 48). Moreover, the police are authorised to enter a dwelling without the consent of the occupant if there is a reasonable suspicion that an alien who is not a lawful resident is staying there (Section 51). In the adjacent area of illegal and undeclared labour, the powers of the Labour Inspectorate have been expanded since 2013 under the Act on Enforcement of Labour and Social Security Law,[8] and a new policy was introduced to focus more specifically on high-risk sectors, which are likely to be sectors with high shares of migrant labour (Renooy 2013). These are all laws, regulations and policy choices that are based on broad powers, which at least open up the possibility that people with a migrant background will run a relatively high risk of being detected when crossing legal boundaries in one way or another.

Equally relevant for the present chapter is the expansion of the Identification Act.[9] Opportunities for identification checks were vastly expanded with the introduction of the 2005 Extended Compulsory Identification Act (WUID), which replaced the more limited act of 1994, based officially on consent (meaning that a person could refuse cooperation). Investigating officers and supervisors were given the power to demand proof of identity from individuals aged 14 or older as part of the performance of their regular duties instead of only under specific instances, as held before. Individuals who do not immediately comply with this demand are guilty of a criminal offence, as they are violating Section 447e of the Dutch Criminal Code[10] and can incur a fine. Whereas in the past, many Dutch citizens strongly opposed identification checks, which were often associated with World War II (Böcker 2002, Pakes 2004), these expansions were accepted without significant protests, presumably as they were seen as crucial in fostering security. Internal rules emphasise that there have to be circumstances that warrant ID checks and that the police should not check identification documents of people whose identity they already know (Van Klink and Zeegers 2008). It is clear that the police are not allowed to check IDs independently of other reasons (Van Kempen 2006). The limit is set by the fact that there has to be a concrete reason to ask for a person's identity; doing so has to be reasonably necessary for enforcing police tasks. Like most expanded powers, the Identification Act was expanded in order to reduce a vague mixture of crime, irregular migration and terrorism (Beck and Broadhurst 1998). As far as it has been evaluated, evidence has shown that compulsory identification was initially applied widely. It was mainly used in the case of regularly occurring minor criminal acts that had to do with public order. Apart from conducting checks in public transport and traffic incidents, papers were, for instance, asked when checking on youths loitering and causing a nuisance in places where such disturbances were common, checking on vagrants, beggars and people who seemed drunk. Contrary to widely expressed fears, no evidence was found of an increase in discrimination after the introduction of the new law (Everwijn, Jongebreur and Lolkema 2009). It should be noted, however, that this latter conclusion was largely based on information from investigating officers, operational staff, supervisory officials and official complaints, which raised some doubts about this conclusion (Eijkman and Schuurman 2011). In 2010, the national government provided more specific criteria for when ID checks were allowed and not.[11]

Several authors have expressed concerns that these rapidly widened powers with respect to legal and policy interventions have transformed the Netherlands into a surveillance society without sufficiently monitoring the consequences and without introducing adequate counterbalances (Den Boer 2007). These concerns deepen with respect to ethnic minority groups (Eijkman and Schuurman 2011). The fear is that when young men with an ethnic background different from the majority population are more likely to be stopped by the police and asked for their identity documents, the already difficult relationship between police and certain ethnic minority groups may worsen (Smith 1997). It is probably not without reason that the debate on selectivity with respect to people with a migrant background started to receive more attention in the Dutch context than in earlier times.

Ever since the late 1990s the political and social discourse on migration has gradually become more excluding and repressive (Pakes 2004, Van der Leun and van der Woude 2011, Van der Woude and Van der Leun 2013). Links among crime, security, migration and integration became more widely seen as social problems than before. Immigrants, and especially irregular migrants and those who cause trouble in cities by being criminally active or causing nuisance, became increasingly targeted (Leerkes, Engbersen and Van der Leun 2012). Dutch legislative reforms in the field of crime and immigration control, as well as the public and political discourse supporting them, fit into a trend often referred to as 'crimmigration' (Stumpf 2006, Van der Woude and Van der Leun 2013): the process whereby criminal law and immigration law become interlinked (Legomsky 2007, Chacón 2012, Sklansky 2012). So far, there have been few reflections on the implications of the expanded laws and enforcement powers in both fields together in practice. Below we will zoom in on the example of ID checks and surveillance of irregular migrants departing from the assumption that both combine elements of crime control and migration control and both will raise the likelihood that people from an ethnic minority background will be stopped by the police when being present in public space, as this may be seen as 'incivility'.

ID checks in urban neighbourhoods

Roughly after 2012, the issue of 'ethnic profiling' by the police suddenly started to attract public and scholarly attention in the Netherlands. Incidents and indications were rapidly translated by NGOs, citizens and scholars into a matter of discrimination, without taking into account broader trends such as selective policy attention in general (Mutsaers 2014, Landman 2015). As part of a broader study into police perceptions and police–citizens relations in urban neighbourhoods, a considerable body of research has attempted to explore the complex relationship between the criminal justice system and ethnic minorities. Views with respect to selectivity vary considerably and there has been little consensus to date between the various studies as conducted in the Netherlands. On the one hand it is clear that members of certain ethnic minority groups, particularly those with a Moroccan and an Antillean background, are disproportionately represented in criminal justice data, which may relate to differences in criminal overrepresentation but also appears to point to biases. On the other hand, studies that directly look into street-level decision making have resulted in diverging outcomes that do not warrant the strong conclusions that are made in public debate. We will not try and solve this debate here, but instead focus on police perceptions and police–citizens relations in urban neighbourhoods with a particular interest in ID checks.

As part of a broader project and with the help of master students in criminology, we conducted 252 street interviews with young adults in the streets of six neighbourhoods in two of the Netherlands' largest cities: Amsterdam (141) and

The Hague (111). We also observed police–citizen interactions during ride-alongs with the police in the same neighbourhoods in The Hague. In the course of this empirical study our attention was drawn towards the issue of ID checks in relation to unwanted behaviour in public spaces, in particular in the accounts of young adults in the streets. Below we will first draw on the street interviews. By going into the streets and spontaneously and informally approaching young people, we aimed at reaching a part of the population that is (*a*) likely to be at risk more than average for being stopped and searched by the police because of their routine activities and (*b*) likely to be underrepresented in general population surveys. In the following section, we specifically focus on the recurrent theme of ID checks, although the study dealt much more broadly with police–citizens relations and was introduced as such to respondents (Van der Leun et al. 2014).

Young people's views

After some opening questions, respondents were asked if they had been approached or stopped by the police in the last 12 months prior to the interview. In Amsterdam, less than half of the respondents (43 per cent, $N = 141$) had been approached and/or stopped, while in The Hague more than half of the respondents (54 per cent, $N = 111$) had been approached and/or stopped by the police. This held more for men than for women, and we found differences across ethnic groups. Respondents with an Antillean, Surinamese or Moroccan background were most frequently stopped. Many people reported to have been stopped more than once in a year. They mentioned being stopped between two and thirty times a year, and some even said twice a week. Many respondents said they had been stopped 'a couple of times', 'quite often', 'too often' or 'too many times to count'. In The Hague, 85 per cent of the respondents who had been stopped said they had been stopped more than once in a year's time.

When asked about the reason for the stops, most people were short or rather vague in their answers: 'Something happened in the neighbourhood and I was stopped for being a suspect'. Others gave more detail on traffic-related incidents (speeding; driving through a red sign; not wearing a seatbelt; not wearing a helmet on a motorcycle; no lights or broken lights on a car, motorcycle or bicycle; and cycling in a pedestrian area) or causing nuisance and creating alcohol- and/or drugs-related incidents in public areas: 'I was stopped for hanging around and smoking weed'. A few others reported general checks for weapons, preventive stop-and-search, checks of vehicles and checks for driving licences.

An aspect that stood out in the interviews was that many respondents spoke strongly about the fact that they were often asked for their IDs. Several respondents said they saw no reason for these checks: 'I had to give my ID, but I did nothing', 'I was standing in the street with friends. They came to ask what we were doing. I had to show my ID'. Although we cannot draw strong conclusions, as we did not witness these cases on a large scale, these stories seemed to indicate that these young adults felt or were heavily policed, or both, and that ID checks played a crucial role in these police checks. In an earlier study in another area of the country, Svensson and Saharso (2015) found similar results for a younger age group. Their survey showed that ethnic minority youths had more often a proactive contact with the police and proactive instruments – including ID checks – used against them. Yet, in a more refined analysis, the significance of ethnic appearance disappeared when various control variables were introduced. This led the authors to conclude that to a considerable extent, outcome inequalities seem to be largely the result of justifiable distinctions, which may be made by the police on other grounds. Yet, they also concluded that this does not eliminate the concern, as young people with an ethnic minority background feel over-targeted and were in practice more often confronted with proactive policing than their counterparts who were native to the country.

Police views

Next to interviewing citizens in the streets, we also conducted observations and interviews with police officers on the beat during ride-alongs, in which the topic of ID checks often came to the fore. Overall, research assistants engaged in ride-alongs during seventeen police shifts (a total of 153 hours of observations) and informally talked to the officers in charge during and after these shifts (cf. Sollund 2005). During the ride-alongs, the research assistants observed actions of thirty-one officers, eight female and twenty-three male. As they were together with the officers for nine hours at a time, they were able to build trust. With approval of the police, the ride-alongs were held in three different neighbourhoods in The Hague, two of which were multi-ethnic. Observations were described during and after the shifts in research memos, which were later analysed. In the present chapter we focus on only the issue of ID checks related to incivilities.

The following interaction, described by one of the research assistants during a ride-along with the police, is an example of a situation that attracts police attention:

> At the moment that we passed a bakery on X Street, a group of youngsters, probably of Moroccan descent, yelled at us ('hey'. . .). The police officer turned the car around and drove by again. She immediately explained that she just wanted to drive by. As soon as we returned, the guys slipped into houses or onto a porch. One guy ran off. We made another round and passed the bakery again, just in time to see the guy running away. After another around, we drove by for a third time to check on the hangout. And after the guys again went inside, we left the area. While driving, one of the officers commented: 'This is just to let them know that we keep an eye on them'. Her colleague added: 'One of the guys ran away just to lure us into going after him. But we are not going to turn this into a cat and mouse game'.

One of the police officers in the situation emphasised that the individuals they checked were OK. They saw them as 'blokes that you can still talk to'. Yet, the officers did feel they had to send a message that they were keeping an eye on them. In the situation above, the officers did this to just 'show authority'. The next step is often asking for identification documents. Police officer: 'We can play with our competencies. To ask for an ID is always a possibility, of course'. In many conversations in our study, police officers described situations in which they express authority – either by asking questions or by asking for IDs – as rather innocent. Police officer: 'Often, it is just a game. Me and a guy, we engage in a fake conversation. Just to let him know I keep an eye on him. Sometimes they throw eggs at us or spit on the ground before us'.

Another officer said: 'I do not know all details by heart. If someone is not able to show an ID, we sometimes take him to the police station. It depends. For example: I have a lot of issues with a young Moroccan guy and I always take him with me. We are never able to catch him and he is always acting in annoying ways. He might be cycling circles around our car, just showing very provoking behaviour. So, in order to antagonise, we will take him along [if he is not able to show his ID – the author]. It is a cat and mouse game.' According to the interviews with police officers, they usually made sure they checked identity papers only when they had a legitimate reason to do so. Circumstances were always taken into account, but then again reasons to engage in an ID check were formulated broadly. Checking papers takes place, for instance, in situations in which young people hang around in places that are designated risk areas or emergency areas and where dispersal powers apply. In these instances, officers are always allowed to ask for documentation. Some respondents in the streets with an ethnic minority background, however, commented that this implied that they were stopped and fined when standing in front of their own house or business, which frustrated them immensely. They saw this as characteristic of the relations in their neighbourhood, which they described as a continuing battle between youngsters and the police. Some of them deliberately go to places where they are not supposed to hang around in order to provoke the police to act. Police officers frequented these places to show their presence and authority. When they indeed take action, they are determined to make clear who is in charge. They therefore prefer to show up with several officers and cars and bring young people to the office without further ado if they do not carry their IDs. They want to make sure they 'win the game'. Whereas many young people feel harassed by the police just for being there, police officers emphasise that they have to uphold norms and prevent disorder. As one police officer said: 'They hang around in the streets, but even if they only talk in these groups of four, they cause disorder. The acoustics of the squares in these neighbourhoods also do not help. For us as police officers it is difficult to explain to the youngsters that they have to leave because of incivilities if they are only talking. Some of them grow more impertinent after every check'.

Most police officers seemed to regard ID checks as a simple procedure without realising what this could mean to those who are checked regularly. Some officers were more critical with respect to the frequent ID checks: 'It is not something we should want, that they are checked so often. We have to make clear their behaviour is wrong, but we should not give them the impression that they are fined for who they are. [. . .] The fines are meant to contribute to self-reflection, but that does not happen, as they do not really understand what they are fined for. And there is no way of explaining this to them, as we cannot even have a normal conversation with them'. Below we will turn to a second example of a policy which is increasingly becoming a mixture of crime and migration policy: the surveillance of irregular migrants.

The surveillance of irregular migrants

In the Netherlands, the police are responsible for the surveillance of irregular migrants. This surveillance used to be a matter of immigration policy and administrative law but has become increasingly intertwined with crime control. Whereas in the 1960s and 1970s migrants could also be 'illegally residing', their presence was not perceived as a particularly worrying or pressing problem. The leniency at the time was closely related to the demand for low-skilled labour in an expanding Dutch economy, which characterised the policy at that time. In the 1980s and 1990s, the discourse on (irregular) immigration became more restrictive, but in reality things changed gradually and incrementally. For instance, it remained fairly easy for irregular immigrants to acquire a tax and social security number with which they could be formally employed in certain economic sectors. After 1991, certain practices continued to be tolerated, but a number of legislative and other measures were taken to combat illegality more effectively. Access to the formal labour market was blocked by imposing sanctions on employers and by establishing a protective ring of documentary requirements around the formal labour market. It became impossible for illegal immigrants to obtain a tax and social insurance number (Van der Leun 2003, Broeders and Engbersen 2007). Subsequently, steps were taken to systematically exclude irregular immigrants from public services (welfare, social security, health care, education and public housing). In 1998, the Benefit Entitlement (Residence Status) Act came into force[12] (Van der Leun 2003). From then on, only immigrants with residence permits could obtain social security and other social rights. The act is also known as the 'Linking Act' because immigration service registration files, census bureau data, tax identification data, and social security and social assistance data can all be cross-checked to verify the validity of a person's immigration and work status.

Linking crime and migration happened only in more recent years, when the Dutch government stated its intentions to put more emphasis on tracing, arresting, detaining and attempting to expel irregular immigrants. A concrete proposal to take the final step and *de jure* criminalise illegal residence was included in two recent coalition agreements. After years of debate, the Dutch government decided in 2012 to make illegal residence in the Netherlands a criminal offence. Foreign national adults who reside illegally would then be guilty of a crime (misdemeanour) when apprehended in the country. They could be sanctioned with a fine of up to 3,800 euros and imprisoned if they failed to pay the fine. In the end this 'crimmigration measure' was rejected.

Remarkably, we know very little about the active surveillance of irregular immigrants in practice. My own work in the mid-1990s showed that police officers were often reluctant to engage in active migration control. They would only intervene in the case of criminal activities. After all, frontline police officers are not only supposed to fight illegal residence, they also have to secure good community relations (Van der Leun and Van der Woude 2011). A more recent empirical work is lacking. In 2011, there was a mediatised case in which bus drivers noticed a number of dark-skinned men and women taking the bus from the Bijlmer neighbourhood to posh areas outside Amsterdam. They suspected illegal practices and contacted the police, who arrested a number of people and praised the bus drivers for helping them in their fight against labour exploitation. Later it turned out that the workers were expelled on the basis of illegal residence and labour, and the issue of labour exploitation was never investigated. The employers were never fined. Much later, the Council of State decided that the police had not been authorised to check the passports of the workers, as there was no 'reasonable cause' to suspect that they were residing illegally.[13] It is difficult to tell whether this case concerns a single incident or whether it illustrates a changing attitude towards detecting irregular migrants. In our recent study on police decision in The Hague we did not have the impression that during regular duties police officers were actively looking for irregular immigrants. We might conclude carefully that there are no indications that the police have become more active in apprehending migrants just for the sake of being in the country illegally. Apprehensions are not particularly high as far as we know (Van der Heijden, Cruyff and Van Gils 2011). Several spokespersons of the police also spoke out against criminalisation of irregular residence and 'razzias' (raids). Yet, at the same time, an independent evaluation in 2004 of the use of immigration control powers under the renewed Aliens Act of 2000 showed that these new powers were increasingly being used (Boekhoorn, Speller and Kruijssen 2004), and in today's highly regulated society with all kinds of regular identity checks, illegal immigrants always run the risk of being detected for one reason or another when they are present in the public space. The only conclusion we can safely draw is that there is little insight into the extent to which irregular immigrants are apprehended by the police merely because they are present in public space.

Conclusions: the expressive impact of criminalising incivilities

Among the powers of the police that were expanded over the years in order to deal with incivilities, crime and migration, the renewed Dutch Aliens Act and the expanded Identification Act and their long-term consequences have received little scholarly and societal attention. Both types of control are examples taken out of a wide context of proactively policing suspect groups and suspect spaces, yet they seem to be telling examples of the consequences of the preventive turn in policing and migration control, and of the intertwining of the two. Both carry the risk of being used selectively against people from an immigrant background. This risk was rather easily dismissed in the political debates that surrounded the law-making process. When the legislation on carrying IDs was changed in 2005, the Ministry of Justice emphasised in the parliamentary debate that the new law did not involve a general obligation to prove one's identity. When the issue of thresholds for checking people's residence status in public spaces was brought up, the mantra that was always used was that there would be 'no razzias'. In both instances, professional ethics was seen as a safeguard against selective implementation. In practice, however, both types of policy seem to contribute to an intensive governing of the behaviour of young men with a migrant background in public spaces (Van Klink and Zeegers 2008), although our explorative analysis seems to suggest that this is fuelled more by worries about immigrant crime than by immigration control rationales. At the same time, we should acknowledge that firm empirical evidence is missing.

Back in 1986, criminologist Fijnaut alluded to potential unintended outcomes of a compulsory ID scheme in the Netherlands by commenting that the groups against whom the police did not have reasonable suspicion and who had a marginal position in society were likely to be those who would become the object of massive police surveillance. He referred to 'foreigners, young people in the squatting movement, and other non-mainstream groups such as itinerant groups and inhabitants of old urban neighbourhoods' (Böcker 2002: 95; Van Klink and Zeegers 2008). Almost three decades later we can conclude that Fijnaut's worries were probably somewhat strongly voiced but not without reason. Whereas police officers often view their practices of asking for IDs as routine and their interactions with groups of young people in the streets as an innocent way of keeping track of what happens and who is doing what, young adults with a migrant background increasingly understand their experiences as unjustified examples of selective police attention and the expression of exclusion and unrestricted state power. This may also intersect with the surveillance of irregular migrants, but there is very little insight into the extent to which this is the case in practice.

In the Dutch debate, selective attention and feelings of being specifically targeted have so far primarily been explained as evidence of ethnic profiling, discrimination or misuse of competencies by the police, but our study suggests that lens is far too narrow. The process of (perceived) selectivity in policing does not develop solely in the streets. The choice of which neighbourhoods or even neighbourhood segments the police shall focus on may have a huge impact on those living and working in these neighbourhoods, and the same holds for the style of policing. And even more generally: the choice of wide discretionary powers and a lack of oversight of how these powers are used are important in fuelling tensions between the police and migrant communities (Mutsaers 2014). The fact that anti-police riots erupted in the summer of 2015 in a multi-ethnic neighbourhood in The Hague shows that trust between migrant communities and the police is unstable and volatile. In October 2015, the mayor of The Hague, Van Aartsen, announced an encompassing Diversity Action Plan as developed by the police.[14] Among many other measures, this included restraint on the side of the police with respect to checking identification documents and more emphasis on explaining why people are subjected to controls if they are, thereby acknowledging the external effects of these checks. This sounds like a good start, but it is crucial that the unintended consequences of official policies are more openly discussed in Dutch society and that we gain better insight into the impact of wide police powers on people with a migrant background. It is equally important to look beyond perceptions and street-level decision making and to take higher-level policy choices – including the choice to focus on incivilities – more thoroughly into account. After all, police–citizen relations are not shaped only in the streets.

Notes

1 Parliamentary Papers, II 2007/2008, 28684, No. 130.
2 Wet Maatregelen Bestrijding Voetbalvandalisme en Ernstige overlast, published at overheid.nl.
3 Gemeentewet, published at overheid.nl.
4 Wet Wapens en Munitie, published at overheid.nl.
5 Municipal by-law documents local rules that apply to everyone within the municipality.
6 Wet Ter Verruiming van de Mogelijkheden tot Opsporing en Vervolging van Terroristische Misdrijven, published at overheid.nl.
7 Vreemdelingenwet 2000, published at overheid.nl.
8 Wet Aanscherping Handhaving en Sanctiebeleid, published at overheid.nl.
9 Wet Uitbreiding Identificatieplicht, published at overheid.nl.
10 Wetboek van Strafrecht.
11 Aanwijzing Uitbreiding Identificatieplicht 2013, published at overheid.nl.
12 Koppelingswet, officially: Wijzigingswet Vreemdelingenwet en enige andere wetten (koppeling aanspraak van vreemdelingen [. . .] en vergunningen aan het rechtmatig verblijf van de vreemdeling in Nederland), published at overheid.nl.
13 http://deeplink.rechtspraak.nl/uitspraak?id=ECLI:NL:RVS:2011:BR2059
14 *de Volkskrant* [National Newspaper] 8 October 2015.

References

Bannister, J. and Kearns, A. (2013) 'Overcoming intolerance to young people's conduct: Implications from the unintended consequences of policy in the UK', *Criminology and Criminal Justice*, 13(4): 380–397.

Beck, A. and Broadhurst, K. (1998) 'Policing the community: The impact of national identity cards in the European Union', *Journal of Ethnic and Migration Studies*, 24(3): 413–431.

Böcker, A. (2002) *Identificatieplicht: Oplossing of oorzaak van problemen?*, Nijmegen: GNI.

Boekhoorn, P., Speller, T. and Kruijssen, F. (2004) *Evaluatie Vreemdelingenwet 2000, Operationeel vreemdelingentoezicht door de politie*. Den Haag: WODC.

Boone, M. and Van Swaaningen, R. (2013) 'Regression to the mean: Punishment in the Netherlands', in V. Ruggierro and M. Ryan (eds.) *Punishment in Europe: A Critical Anatomy of Penal Systems*, London: Palgrave Macmillan.

Broeders, D. and Engbersen, G. (2007) 'The fight against illegal migration: Identification policies and immigrants' counter strategies', *American Behavioral Scientist*, 50(12): 1592–1609.

Buruma, Y. (2007) 'Dutch tolerance: On drugs, prostitution, and euthanasia', in M. Tonry and C. Bijleveld (eds.) *Crime and Justice in the Netherlands* (Crime and Justice Series, Vol. 35), Chicago: University of Chicago Press.

Chacón, J. M. (2012) 'Overcriminalizing immigration', *Journal of Criminal Law and Criminology*, 102(3): 613–652.

Collins, R. (2007) 'Strolling while poor: How broken-windows policing created a new crime in Baltimore', *Georgetown Journal on Poverty Law and Policy*, 14: 419–439.

Crawford, A. (2008) 'Dispersal powers and the symbolic role of anti-social behaviour legislation', *Modern Law Review*, 71(5): 753–784.

Daems, T. (2009) *De bestraffingssociologie van David. W. Garland*, Den Haag: Boom Juridische Uitgevers.

Dekkers, T.J.M. and Van der Woude, M.A.H. (2014) 'Staring at the felony forest: de complexiteit van risicoprofilering nader in kaart gebracht', *Proces, tijdschrift voor strafrechtspleging*, 93(1): 52–70.

De Leeuw, T. and Van Swaaningen, R. (2011) 'Veiligheid in veelvoud: Beeld, beleid en realiteit in Rotterdams Oude Westen', *Tijdschrift voor Veiligheid*, 10(1): 26–42.

Den Boer, M. (2007) 'Wake-up call for the Lowlands: Dutch counterterrorism from a comparative perspective', *Cambridge Review of International Affairs*, 20(2): 285–302.

Downes, D. and Van Swaaningen, R. (2007) 'The road to dystopia? Changes in the penal climate in the Netherlands', in M. Tonry and C. Bijleveld (eds.) *Crime and Justice in the Netherlands* (Crime and Justice Series, Vol. 35), Chicago: University of Chicago Press.

Eijkman, Q. and Schuurman, B. (2011) *Preventive Counter-Terrorism and Non-Discrimination in the European Union: A Call for Systematic Evaluation*, The Hague: International Centre for Counter-Terrorism.

Engbersen, G., Van der Leun, J. P. and De Boom, J. (2007) 'The fragmentation of migration and crime in the Netherlands', in M. Tonry and C. Bijleveld (eds.) *Crime and Justice in the Netherlands* (Crime and Justice Series, Vol. 35), Chicago: University of Chicago Press.

European Commission (2000) *The prevention of crime in the European Union – reflections on common guidelines and proposals for community financial support [COM/2000/0786 final]*. Brussels: European Commission.

Everwijn, H., Jongebreur, W. and Lolkema, P. (2009) *Het functioneren van de WUID in de Praktijk: Evaluatie van de Wet op de uitgebreide identificatieplicht*, The Hague: WODC.

Feeley, M. and Simon, J. (1992) 'The new penology: Notes on the emerging strategy of corrections and its implications', *Criminology*, 30(4): 449–474.

Garland, D. (2001) *The Culture of Control: Crime and Social Order in Contemporary Society*, Oxford: Oxford University Press.

Hunter, A. (1978) 'Symbols of incivility', paper presented at the annual meeting of the American Society of Criminology, Dallas, Texas.

Koemans, M. L. (2010) 'The war on "street terror": Why tackle anti-social behaviour?', *Crime, Law and Social Change*, 53(5): 477–491.

LaGrange, R. L., Ferraro, K. F. and Supancic, M. (1992) 'Perceived risk and fear of crime: Role of social and physical incivilities, *Journal of Research in Crime and Delinquency*, 29(3): 311–334.

Landman, W. (2015) *Blauwe patronen. Betekenisgeving in Politiewerk*, Den Haag: Boom Lemma.

Leerkes, A. S., Engbersen, G. and Van der Leun, J. P. (2012) 'Crime among irregular immigrants and the influence of internal border control', *Crime, Law and Social Change*, 58(1): 15–38.

Legomsky, S. H. (2007) 'The new path of immigration law: Asymmetric incorporation of criminal justice norms', *Washington and Lee Law Review*, 64(2): 469–528.

Mutsaers, P. (2014) 'An ethnographic study of the policing of internal borders in the Netherlands: Synergies between criminology and anthropology', *British Journal of Criminology*, 54(5): 831–848.

Pakes, F. (2004) 'The politics of discontent', *Howard Journal of Criminal Justice*, 43: 284–298.

Pakes, F. (2005) 'De Britse aanpak van antisociaal gedrag', *Tijdschrift voor Criminologie*, 47(3): 284–289.

Renooy, P. (2013) *Labour Inspection Strategies for Detecting Undeclared Work in Europe: The Netherlands*, Amsterdam: Regioplan.

Peršak, N. (2014) 'Norms, harms and disorder at the border: The legitimacy of criminal law intervention through the lens of criminalisation theory', in N. Peršak (ed.) *Legitimacy and Trust in Criminal Law, Policy and Justice: Norms, Procedures, Outcomes*, Farnham, Burlington: Ashgate.

SCP [Sociaal en Cultureel Planbureau] (1995) *Rapportage minderheden: concentratie en segregatiex*, The Hague: The Netherlands Institute for Social Research.

Sollund, R. (2005) 'Obstacles and possibilities in police research', *Outlines*, 7(2): 43–62.

Sklansky, D. A. (2012) 'Crime, immigration and ad hoc instrumentalism', *New Criminal Law Review*, 15: 157–223.

Smith, D. J. (1997) 'Ethnic origins, crime and criminal justice in England and Wales', in M. Tonry (ed.) *Ethnicity, Crime and Immigration: Comparative and Cross-National Perspectives* (Crime and Justice Series, Vol. 21), Chicago: University of Chicago Press.

Stumpf, J. P. (2006) 'The crimmigration crisis: Immigrants, crime, and sovereign power', *American University Law Review*, 56: 367–419.

Svensson, J. and Saharso, S. (2015) 'Proactive policing and equal treatment of ethnic-minority youths', *Policing and Society: An International Journal of Research and Policy*, 25(4): 393–408. doi: 10.1080/10439463.2013.875015.

Tonry, M. and Bildsten, H. (2009), 'Antisocial behaviour', in M. Tonry (ed.) *Crime and Public Policy*, Oxford: Oxford University Press.

Uitermark, J. (2003) '"Social mixing" and the management of disadvantaged neighbourhoods: The Dutch policy of urban restructuring revisited', *Urban Studies*, 40(3): 531–549.

Van der Heijden, P.G.M., Cruyff, M. and Van Gils, G.H.C. (2011) *Schatting illegaal verblijvende vreemdelingen in Nederland*, Den Haag: WODC.

Van der Leun, J. P. (2003) *Looking for Loopholes. Processes of Incorporation of Illegal Immigrants in the Netherlands*, Amsterdam: Amsterdam University Press.

Van der Leun, J. P. and Koemans, M. L. (2013) 'Down these mean streets: An analysis of the local public discourse on antisocial behaviour in disadvantaged urban neighbourhoods in the Netherlands', *Urban Studies*, 50(16): 3342–3359.

Van der Leun, J. P. and Van der Woude, M. A. H (2011) 'Ethnic profiling in the Netherlands? A reflection on expanding preventive powers, ethnic profiling and a changing social and political context', *Policing and Society*, 21(4): 444–455.

Van der Leun, J. P., Van der Woude, M.A.H., Vijverberg, R. D., Vrijhoef, R.P.M. and Leupen, A. J. (2014) *Etnisch Profileren in Den Haag? Een verkennend onderzoek naar beslissingen en opvattingen op straat. Veiligheid en Samenleving*, Den Haag: Boom Lemma.

Van der Woude, M.A.H. (2010) *Wetgeving in een Veiligheidscultuur. Totstandkoming van antiterrorismewetgeving bezien van maatschappelijke en (rechts)politieke context*, Den Haag: Boom Juridische Uitgevers.

Van der Woude, M.A.H. and Van der Leun, J. P. (2013) 'De Nederlandse veiligheidscultuur als katalysator voor etnisch profileren?', *Tijdschrift over Cultuur en Criminaliteit*, 3(2): 123–136.

Van Klink, B. and Zeegers, N. (2008) 'De identificatieplicht als middel tot de-anonimisering en disciplinering', *Recht der Werkelijkheid*, 29(2): 35–55.

Van Kempen, P. H. (2006) 'De Wet op de uitgebreide identificatieplicht in het strafrecht', in B. van Klink en N. Zeegers (eds.) *Hoe maakbaar is veiligheid? Over de Wet op de uitgebreide identificatieplicht*, Breda: Uitgeverij Papieren Tijger.

Van Kempen, R. (2000) Big cities policy in the Netherlands, *Tijdschrift voor Economische en Sociale Geografie*, 91(2): 197–203.

Van Stokkom, B. (2007) 'Regulering van antisociaal gedrag', *Tijdschrift voor Veiligheid*, 6(3): 36–50.

Van Swaaningen, R. (2008) 'Sweeping the street: Civil society and community safety in Rotterdam', in J. Shapland (ed.) *Justice, Community and Civil Society: A Contested Terrain Across Europe*, Cullompton: Willan.

Van Swaaningen, R. (2005) 'Public safety and the management of fear', *Theoretical Criminology*, 9(3): 289–305.

Part III

Concluding thoughts

10 Dimensions, concerns and effects of addressing uncivil behaviour through punitive law

Nina Peršak

This book has addressed the pertinent issues surrounding the current (penal) regulation and social control of incivilities (disorder, nuisance, public order offences, quality of life crimes), their trends, criminological explanations, representations, political, spatial and cultural dimensions, as well as the underlying behaviour such regulation targets. Although some such offences may be harmful and legitimately proscribed (those have mostly already been criminalised in some way or another), some others represent only trivial and fleeting annoyance (a subjective feeling) to others or a simple violation of a rule, without causing any harm or objective setback to one's interests. Preceding chapters have shown the several regulation types and measures that various European countries – so far largely underexamined or underrepresented in the English-language literature – employ to manage incivilities.

Furthermore, the spreading of punitive regulatory measures targeting incivilities across Europe raises important issues regarding the legitimacy, effectiveness and impact of such formal social control. These issues have also come to the fore in the book – albeit to varying degrees across chapters – and raised important concerns, which will be further discussed in the second part of this chapter.

As there is no common vocabulary, no uniform term or common meaning of incivilities (Blasko, Gouvis Roman and Taylor 2015), nor one common term for the low-level criminal law with many administrative-law elements, which is often used to tackle incivilities, we have let each contributor choose his or her own term or English translation that, according to them, the most corresponds to the original version (in their own language) or is the most used in their own legal doctrine.

Different cultures and EU states have their own ways of dealing with such issues. Although a worrying trend of repressive use of either existing or new tools against incivilities has been recognised, and to some extent the general theories and explanations for it (see, for example, Chapter 2) can be used, the local specifics and the moulding of general explanations to fit into the local environment (be it national, regional or municipal) allow no single grand narrative to be used to encapsulate some sort of 'European way' of dealing with incivilities. Despite the missing grand narrative or the fact that no one theory could subsume the developments in all these countries under one roof, there are some commonalities that cut across different dimensions of the phenomenon.

The incivility prism and its various dimensions

Looking at the regulation of incivilities, one necessarily starts by focusing on the legal or social control aspects of it. The societal dimensions that came to the fore in many chapters in this book, however, revealed many other faces of the 'incivility prism', dimensions linked to space, politics, morality, visibility, physicality and culture.

Social, physical and cultural dimensions

Some claim we should distinguish between the social and the physical aspect of incivilities or between the social and the physical or environmental incivilities. Some even use different terms for it. While recognising that in the UK 'incivilities' and 'disorder' are often used interchangeably, generally 'incivilities' is a term that is used to refer to both physical and social phenomena, while 'disorder' tends to refer mostly to social phenomena (Matthews 1992). 'Incivilities' could therefore be a broader term than 'disorder'. Some others, however, distinguish between physical disorder (graffiti, broken windows, litter, etc.) and social disorder, linking 'incivilities' to the 'visible evidence of disorder' (Sampson and Raudenbush 1999: 604, citing Hunter). On this view, 'incivilities' are then a narrower term compared with 'disorder'.

Despite the trend of merging both categories, the distinction between social incivilities and environmental or physical incivilities may be useful to keep when it allows one to tackle a certain type of socially undesirable phenomena in a more focused and effective way. Those who take out rubbish on the wrong day (that is, on the day not designated for picking up that sort of rubbish) may not be rude in general. Tackling social incivilities may require different (socialising) techniques than tackling physical disorder. One (probably the latter) might be more amenable to change through fines than the other.

Although 'physical incivilities' are more environmental, space matters to all types of petty offences committed in the neighbourhood, as highlighted already by the Chicago School and its theory of social disorganisation. Shaw and McKay (1942) have demonstrated that social disorganisation, particularly widespread in urban areas, correlates with crime and delinquency. Modern cities, characterised by gentrification of city centres, tackle various (potentially nuisance) conduct accompanying the night-time economy by designating specific locations where certain activities (e.g. sex work, gambling, entertainment) may take place (Hayward 2004). The 'geography of anti-social behaviour' (Atkinson 2006) therefore matters. Physical characteristics of certain areas can stimulate or hamper the occurrence of crime as well as influence its law enforcement (see Chapter 7). The same act committed in one part of the city may be classified as incivility, while being acceptable behaviour in another part of the city. Certain behaviour of the homeless, namely using public places for living purposes, is, for example, prohibited in the 'protected zones' of Budapest, while in others it is not an offence (see Chapter 5). Police officers may tolerate certain nuisances (e.g. drinking-related noise) on their own but react and enforce the nuisance law when they receive a complaint by local residents about the same behaviour. Moreover, cultural differences play a role in how incivilities are perceived (or even whether some behaviour is perceived as an incivility) and how they are enforced (Chapter 7).

The problem of (physical) incivilities seems to be connected a lot to the visibility of 'dirt'. Even though 'dirt' with respect to incivilities is largely in the eye of the beholder or, as Bauman (1997) observes, not an intrinsic characteristic of things but rather their location in the order of things, their out-of-placeness, it is their visibility that bothers the most. Several chapters in this book refer to the visibility elements of incivilities, such as aesthetics of the 'offenders' (Chapter 7), urban attractiveness (Chapter 5) and visibility of the homelessness that led to the 'purification' of city centres (Chapter 6). The visibility offends the eye, shocks and exposes us to the uncivil element. Why the mere visibility should be problematic could perhaps be explained through the notion of 'visible exposure'. Although we can clearly be exposed to X even if we do not 'see' it, we fear the invisible less, as if it is therefore less real. Particulate matter that causes particle pollution is, for example, a source of many serious respiratory diseases and over 5 million deaths each year (Amos 2016), yet never amounts to the sort of security or moral panic or indignation that, for example, rubbish or beggars on the streets or a person occupying two seats or talking loudly on the train seem to.

When it comes to germs, scientists claim that early exposure to them in childhood, rather than obsessive avoidance, has lasting benefits in terms of building our immune systems (Thompson 2012). Perhaps a similar approach should be taken with respect to more 'social' issues that deviate from the norm of purity. Even if the cities are a bit dirty, exposure to some dirt (be it litter, dirty clothes or other people and their germs) can be good. The more we are exposed to the difference, be they homeless, hygienically challenged or simply culturally different types of people with their own habits, the more used to them, the more tolerant and accepting we become. Those who travel and live in different countries learn this lesson rather soon. A bit of traveling also 'encourages efforts to avoid parochialism and ethnocentrism' (Tonry 2015: 508).

People often make a link between dirtiness and immorality (or cleanliness and morality), connecting physical disorder to moral disorder or depravity, but is there any link between the two? Some such link may exist, although not in the sense one might imagine. The 2008 psychological study suggested that judgements of moral purity were linked to concepts of physical cleanliness. After having the cognitive concept of cleanliness activated or after physically cleansing themselves after experiencing disgust (i.e. washing hands), participants' moral judgements were less severe. In other words, participants who were exposed to a cleanliness manipulation found certain moral actions to be less wrong than did participants who had not been so exposed (Schnall, Benton and Harvey 2008). However, when the study was recently duplicated, the effect was found to be substantially smaller than in the original study (Carey and Roston 2015).

Legal, political and moral dimensions

Regulation targeting incivilities leads in some cases effectively to the 'criminalisation of status'. Looking at the Hungarian approaches to the homeless (see Chapter 5), for example, it is difficult to conclude otherwise, even if, on the face of it, the criminal-law prohibition expressly targets certain conduct. If all or most of the usual activities of the homeless are prohibited, this *de facto* prohibits being homeless. Homelessness is thus driven away from certain zones and sanctioned by community work or fines and even imprisonment if fines cannot be paid.

Another interesting legal dimension of incivilities regulation is its porousness. Incivilities easily cross between different types of laws. There are already criminalised and non-criminal incivilities. For the already criminalised, further legal questions as to the double penalisation, the justification for such a regime, legal certainty, as well as questions about the discretion of prosecution, e.g. who makes the decision, and why, on whether to prosecute X as a crime or as an administrative offence, come to the fore. However, there is a lot of confusion and overlap between anti-social behaviour and crime in, for example, media representations of the phenomenon (Chapter 8). A 'shifting' dividing line between incivilities and crime partly arises out of the vague and confusing legal categorisation of the two types of deviance or undesirable social behaviour. As Burney (2005: 8) noted, 'most behaviour which has given rise to ASBOs could in law have been prosecuted as an offence'. Moreover, the overlap is possible also due to the fact that anti-social behaviour often accompanies crime and because 'in reality the two cannot be separated, as they present a spectrum of deviance' (Burney 2005: 60). This makes gauging incivilities as a separate set of phenomena rather difficult.

This fluidity of incivilities, however, enables social control to be widely dispersed – horizontally as well as vertically. Some incivilities are criminalised in the criminal law proper, some in the law on violations (low-level penal law), some in the administrative law. Sometimes they are proscribed by the national legislator, other times or some others (or even the same ones) by local authorities. As can be observed, the anti-nuisance tool is clearly an important weapon in the arsenal of local authorities. For many mayors, local ordinances and other anti-incivilities measures became a way – to paraphrase Simon (2007) – of 'governing through disorder'. The spill-over regime and the proliferation of offences makes it, however, almost impossible for the individual to keep track of all that is now prohibited.

Another political and legal dimension is the policy transfer that happens not only on the level of political rhetoric (or politicians) but also law transplantations arising from work of various government officials and desk officers, often in search of best practices or persuasive argumentation. Although big narratives, such as culture of control, have not been proved as being applicable across all countries (Devroe 2012, Tonry 2015; observed also in this volume), nor is the culture or fear and penal populism present to the same extent in all of the countries studied, contributors have recognised that there is a mutual learning and importation of models taking place: officers travel to another country to learn police techniques of control, lawyers when drafting statutes look at the comparable laws and articulation of offences in other countries. In some cases, the transportation of control is even stronger: the Western logic of the 'culture of control' is said to better explain current Spanish controlling techniques than historical particularities of Spain (see Chapter 4).

Despite the seemingly neutral security rhetoric that drives the social control of incivilities, there is also a moral dimension to it. Examining the politics of anti-social behaviour, Waiton (2008) has argued that morality has been replaced by the amoral concept of security. This is an interesting claim and it is true that 'security' sounds rather neutral. However, through its employment, has it not become an emotive word? Has the security discourse not, in the meantime, become a moral concept? These days – be it on the children's playground or at the workplace – it seems that not arguing for more security makes you suspect, makes you pro danger, makes you in the eyes of pro-security others immoral. Particularly when children or some other widely recognised vulnerable group is concerned, one is quickly shamed if one raises doubts about the new security measures or the speed with which they are to be put in place. Conversely, one is rewarded if one contributes to the indignation, fear-mongering and moral panic about some 'breach of security', no matter how minor. The security discourse silences opposing voices. The morality of security has in fact been so successful in achieving its goals and silencing opposing voices that it is now readily employed also by the more old-fashioned moralist groups.

Because of the moralising tendency present also in the social control of incivilities, it may be useful – as a best practice – to look at the distinction Belgium makes as regards public order (see Chapter 6), namely the distinction between 'moral public order' and 'material public order'. While, for example, the Belgian Council of State has no trouble upholding measures taken by authorities to protect the latter, the former (used, for example, to close establishments that upset some people or disturb their emotions without the external element of harm to the public order) is in itself not considered a legitimate foundation for punitive regulation or restrictive measures, such as the Belgian regulation of incivilities through the system of administrative sanctions.

Concerns and effects

Examining the measures employed against anti-social people, i.e. fines, imprisonment, banishment from certain areas, it is not difficult to see the punitive and exclusionary character of such social control. A good citizen is a moving citizen; moreover, he or she is a buying moving citizen, a mobile consumer. Those who fail to act in this manner are unwelcome in many city spaces. One can enjoy public space only *en passant*; those who linger better be buying something, lest they be charged with 'loitering' or 'hanging about'.

Criminalisation is, of course, a smoke screen, meant to disguise the state's identity fears. As many notice, only weak(er) states rely on punitiveness and law-and-order policy (Durkheim 1973, Garland 1996, Sparks 2000, Nietzsche 2006).

The stronger the state, the lesser the need for social control and preservation of 'order'. The display of punitiveness is a sign of weakness, 'an attempt to recover the state's eroded powers of sovereign command' (Sparks 2000: 135).

The main concerns flagged by our authors were related to issues of legitimacy or justifiability of measures used to tackle incivilities, effectiveness of such laws and measures and the negative impact they have on society.

Concerning the *legitimacy* of anti-incivilities laws and measures: first of all, it has to be recognised that non-involvement of the state in tackling anti-social behaviour may be problematic as well. Law, and criminal law in particular, carries with it a certain symbolic, expressive character (see Chapters 2 and 9). Van der Leun in Chapter 9 mentions the expressive character of the anti-incivilities agenda pursued in the Netherlands. Not doing anything about uncivil petty offences can jeopardise the legitimacy of criminal justice, as we have seen in the case of Belgium, where nuisance legislation (GAS) has garnered support on the basis of people's indignation against the impunity that petty offenders received when their offences remained unprocessed. Some criminalisation of incivilities in the broad sense (e.g. via administrative or low-level criminal law) also resulted in decriminalisation, i.e. removing of certain acts from the Criminal Code, thereby resulting in their not being classified as criminal offences in the strict sense (see Chapters 4, 5 and 6).

However, this does not mean that any law, measure or procedure adopted against undesirable behaviour is therefore *a contrario* legitimate. The issues that had many contributors concerned included the impact on human rights (e.g. positive right to housing – see Chapter 5), relaxed procedural guarantees (see, for example, Chapter 4), weakened traditional criminal-law principles, such as the principle of legality (vague definitions), the principle of last resort (always the first victim of the widening of the net of social control) and the harm principle (as many such criminalisations do not contain wrongfully harmful conduct).

Effectiveness of such measures depends on what the goal is – if it is to displace a certain group, e.g. homeless, somewhere else or remove them from the visible urban spaces, then some such measures are clearly, unfortunately effective (albeit not legitimate). If it is to raise the number of arrests, which are often used as an indicator of the effectiveness of the police (see Chapter 5), then likewise it is 'effective'. Administrative sanctions in Spain have proved themselves to be 'an effective dissuasive tactic against social mobilisation' (Maroto Calatayud in Chapter 4). However, the legislation may not be effective if it is counterproductive. Repression of protests can, for example, raise new resistance, lead to further protests or represent a new 'mobilising opportunity' (Chapter 4). Podoletz (in Chapter 5) shows how criminalisation of homelessness can be counterproductive by actually increasing people's fear of crime when they encounter such, now criminalised, behaviour, as criminalisation 'carries the message that an act poses a danger to society'. Although effectiveness is the mantra of many governments and politicians, who fear being perceived as ineffective (Chapter 5), it is often the case that the effectiveness of the measures they adopt is not even evaluated. Usually, post-adoption of a law, the issue is rarely raised and even more rarely tested (for one such rare enterprise, see Chapter 3).

(Additional) *negative impact* or detrimental societal effects include the discriminatory impact the legislation and its execution or implementation and enforcement have on certain groups of people, such as the young, immigrants, homeless – who seem to be the prototypical 'rude, bad and ugly' of incivilities legislation. The shift of the criminalising gaze from the 'conduct' of adults to the 'behaviour' of children (Pickard 2014), and increasingly younger children (see, for example, Chapter 6), is a tell-tale sign of the changes in our society. If the behaviour of children can be linked to the weakening of the societal fabric, this, as Waiton (2008: 7) put it, 'perhaps tells us more about the fragile nature of that society than about the behaviour of children itself'. Homeless or, more generally, the poor have always been targeted, particularly when they are visible. They are perceived as unsightly (and thereby having the potential to upset tourists, shoppers and post-gentrification residents as well as affect the general attractiveness of the city) and they do not participate in mass consumption (which may be the biggest 'sin' in consumerist societies). In some countries, police seem to disproportionately or selectively target certain ethnic groups. When police methods, such as ID checks, are applied in a way that targets (or is perceived as targeting) a certain group not otherwise engaged in any wrongdoing (i.e. for 'prevention' reasons) – for example, certain groups of immigrants and their offspring – this also contributes to the mistrust and resentment on the part of the latter. In turn, such police selectivity has negative repercussions for police legitimacy (Chapter 9).

Coming down hard on those who temporarily upset the order of things to make a statement has also a 'chilling effect' on citizen engagement and their legitimate exercise of rights (see Chapter 4). Democracies in particular should be capable and willing to integrate dissent and a certain amount of civil disobedience. Furthermore, in view of the dispersed nature of the social control measures against incivilities, there is a danger of a slippery slope, i.e. of the measures being progressively used as a tool against refugees, which is of particular relevance in today's time with over one million refugees from Syria and immigrants from other countries (BBC 2016) entering (rather unprepared) Europe and Europe's currently (in January 2016) rather unsuccessful way of dealing with the situation uniformly and keeping populist sentiment at bay.

Some ways ahead

Many chapters in this book are descriptive as well as normative, aiming to help the law maker and policymaker by pointing out the Scylla and Charybdis and suggesting possible solutions. This 'normative' element is an added value, as without contemplation of 'what can be done' and 'what should be done', one is left with nothing but a description of the problem, no matter how precise and articulated the latter might be. However, it is often the case that people easily agree on what the problem is but find it much more difficult to find or agree on solutions. Yet, despite being a difficult task, it is one worth pursuing. So, what may be some ways ahead in terms of regulation and thinking about (the regulation of) incivilities?

In addition to those fleshed out in the preceding individual chapters, mostly focused on the problems of (and explicitly or implicitly suggested solutions to the problems of) the regulation against incivilities, we shall here mention also a few ideas regarding the problem of incivilities as such. Even though many chapters have mostly focused on the critical, problematic points of the social control of nuisance, expressing concerns about the social development in this area and about increasing societal intolerance, this does not mean they have not acknowledged that incivilities are a social issue in their own right. They may even be a social problem, just not necessarily one that should be tackled by punitive law.

The first thing anyone notices is that incivilities come in different shapes and sizes and as the term covers a wide variety of conduct, they naturally require different solutions. While protests and certain social disorder caused by exercising one's rights or civil disobedience should to a large extent be tolerated, otherwise they can render certain human rights void (see the European Court of Human Rights case *Ashughyan v. Armenia* [2008] concerning the right to freedom of peaceful assembly [Art. 11]), some other uncivil behaviour may be better tackled through different channels. While criminalisation could be justified for harmful incivilities, it ought in principle stay away from the harmless ones. A bottom-up approach to civilising people – as opposed to the top-down criminalisation – would be through strengthening social solidarity and allowing informal social control to do its work. This approach ought to be primarily resorted to when tackling harmless incivilities. It may also turn out to be the most effective. A while ago, two videos went 'viral', meaning they were looked at and shared by a large number of people across the world in a relatively short time span. One was made in Brazil and featured a car wrongly parked in the space for the handicapped. When the young owner or driver returned, he found his car completely covered with blue-and-white Post-it notes arranged into a handicapped access sign, similar to that in the space in which he parked. He was angry and rather unsuccessful at removing them, and tried quickly to drive away while passersby stopped to laugh at him, take pictures and make videos – a successful, albeit harmless, shaming that seemed to have been successful in getting the message across to the 'offender' as well as educating thousands of people who watched this video. The other viral video was posted on Facebook in September 2015 featuring a young Scotsman playing bagpipes, thereby drowning some rude person shouting homophobic statements – a peaceful, musical response against hatred, which many passersby visibly enjoyed and approved of (as well as all those sharing or 'liking' the video on social media). An informal, yet extremely powerful 'civilising' message to an uncivil individual is also a message to us all, teaching us how to best respond to many such rude, offensive people. It does require us, however, to speak up, to intervene, to tut-tut, to say something, to share positive responses and ideas. In this day and age of fear, such acts (of social solidarity) take courage, but the price of doing nothing or using the wrong tool (criminalisation) is in the long run too high to pay. Using informal social control is important not only because it is a finer tool to achieve a goal (if the goal is to re-socialise or change one's undesirable behaviour on a more permanent basis), it also helps communities and the individual to regain the power. In fact, there is an interesting paradox here. The decline of informal social control tends to cause an increase (or the demand for an increase) of formal social control; however, this at the same time negatively affects the effectiveness of informal control, as more formal control tends to 'further erode informal social control mechanisms' (Van den Broeck 2012: 320). Not letting go of the reins entirely is therefore the only way to maintain the capacity of a community to counter incivilities itself (through informal social control) and not go down the slippery slope of heavy top-down policing from outside.

Next, using the knowledge of other disciplines, such as social psychology, can help us examine what exactly offends us, how and why we (or some of us) react negatively to certain behaviours and under which conditions (for example, research on the contribution of 'urbanophilia', referred to in Chapter 1, and on the contribution of residents' individual characteristics and neighbourhood social structure to subjective perceptions of disorder [Franzini et al. 2008]). Urban planning, geography and architecture should not be usurped for the services of stricter social control, but rather used to explore alternative, more humane, ways of strengthening communities in the city and in finding more benevolent, yet effective, ways of 'civilising' its residents (for example, the city of Hamburg's use of hydrophobic paint, mentioned in Chapter 2, endnote 3). Civil initiatives (citizens 'pushing back') could be employed for engaging residents in saying no to antisocial initiatives driven only by financial considerations (for example, initiatives that upon the entrance of certain groups of people [e.g. refugees] confiscate their money and belongings).

Civic education (of all residents) should include tolerance-building exercises. Uncivil behaviour, especially that which gets more media coverage or upsets a larger community, should also be reprimanded verbally in the political, non-governmental, public arena through the means that a democracy should primarily resort to – prior to any criminal-law intervention. Such a public response should remind everybody that 'values of the democratic society' include 'pluralism, tolerance and broadmindedness'. This statement, uttered by the European Court of Human Rights in the landmark case of *Handyside v. UK*, clearly flies in the face of the xenophobic and even racist sentiment spreading through Europe in the wake of the current refugee crisis.

In terms of future research, more comparative work is to be encouraged. Shedding light on the possible relevant practices in different systems or representing them as accurately as possible, explaining differences or similarities between various systems and trying to improve the practice in one system through lessons taken from another system, which are the three main aims of comparative research according to Nelken (2015: 519), gives us not only knowledge but also tools to tackle any domestic issue that may have been successfully resolved in a similar system elsewhere. Further, research on people (what they really think about certain incivilities, what they are bothered by and how much), on media (particularly new, social media – a still rather untapped territory) and its role, on actual practices (e.g. differences in the police enforcement of regulations on social incivilities) and on practical considerations and problems as they arise in day-to-day situations when implementing or executing anti-incivilities laws, would also be desirable. After all, the social control of incivilities may not happen *only* on the streets, but it *also* happens on the streets.

References

Amos, J. (2016) 'Polluted air causes 5.5 million deaths a year new research says', *BBC News*, 13 February 2016. Online. Available at: www.bbc.com/news/science-environment-35568249 (accessed 13 February 2016).

Atkinson, R. (2006) 'Spaces of discipline and control: The compounded citizenship of social renting', in J. Flint (ed.) *Housing, Urban Governance and Anti-Social Behaviour*, Bristol: The Policy Press.

Bauman, Z. (1997) *Postmodernity and Its Discontents*, Cambridge, Malden: Polity Press.

BBC (2016) 'Migrant crisis: Migration to Europe explained in graphics', *BBC News*, 28 January 2016. Online. Available at: www.bbc.com/news/world-europe-34131911 (accessed 29 January 2016).

Blasko, B., Gouvis Roman, C. and Taylor, R. B. (2015) 'Local gangs and residents' perceptions of unsupervised teen groups: Implications for the incivilities thesis and neighbourhood effects', *Journal of Criminal Justice*, 43: 20–28.

Burney, E. (2005) *Making People Behave: Anti-Social Behaviour, Politics and Policy*, Devon: Willan Publishing.

Carey, B. and Roston, M. (2015) 'Three popular psychology studies that didn't hold up', *New York Times*, 28 August 2015. Online. Available at: www.nytimes.com/interactive/2015/08/28/science/psychology-studies-redid.html?_r=0 (accessed 28 August 2015).

Devroe, E. (2012) *A Swelling Culture of Control? De genese en toepassing van de wet op de gemeenteljike administratieve sancties in België*, Antwerp, Apeldoorn: Maklu.

Durkheim, E. (1973) *Moral Education*, New York: Free Press.

Franzini, L., O'Brien Caughy, M., Murray Nettles, S. and O'Campo, P. (2008) 'Perceptions of disorder: Contributions of neighbourhood characteristics to subjective perceptions of disorder', *Journal of Environmental Psychology*, 28: 83–93.

Garland, D. (1996) 'The limits of the sovereign state: Strategies of crime control in contemporary society', *British Journal of Criminology*, 36(4): 445–471.

Hayward, K. J. (2004) *City Limits: Crime, Consumer Culture and the Urban Experience*, London, Sydney, Portland: GlassHouse Press.

Matthews, R. (1992) 'Replacing "broken windows": Crime, incivilities and urban change', in R. Matthews and J. Young (eds.) *Issues in Realist Criminology*, London: Sage Publications. Available at: http://rogermatthews.net/images/papers/replacing_broken_windows.pdf (accessed 10 May 2015).

Nelken, D. (2015) 'Foil comparisons or foiled comparisons? Learning from Italian juvenile justice', *European Journal of Criminology*, 12(5): 519–534.

Nietzsche, F. (2006, orig. 1887) *On the Genealogy of Morality*, Cambridge, New York: Cambridge University Press.

Pickard, S. (2014) 'Introduction', in S. Pickard (ed.) *Anti-Social Behaviour in Britain*, Basingstoke: Palgrave Macmillan.

Sampson, R. J. and Raudenbush, S. W. (1999) 'Systematic social observation of public spaces: A new look at disorder in urban neighbourhoods', *American Journal of Sociology*, 105(3): 603–651.

Schnall, S., Benton, J. and Harvey, S. (2008) 'With a clean conscience: Cleanliness reduces the severity of moral judgments', *Psychological Science*, 19(12): 1219–1222.

Shaw, C. R. and McKay, H. D. (1942) *Juvenile Delinquency in Urban Areas*, Chicago: University of Chicago Press.

Simon, J. (2007) *Governing Through Crime: How the War on Crime Transformed American Democracy and Created a Culture of Fear*, New York: Oxford University Press.

Sparks, R. (2000) 'Perspectives on risk and penal politics', in T. Hope and R. Sparks (eds.) *Crime, Risk and Insecurity*, London, New York: Routledge.

Thompson, H. (2012) 'Early exposure to germs has lasting benefits', *Nature*, 22 March 2012. Online. Available at: www.nature.com/news/early-exposure-to-germs-has-lasting-benefits-1.10294 (accessed 15 July 2015).

Tonry, M. (2015) 'Is cross-national and comparative research on the criminal justice useful?', *European Journal of Criminology*, 12(4): 505–516.

Van den Broeck, T. (2012) 'Mind the gap – changes in social control and two decennia of community-oriented policing and local governance of crime', in P. Ponsaers (ed.) *Social Analysis of Security: Financial, Economic and Ecological Crime – Crime, (In) security and (Dis)trust – Public and Private Policing*, The Hague: Eleven International Publisher.

Waiton, S. (2008) *The Politics of Antisocial Behaviour*, London, New York: Routledge.

Index

For Product Safety Concerns and Information please contact our EU representative GPSR@taylorandfrancis.com Taylor & Francis Verlag GmbH, Kaufingerstraße 24, 80331 München, Germany

Batch number: 10725973

Printed by Printforce, the Netherlands